Quiz: Are You

1. Are you curious about a variety of religions and philosophies such as Kabbalah or Celtic Christianity? Do you ever use the saying "many paths, one mountain?"

2. When asked for your religious preference, do you prefer to use the term "spiritual?"

3. Do you believe that you should blaze your own spiritual path?

4. Do you assume there is more to the world than meets the eye—that it is a manifestation of a greater spiritual reality?

5. Do you try to listen for the voice of that spirit in your daily life? Do you feel drawn toward contemplative practices such as qigong or yoga or meditation?

6. Do you try to recognize the difference between the quiet soul and noisy ego?

7. Do you ever feel somehow connected to all other people on the planet, or feel that we are interrelated parts of a greater whole?

8. Do you suspect that the battle between good and evil is, in reality, a struggle between ego and soul, fear and love?

9. Do you feel that true morality comes through an accurate grasp of our unity?

10. Do you think that if more people would "awaken" to a more enlightened view of reality, then many of our social and political problems would be answered?

If you answered yes to five or more of these questions, then you most likely share the idealism of the New Age—the latest version of the world's oldest, wisest, most empowering, and most transformative philosophy.

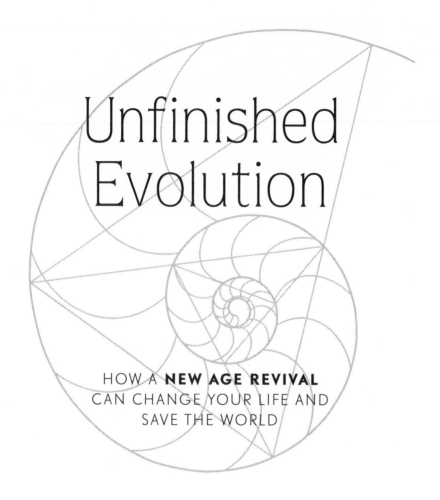

Unfinished Evolution

HOW A **NEW AGE REVIVAL** CAN CHANGE YOUR LIFE AND SAVE THE WORLD

TEENA BOOTH

It takes two to speak the truth;
one to speak, another to hear.

— HENRY DAVID THOREAU —

Published by:
Scotalyn Press
PO Box 51270
Phoenix, AZ 85044
newagepride.org
teena@newagepride.org

Editor: Gail M. Kearns, topressandbeyond.com
Cover and logo design: Diane McIntosh, brightideasdesign.net
Interior design and production: John McKercher, studioxen.com
Book production coordinated by To Press and Beyond
Set in ITC Veljovic

Publisher's Cataloging-In-Publication Data
(Prepared by The Donohue Group, Inc.)

Booth, Teena.
Unfinished evolution : how a New Age revival can change your life and save the world / Teena Booth.
p. ; cm.
Includes bibliographical references and index.
ISBN-13: 978-0-615-22972-0
ISBN-10: 0-615-22972-7

1. New Age movement. 2. Spiritual life—New Age movement. I. Title.
BP605.N48 B66 2010
299/.93 2009903402

Printed in the United States of America

Contents

Foreword

by David Spangler

In 1976, my friend Mark Satin published a groundbreaking book, *New Age Politics: Healing Self and Society*. It was a slim volume, privately published, lacking the polish that a large, mainstream publisher could have given it. But for all its modest appearance, it was a revolutionary document, the first attempt to marry the idealistic philosophy of the New Age movement with a political vision. The purpose was to provide a means by which the good will and visionary ideas of the New Age could be translated into effective public policy and social change; it was a manifesto for a movement.

An attempt was made to translate Satin's ideas into a political party. Alas, this effort foundered, in part because as we entered the Reagan years, the New Age movement turned away from being a transformative social movement. Attention turned inward to explore self-development and personal states of consciousness rather than outward to grapple with issues of societal wellbeing and wholeness. Instead of remaining a symbol for positive change and a hopeful future, the New Age became an image of narcissism that invited ridicule.

Now Teena Booth is daring to pick up the tattered and torn banner of the New Age and restore to it the meaning it once had. Once again, a passionate advocate for a better, more holistic future is seeking to marshal a transformative spirit to empower a movement for change. This book seeks to do for our time what Mark Satin's book did thirty years ago. It calls us to remember why many of us were attracted to the idea of a new age in the first place and the promise it held to make a difference in the world. It once again calls us to heal self and society.

The New Age may seem like a strange candidate for such a calling. In recent years, if we hear about it at all, it's usually in a way intended to dismiss a person or group as self-indulgent or out of touch with the "real world." To be New Age is to be at the fringe of society, engaging in marginalized beliefs or practices.

But the idea of a New Age is hardly marginal. It is an idea as old as humankind, found in all our visions of a better future. It may spin off into utopian fantasies but it's also present in all the dreams that ultimately lead to human progress. It is at the heart of our power to imagine; it embodies our human capacity to revision the present in ways that open the doors to new possibilities and potentials. In essence, the New Age idea says simply that the past need not determine the future. Positive change is possible.

Fertile ground for a movement

The modern New Age movement has numerous roots. Many of them are in Christian millenarianism, the expectation of the Second Coming of Christ and the end of history as we know it. Indeed, as far back at the Twelfth Century, the mystic and monk Joachim of Fiore was prophesying, using words that would parallel those of many modern authors, about the birth of a new age that would usher in a whole new spiritual consciousness for humanity.

More recently, parts of what have become New Age thought can be found in the Transcendentalism of Emerson and Thoreau. Likewise, the New Thought movement that grew out of the work of Phineas Quimby, Mary Baker Eddy, and Ernest Holmes fed significant ideas into the mix. The American Theosophist Alice Bailey was also writing about a coming New Age in the early years of the Twentieth Century. And decades before the performers in the musical *Hair* sang about the dawning of the Age of Aquarius, astrologers were anticipating this transition from one astrological age to another.

So the New Age is not a new idea, but it *is* an evolving one. This I can testify to at first hand for in one way or another I have been associated with the modern New Age movement for the past fifty years, even before it was known as such. I have seen it go through many phases, rising and falling in public estimation. If Teena Booth has anything to say about it, it's time for it to rise again, but if it does so, it will be in a new way yet again.

I first encountered the idea of the New Age in the late 1950s, at the age of fourteen, when the Cold War was heating up and fears of a nuclear war were rampant. Some were building backyard bomb shelters, but others were paying attention to prophecies received by psychics like Edgar Cayce, the "Sleeping Prophet," who proclaimed that a New Age was about to be ushered in by an apocalyptic event that would devastate the old order. This event could be catastrophic earth changes, or World War III, or even the arrival of beings from another world in UFOs.

The linking of prophecy, disaster, and the expectation of a new era is common in Western civilization. There have been apocalyptic millenarian movements at various times in European history, all of them originating, not unsurprisingly, among the dispossessed classes, the ones who had nothing to lose and much to gain if the existing power structure and social order were to be overturned. Lacking the power to bring about such radical changes themselves, the poor could only envision some form of divine or natural intervention in the form of some disaster that would bring the expected new age into being.

Our time is not so different. While we no longer have classes of serfs and peasants, most people still feel disempowered by the largeness of existing social, political, and economic powers and by the challenges that the world faces. So the idea of change brought about by the intervention of powerful outside forces—spiritual, natural, or extraterrestrial—remains attractive. So does the idea of apocalypse, as witness the current rising interest in the so-called Mayan prophecies of 2012 as an end date for civilization. It's as if we can't quite grasp our power to change things ourselves so we must look to disasters and extraordinary forces to intervene and make changes on our behalf.

The New Age comes together

In 1965, I became a spiritual teacher and lecturer. All my life I have been in communication with non-physical beings, and from them I learned that yes, humanity was in a time of profound and historic transformation, and a new age was indeed emerging, but it would not come about through any form of apocalypse. I learned that the New Age was not an event at all—certainly not a world-changing disaster—but a symbol of humanity's creative power to shape its future. In other words, the New Age was an invitation to understand and use an innate capacity for change.

I lived and taught in the San Francisco area, the heart of several major social movements emerging at that time. There was the anti-war movement that had one of its major centers at the University of California at Berkeley. There was also the drug and hippy counterculture centered in the Haight-Ashbury region of San Francisco whose slogan was "turn on, tune in, and drop out." Further down the peninsula around Stanford University in Palo Alto, humanistic and transpersonal psychologies were evolving as well, giving birth to the human potential movement.

The convergence of these movements created a different kind of womb for the New Age. When the movement was considered the result of some prophesied disaster, there was no room for human agency or creativity. One simply waited until the apocalypse came to usher in the new era. Yet, both the civil rights and anti-war movements were demonstrating the power of individual citizens to make a difference. Likewise, the human potential and counterculture movements were proclaiming the innate power of the individual to make radical changes in consciousness and behavior. Under the influence of these ideas, the New Age metamorphosed into something very different from what it had been. It became a vision for culturally creative and visionary individuals to remake society in a more humane and holistic image. In other words, the New Age wasn't something we waited for; it was something we could bring into being.

As the 1970s began, the New Age sought to bring a visionary spiritual element to the forces of change represented by the antiwar, civil rights, and counterculture movements. In a similar way, though this might seem strange today given its current reputation for narcissistic self-involvement, the movement took the self-development focus of the human potential movement and put it into a cultural, collective and visionary context. It proclaimed the power of self-development as a way of unleashing our creative power to imagine and work for social change.

This movement took on a new energy in the 1970s with the Arab oil embargo which raised petroleum prices to unheard of heights. Ever since Rachel Carson published her landmark book, *Silent Spring*, in 1962, an environmental movement had been growing. With lines at the gasoline stations stretching around the block in many American cities, the need for conservation took center stage, which in turn bolstered ecological awareness. Sustainability became a buzzword as various forms of alternative energies began to be explored with greater social support. This in turn gave the New Age a more ecological and earth-oriented character as well.

In 1971, a cultural historian from M.I.T., William Irwin Thompson, published a book, *At the Edge of History*, about the transformation of modern culture. It was a finalist in 1972 for the National Book Award (the *Whole Earth Catalog* was the winner that year). It was followed three years later in 1974 by *Passages about Earth: an Exploration of the New Planetary Culture*. These two books cemented Thompson's reputation as a literate and scholarly spokesperson for the possibilities—indeed, the need—for a global social transformation. In 1974 he founded the Lindisfarne Fellows, a gathering made up of various disciplines that would meet once or twice a year to discuss and collaborate with each other's ideas and projects, all in pursuit of a more holistic and planetary vision of human culture. A list of the fellows is like a Who's Who of the leading edge thinkers of that time: microbiologist Lynn Margulis, economist E. F. Schumacher, poet Wendell Berry, scientist James Lovelock, mathematician Ralph Abraham, anthropologist Gregory Bateson, futurist Stewart Brand, monk David Steindl-Rast, architect Paolo Soleri, ecologists John and Nancy Todd, and composer Paul Winter among others.

As one of the fellows, I came to realize that this group of individuals and their work collectively represented the very heart of what the New Age was about. For this group, as for many others during the 1970s, the guiding image of the New Age was not an apocalyptic prophecy but the development of a planetary consciousness and the emergence of a holistic society. The catchphrase was to "think globally but act locally" in order to create a better future. It was in this context that Mark Satin published his book *New Age Politics*.

This was the New Age I knew best and the one I lectured on continuously for over ten years as co-director of the Findhorn Foundation Community in Scotland and beyond. And it seemed for a time, particularly during the years the Carter Administration was actively supporting alternative energy research and application, that a real cultural transformation was at hand. For example, Belden and Lisa Paulson created the High Wind ecological and alternative energy community and center in central Wisconsin, an overtly New Age center, the story of which has been recently published in *Odyssey of a Practical Visionary*. (For anyone interested in the history of the New Age movement as a social, environmental and political force in the 1970s, I recommend it highly.)

But everything changed during the 1980s. It was as if America's collective spirit took one look at the possibility of transformation and said, "Um, maybe later." With the Reagan years and the return of cheap oil, many pulled back from efforts at conservation and research into alternative energies. The New Age movement changed, too, slowly at first, but then more rapidly as interest in cultural transformation shifted to interest in psychic phenomena and personal development. This change in emphasis became cemented in the public awareness with the TV airing of Shirley MacLaine's miniseries, *Out on a Limb*. MacLaine's adventures with channels and psychics, past lives and power points, and esoteric spiritualities suddenly defined the meaning of New Age for most people from that moment on.

The wind shifts

The effects of the change in public perception were immediate and dramatic for me. Literally the day after the *Out on a Limb* miniseries ended, I went into my local bookstore, part of a national chain, and discovered that the label "New Age" had been removed that morning from the shelves that contained books on alternative energy, ecology, new science, and cultural change—and placed on the shelves that held books on astrology and psychic development. Within a matter of weeks, organizations that had hired me to give talks on the New Age wrote either to cancel the engagements or to ask that I drop the term "New Age" from my title. In a stunningly short period of time, New Age went from meaning a positive, transformative social movement for a better future—the kind of New Age Teena writes about so eloquently in this book—to a private quest for esoteric spiritual development.

Of course, the real impetus and work for cultural change continued under other names. The desire to envision and work towards a better future is innate in human beings and is unaffected by labels as such. But as Teena describes, the shift in direction for the New Age movement did have a dampening effect on many thousands of people who might otherwise have played a more significant role in the political and social events of the past twenty years.

It's possible to look at the story I've told and say that the New Age failed. Indeed, in the mid-1980s, the leader of a successful New Age center said to me in some despair, "the New Age is dead." It's also possible to say that when economic times are tough, as they were in the 1970s, people look for transformation, but when times get better and everything is going along fine, as they were for many in the 1980s and 90s, people simply want to keep the status quo. But I think there is a cyclical movement to changes in consciousness and society.

From my point of view, the modern New Age movement was the result of a powerful influx and stimulation of spiritual energies beginning in the mid-1950s, setting in motion changes in human consciousness. I think of it as a tide coming in to shore and reaching a high water mark in the late 1970s and then, as tides do, receding. A time of activity and turmoil was replaced by a time of consolidation. It's a natural cycle and gives an organism a chance to reflect, digest, and assimilate.

In effect, what became known as the New Age movement in the late 1980s is in some ways only the surface moisture left on the land after the water receded. Yet, underneath the surface, largely out of sight, water is still soaking the land and germinating seeds. New Age ideas have taken root in society in forms such as holistic healing, yoga, health food stores, meditation, and a greater ecological awareness. Also, as Teena points out, the efforts to transform society in positive ways haven't disappeared; the people involved with them just don't want to call them "New Age" anymore for fear of not being taken seriously.

Still, in one important way, the shift in perception of the New Age from that of a William Irwin Thompson or a Findhorn to that of a Shirley MacLaine is more apparent than real. The real New Age has always been more about capability than about content, a point often overlooked in discussions of the "death" of the New

Age. What changes—what has changed—is largely content, what people talk about when they say they are New Age. What has not changed is the sense that we have a power to keep the future from being simply a rerun of the past. We have the innate capacity to choose and implement transformation.

This capacity doesn't by itself determine the nature of that transformation. We can make things worse as well as better. Intelligence, wisdom, love, compassion, a sense of the larger wholes of which we are a part, and skill in action are all required to shape our creativity in positive directions. But we don't and won't bring these qualities into play unless we first understand and believe that we each, through our attitudes and our actions, can truly make a difference in our world. That is what the New Age is really about.

Which brings me to *Unfinished Evolution*, Teena Booth's outstanding new book. In this volume, she seeks to recover that power, to bring back the possibility that the New Age can again inspire people to engage with society and act with vision to create a safer, saner, healthier future. She links the valuable work of self development with an engagement with society that can be healing and transformative.

Is this possible? Can she succeed? Certainly, the times are ripe. As in the 1970s, we again face rising oil prices and the need to rethink and change our lifestyles. The environmental challenges are more threatening than they were thirty years ago, largely because we let slip the opportunities that we had then to make meaningful changes. A spirit of anxiety and anticipated apocalypse is again rising in the land. Clearly, all the elements are there to make a call for the creation of a new age once more meaningful.

Yet, can the New Age overcome twenty years of ridicule and marginalization? Can its adherents overcome twenty years of focus on the self to embrace once more a larger vision and the challenges and responsibilities that come with it? These are vital questions, for which I do not have an answer. It's possible that the term "New Age" has had its day, shot its bolt, and now some newer term must appear to galvanize the spirit and focus our energies. But as Teena points out, none of the candidates so far have made the grade. And like her, I believe there is inherent in the term New Age a simplicity and a directness that is hard to beat when it comes to talking about new visions for the future. For that is what the work is about. Put simply and directly, we must create a new age for the benefit of our children and all our descendents, or we are lost.

Having lectured on the New Age for many years, in recent time I have been focused on developing what I call an incarnational spirituality. This looks at the inner, creative resources we have as individuals to make a difference in our lives and in the life of our world. I have not written or spoken on the New Age hardly at all for ten years. It wasn't that I had given up on it; I simply had other work to do. But when I received Teena's manuscript and went to her Web site, I felt a thrill and a passion I had not felt for some time. I felt like an old New Age workhorse that was ready to wear the saddle again. I was inspired. It honored the work that I and colleagues of mine such as Belden Paulson and William Irwin Thompson have done over the years on behalf of the movement.

This book says the New Age as an idea—as a call to service, as a vision of constructive and compassionate change, and as a statement of human possibility—has a future, not just a past. I endorse that heartily. It's what I believe as well. But Teena is the one who has done the work to say so and to say it thoughtfully, eloquently, and passionately. I am grateful for it.

So I end by saying again what I said in *A Pilgrim in Aquarius*, a book I wrote many years ago at Findhorn's request.

I am proud to be a New Ager.

— David Spangler
June 2009

OCTOBER 21, 2008

Writing Stories

BLOG
Looking for the New Age

I am often amused and bemused to realize I've been working on different versions of this same project for close to twenty years—revising and reworking the narrative for who I am today. This endless task has kept me sane in many ways, allowing me to organize the meaning of my life into twenty-seven chapters.

It doesn't seem all that different from my day job, writing scripts for television, narratives "inspired by real events," fictional versions of the truth, which are organized into eight acts.

I used to think spiritual effort was supposed to help us "wake up" from the stories we tell ourselves about reality, supposed to help us live here in this moment, free and unfettered by our fictional versions of truth. But it has become clear to me that just like meditation does not stop thoughts, we cannot stop our own story-making. In the act of setting one story aside, another automatically composes itself along the structure of new insights, new emotions.

It has also become clear to me this is exactly why we are here, why the universe peopled itself. We are here not to wake up but to dream—dream up stories of meaning, revise with new insights, until we dream up a story that rings true, a story that connects us.

"Restoration," writes Peter Block, "is the willingness to complete the current story we have of our community and our place in it. This creates an opening to produce a new collective story. A new story based on restorative community, one of possibility, generosity, accountability."

I so much hope to help write a new story with this book.

Introduction: My New Age Journey

I still remember—vividly—the first time I read Shirley MacLaine's *Out on a Limb*. I was 19 years old and full of questions about reality and meaning and my purpose in being alive, questions that seemed unrealistically (and depressingly) answered by my family's version of Christianity-from-the-cradle. I'd never been exposed to any other worldview, and as I read through MacLaine's New Age experience, I had to set the book down every few pages to catch my breath and hold my swimming head.

She wrote that God is energy, the divine energy that makes up everything that exists. She wrote that physical reality is an illusion, the surface reflection of a deeper spiritual reality. She wrote that we each may have lived before, past lives in which we probably knew our loved ones. And I thought, is she serious? Are such things *possible*?

From that moment on, I was a New Ager. Not because I swallowed whole everything MacLaine wrote in her book (I didn't). But because encountering the ideas in her book was like being grabbed and spun around to look at the world from a different direction, a direction that, as it turned out, felt natural and right to me.

Growing up, the religious dualism I learned at church, along with the scientific materialism I learned at school, had been so confidently presented to me that it never occurred to me there might be another window from which to view the world. This other window is idealism—the philosophy of "spirit as the ultimate reality" first given form in the East by the Hindus and in the West by Plato. And it quite literally saved me to discover a way out from between the mental rock and hard place of the West's two mainstream points of view.

I loved the New Age. I loved that it took a basic and beautiful philosophy and braided it together with humanistic psychology, quantum physics, and mystical religion, along with a thread of the occult for color. I loved that it was inclusive and respectful and supportive, and how it illuminated the difference between right and wrong. I loved how it helped life make sense to me—and gave me a sense of balance that allowed me to navigate through intense challenges and difficulties.

More than anything, I loved the sense of hope it gave me for the world in which I was raising three children. I wholeheartedly embraced the vision of the future presented by the New Age, in which more people would awaken to a greater spiritual reality, one individual at a time, until we reached critical mass and tipped the planet into an actual new age of harmony.

Life is change

And then, sometime in the early 1990s, I first read the news in *Publishers Weekly*: "The New Age is dead." People I knew, and read about, were not just dropping the term, but were suddenly embarrassed by it. They now preferred to be just plain "spiritual," or "holistic." They preferred to shop for books marked "Mind/Body/Spirit." Once thriving New Age magazines like *Magical Blend* and *Body Mind Spirit* folded, while others, like *New Age Journal*, changed their names to something bland and generic.

By the turn of the millennium, the entire movement was declared over and done. The vehicle that was supposed to be carrying us toward the next quantum stage of evolution had been entirely abandoned. Over the next several years, there would be studies published that questioned whether there had ever been such a thing as a New Age movement at all.

Of course, the movement wasn't really dead. Spiritual idealism was still very much alive and well in the hearts of millions. Web sites by the thousands about "cultural creatives" and "emergent culture" popped up all over the Internet. And many of the authors connected to the movement continued to publish books that enjoyed brisk sales. Yet it seemed to me these books arrived unconnected from their rightful context. They were addressed to the individual concerns of the individual reader, and not an audience with a collective identity and the means to join together and effect change.

Still, many seemed glad to be rid of a label that had become heavy with too much baggage. And although I wasn't one of them, I tried to practice be-here-now acceptance, along with detachment from outcomes, and moved on with the times like everyone else. But now and again, I would be surprised by feelings of dismay—even anger—at the loss. One minute I had been one of millions, riding the leading edge of a transformation sweeping over society; the next minute I was sitting alone in the dry corner of an abandoned movement.

For years I had proudly called myself a New Ager. Now what was I going to call myself? How would I identify and explain my beliefs to others?

Like most, I didn't call myself anything at all. I felt denied an identity. When filling out a form that asked my religious preference, I would check the box marked "Other," then sigh at the blank line beside it. There wasn't enough room to scrawl in "The spiritual idealism briefly known as New Age."

While I still nurtured my dream of the gradual awakening of

society—the same dream passed on like a torch by idealists of every society, in every century—I could not help but notice that even the most hardcore idealists I knew, including myself, were becoming more preoccupied with materialistic goals.

Something's wrong with this picture

In 2001, Shirley MacLaine, the person who first introduced me to New Age ideas, the person who had represented "New Age" like no one else, traveled the country on a speaking tour. I bought a ticket for her well-attended stop in Phoenix, and went with the hope of hearing her say something about the passing of the New Age label. Did she mourn it as well?

But MacLaine did not mention the phrase "New Age" at all; instead, she referred to herself as a "Cultural Creative." In the Q&A session that followed her speech, a woman stood up to talk about how lonely she felt in her spiritual quest, how difficult it was to find others who shared her beliefs. MacLaine said something about how we all need to become complete within ourselves, something smart and true. Still, I'm sure the woman left feeling no less lonely.

Truly astonishing and horrifying events soon followed: The attacks of 9/11. The march to war in Iraq. The rise of fundamentalist fervor and conservative power. All of which gave a severe shaking to my idealistic notion that humanity is evolving toward higher consciousness.

And then came the election of 2004.

As far as I was concerned, this was it—our big defining moment. This was the test to answer the question posed to us by the events of 9/11 about who we are, and how we planned to manage the problem of hate versus love. If there was any validity to the assumption of a steady awakening and enlightening of society, and any hope at all for a new age of harmony, then surely this was the time, and this was the election, when it would become apparent.

Along with so many others I knew, the choice seemed so clear to me, so obvious, that I was sure that George W. Bush's conservative politics of fear and force could not possibly carry the day.

Except that it did. On November 2, 2004, long after the dawning of the Age of Aquarius in the most enlightened society on earth, the idealism of "we are all one" failed. Instead, the materialism of greed and the dualism of good vs. evil was voted back into power. If American society was moving in any direction at all, it was clearly, tragically, backwards.

Face to face with my convictions

Now, it may seem that I have wandered from my New Age subject with this digression into presidential politics. But for me, the election of 2004 brought me face to face with my convictions in a way no personal crisis ever had.

Of course, all progressives were depressed about the outcome of the election, and many made half-joking plans to leave a country that suddenly seemed like hostile territory. But my own depression over the election settled into a much deeper disillusionment that put my entire way of thinking into question.

On the surface, I tried to comfort myself with idealistic notions of dialectic progress, which says that every expansion is necessarily followed by a contraction. I told myself that one step back after the two steps forward does not mean that progress is not being made. And, like any good idealist, I tried to practice detachment from outcomes.

But down deep, I could not shake the feeling that my philosophy was somehow inadequate, that I was missing an important piece of the puzzle, maybe even the most important piece. And I couldn't stop myself from thinking that maybe idealism as I understood it was not *the* answer after all.

Today I know that during those months after the election, I was coming to terms with the limits of *flatland* idealism, which says that all views are created equal. This brand of relativistic idealism, delineated for me by the integral philosopher Ken Wilber, formed the core of the New Age movement and was ultimately responsible for its demise. It was also responsible for my post-election pain.

You see, my shallow understanding of idealism had made it so that even when I believed the re-election of George W. Bush would be an unmitigated disaster for our country and the world, I did not do a thing beyond stepping into the ballot box to help the more enlightened candidate win. My brand of idealism had encouraged my belief, but allowed me to sit out on the action because, after all, my little belief was no better or worse than any other.

Ultimately, my depression over the election was not about the lack of vision in others—or what others failed to do. My depression was over my own lack of vision—and what *I* had failed to do. And I felt absolutely wretched with the burden of my responsibility. And not just for the outcome of the election. I was finally starting to grasp my responsibility for all the other dire problems that plague us as a society, problems that I had done almost nothing to alleviate, year after year, day after day.

For yet another painful stretch of time, I wondered if the New Age was indeed guilty of leading us all into do-nothing narcissism, as many critics accused, and wondered if we were better off without it. But the more I have thought and read and contemplated, the more I have come to understand that it is the disappearance of the New Age as a communal movement, and our abandonment of it, which left us stranded in flatland idealism with no way out. The New Age had promised to take us on an evolutionary journey. But when we idealists hopped off the movement to strike out on our own individual spiritual paths, our collective evolution was left unfinished.

Today I feel unreasonably certain that if the New Age had not been allowed to drift away like a fashion trend without value, but had been supported and refined and encouraged to mature into a fuller expression of idealism—and its ideas passed along as the saving instruments they are—the world would be a much different place right now.

A clear purpose

I want the New Age back. Not exactly as it was—it generated a lot of superfluous fluff that unhelpfully distracted us. (Okay, that's an understatement. The New Age generated such copious amounts of fluff that years after it helped suffocate the movement, much of it still floats around like wilting balloons that hang around days after the party is over.)

But with our planet in immediate peril from global warming and terrorism and economic collapse, we are now, more than ever, in need of a vehicle to help us make that long-awaited leap to the next stage of our evolution. We are now, more than ever, in need of tools and inspiration and social capital to change our lives and save the world.

Fortunately, the hopeful election of Barack Obama in 2008 has restored the bright sheen of possibility to the prospect of transformation. And I believe that the New Age—accurately understood and collectively supported—is still the right vehicle to get us there. So I intend to do what I can to dust off all the fluff and see if it will start up again, this remarkable vehicle that once made it possible for me and so many others to explore reality, share ideas, and join together for the purpose of transforming society.

Of course, the New Age may well be dead, and I may simply need to better learn to let go and move on, learn to be plainly spiritual, or humbly holistic. But just in case it's still there, hiding quietly in the hearts of idealists everywhere, waiting for this moment of expansion to make itself known and take up its vital work, I am going to make my case in this book and get it out into the world. And I am going to ask you, and anyone who will listen, to help.

Although I do admit, when I present this intention to some of my spiritual friends, they often squinch their faces in confusion or annoyance. They are the ones that live in places like Santa Cruz, California, or Ashland, Oregon, and have jobs like "Reiki healer" or "yoga instructor," and as far as they can tell, the movement is doing just fine, thank you very much. And in those places, they are right, spiritual idealism thrives, unnamed and unspecified, and is well integrated within their local culture. Thanks to Oprah and her New Age-y focus on spiritual matters, they can even see bits and pieces of it gaining traction in the mainstream.

However, I suspect my friends are mistaking their local view for the world at large. The view outside of our far-flung liberal communities is much, much different. True, a new paradigm holds sway on movie sets and in yoga studios and alternative medicine clinics and new green start-ups and a number of wonderful, forward-thinking organizations. But start moving away from the coast, and one rarely stumbles across any signs of it. The old paradigm still holds sway across the land, is still firmly entrenched in school rooms and corporate boardrooms, in religious chambers and legislative chambers. The old paradigm still makes public policy and builds formidable obstacles to all our good intentions. And whatever cracks we might be able to perceive in the old structures, the fact remains, the old paradigm today threatens the future like never before.

Our collective evolution, which seemed to be advancing in great leaps a few decades ago, has clearly stalled. The old paradigm will not, and cannot, go away until more of us understand and embrace a well-defined alternative paradigm. The problem is, the new paradigm is anything but well-defined and is, in fact, widely *mis*understood. The problem is, the new paradigm no longer even has a name.

"It is hard to focus attention on the nameless," wrote William James, the famous philosopher-psychologist. Without a label to represent them, the ideas that exist so vibrantly in our hearts and in our personal pursuits exist barely at all in the popular culture we all share. In my opinion, we spiritual idealists need to bring back the New Age label so that the world will be better able to embrace a new paradigm.

It could be that I am choosing the wrong battle. It could be that in my stubbornness, I will find that in holding up my banner with "New Age" printed in bold purple letters, few others will care to join me, let alone pay me any attention. But I will, at least, have saved myself from being another lonely "other," stripped of designation and cast adrift on a sea of vague and nameless spirituality. And if nothing else, I will hopefully discover a few others who see the world the same way and might enjoy sharing a conversation.

I am a New Ager and proud of it. In these pages I explain what it means to me, and what I believe it once meant to others. I explore what may have happened to cause the label's demise, and why I believe it can still hold vital meaning and value for us today. Most important, I ask you to consider the implications of reviving the movement and its label so that it may help us continue to grow in our unfinished evolution.

PART I

What Is the New Age?

These are the thoughts of all men in all ages and lands,
they are not original with me,
If they are not yours as much as mine they are nothing
or next to nothing,
If they do not enclose everything they are next to
nothing,
If they are not the riddle and the untying of the riddle
they are nothing,
If they are not just as close as they are distant
they are nothing.

This is the grass that grows wherever the land is
and the water is,
This is the common air that bathes the globe.

This is the breath of laws and songs and behavior,
This is the tasteless water of souls...
this is the true sustenance.

— WALT WHITMAN —

1 New Age in a Nutshell

What is the New Age? Rarely has a question caused such head-scratching confusion and voluminous guesswork among social observers. Go back through hundreds of magazine and journal articles, dozens of books, encyclopedia entries, and who-knows-how-many Web site posts, and you'll never find the New Age defined the same way twice.

Well, here's my definition, short and sweet:

> *The New Age is the most recent social expression of the Perennial Philosophy—the philosophy of idealism—which says that One Spirit is the essence of all reality.*

That's it.

Each New Ager works out the details of "All Is One Spirit" in different ways. Still, that's pretty much it—the New Age in a nutshell.

Wait a minute, some might say. That's it? What about crystals? And Tarot cards and near-death experiences and all that occult stuff on the New Age shelf at Barnes & Noble? Everyone knows that stuff is what the New Age is about, right?

The New Age spectrum

The list of New Age interests is nearly limitless, wandering all over the spectrum from the holy and profound to the irrelevant and ridiculous.

Alternative and holistic medicine, Eastern and Native American religions, transpersonal psychology, pagan spirituality, Gaia environmentalism, the "new" physics, myths, and archetypes—all these subjects can be found in a New Age bookstore. And yes, there are also books on crystal healing and astrology and ESP and the occult.

Turn around and you will find sitting Buddhas, dancing Shivas, angel pendants, yin-yang symbol earrings, candles for Wiccan rituals, cushions for meditating, "Give Peace a Chance" bumper stickers, aromatherapy oils, and CDs of music made to sound like rain. It's no wonder that New Age pioneer David Spangler, one of the founders of the Findhorn spiritual community, compared the New Age to a country fair with its combination of wares and amusements for sale.

To some observers, this anything-and-everything laundry list of subjects makes the New Age too slippery to pin down. In his book, *The Children of the New Age: A History of Spiritual Practices*, religion historian Steven Sutcliffe complains about the lack of boundaries in the New Age and refuses to grant it the status of a social movement. The New Age, he declares, is nothing but "a diffuse collectivity of questing individuals."

I've never understood why so many observers are so determined to define the New Age by the scattered interests of its adherents. No one would try to define Christianity by the ability to speak in tongues or the use of rosary beads. Such practices are beside the point. Christianity is defined by a particular set of beliefs about the nature of reality; namely, that there is a division between spirit and matter, God and man, heaven and hell—and the bridge between them is belief in the resurrection of Jesus Christ.

Yes, occult subjects are popular in the New Age; in an All Is

One Spirit reality, communication with the dead is theoretically not outside the realm of possibility. And how will you ever know if you don't at least test that possibility? But the majority of spiritual idealists have little interest in the occult. Meanwhile, many a Christian dualist has been known to try to communicate with their own dearly departed through a psychic or medium, which tells us an interest in the occult is not particular to the New Age.

In the same vein, New Agers may come upon a practice or tradition that expresses their idealism "just right," such as Buddhist meditation or Wiccan ritual. And more than likely, the Buddha-curious or the Wiccan practitioner is also a New Age-style idealist. But it does not work in reverse. Just because all Catholics are Christians, doesn't mean all Christians are Catholics. And just because most Wiccans are New Agers doesn't mean all New Agers are trooping off to join a coven.

Sutcliffe may be right that the New Age is comprised of a collectivity of questing individuals, but he's wrong about the movement being *only* that. New Agers do pursue divergent interests, but what they practice is not nearly as important as *why* they practice it.

Why do holistic health consumers believe the mind can heal the body? Why do psychics claim it is possible to see into the future? Why do some scientists believe quantum physics supports the worldview of Eastern religions? What kind of picture of reality allows such divergent beliefs?

Beneath the surface flash of the New Age, beneath all the faddish practices and commercial pitches, the basic principle of All Is One Spirit holds the whole movement together. This principle is what connects one New Age seeker to the other, from the physicist who sees Zen principles reflected in the behavior of subatomic particles, to the psychic who finds wisdom in her Tarot cards.

In other words, the New Age is a movement fueled by a philosophy—a working hypothesis about what is real, and what that reality makes possible in our lives.

Under the New Age Umbrella

Just as the basic principles of a Christian worldview are expressed in seemingly countless number of denominations and interpretations, so do the idealistic principles of a New Age worldview take on many different configurations and flavors. In fact, a diversity of beliefs is a hallmark of the New Age.

The essential element of New Age philosophy is the idealistic notion that All Is One Spirit, and that we are all interrelated parts of one whole. Numerous belief systems grow from this premise and naturally fit under the New Age umbrella. Virtually all of the following belief systems and practices are philosophically consistent, and complement each other to varying degrees. All are popular in the New Age today, and while many New Agers strongly identify with one or two paths or disciplines, most of us mix and match any number of them to suit our own particular lives.

- **Hinduism**—Yoga, The Vedanta Society, Swami Vivekananda, Rabindranath Tagore, Sri Aurobindo, Mahatma Gandhi, Ram Dass.
- **Buddhism**—Zen meditation, the Dalai Lama and Tibetan Buddhism, Alan Watts, Thich Nhat Han, Jack Kornfield, Jon Kabat-Zinn, Pema Chodron, Genpo Roshi and Big Mind, *Shambhala Sun*, *Buddhadharma*, *Tricyle Review.*
- **Advaita** (non-duality)—An offshoot of Vedanta that says truth is a pathless land, and we don't need any particular path or practice to wake up. J. Krishnamurti, Nisargadatta Maharaj, Sri Ramana Maharshi, Adyashanti, Gangaji, Radiant Mind, Jeff Foster, Joan Tollifson, Eckhart Tolle.
- **Taoism**—Lao Tzu, the practices of t'ai chi or qigong, the recent work of Wayne Dyer.

- **Aboriginal Spirituality**—Native American shamanism, Miguel Ruiz and Toltec Wisdom.
- **The Transcendentalists**—Ralph Waldo Emerson, Henry David Thoreau.
- **Pagans and Wiccans**—Nature-based idealism and mysticism, magick-oriented, all things Celtic and Druid.
- **Jewish Idealism and Mysticism**—Kabbalah, *Tikkun Magazine*, Rabbi Michael Lerner.
- **Muslim Idealism and Mysticism**—Sufism and the poetry of Rumi.
- **New Thought Religions**—Religious Science, Christian Science, Unity, "The Secret," Dr. Michael Beckwith, and the entire manifestation crowd.
- **Christian Idealism and Mysticism**—Meister Eckhart, Tielhard de Chardin, Thomas Merton, Thomas Keating and Centering Prayer, Anne Lamott, Huston Smith, Matthew Fox and Creation Spirituality.
- **Theosophy**—Madam Helena Blavatsky, Annie Besant, Quest Books.
- **The Mystery Schools** (Idealism as secret knowledge passed down)—Gnosticism, Esoteric Christianity, Alchemy, Hermeticism, Rosicrucianism, Freemasonry, Knights Templar, Manly P. Hall and *The Secret Teachings of All Ages.*
- **The Healers** (Idealism in health and medicine)—Holistic living, Reiki, Deepak Chopra, Carolyn Myss, Judith Orloff, alternative medicine, vegans, raw foodists.
- **The Transpersonal Psychologists** (Idealism from a psychological perspective)—Carl Jung, Abraham Maslow, Carl Rogers, M. Scott Peck and *The Road Less Traveled*, Clarissa Pinkola Estes, Joan Borysenko, Cheryl Richardson, Debbie Ford.
- **The New Physicists** (Idealism meets science)—Fritjof Capra and *The Tao of Physics*, *What the Bleep*

Do We Know?, Fred Alan Wolfe, Gary Zukav and *The Dancing Wu Li Masters*, Rupert Sheldrake, Bruce Lipton (cell biologist), Joe Dispenza.

- **The Culture Contingent** (Idealism in society)—*The Aquarian Conspiracy*, Paul Ray and Sherry Ruth Anderson and *The Cultural Creatives,* "emergent culture," "wisdom culture," futurists like Buckminster Fuller, Barbara Marx Hubbard, Jean Houston, *EnlightenNext* magazine.
- **The Greens** (Idealism from a political/environmental perspective)—Deep Ecology, Worldchanging.com, sustainable development, Gaia Hypothesis, Joanna Macy.
- **Do-It-Yourself Spirituality** (Generic Idealism)—Oprah Winfrey, James Redfield and *The Celestine Prophecy*, Byron Katie and *The Work*, Unitarian Universalism, Sara Ban Breathnach, Beliefnet.com, the LOHAS market, *Body + Soul* magazine.
- **The Channelers**—Edgar Cayce, Seth, Neale Donald Walsch, Ramtha, Emmanuel.
- **A Course in Miracles**—A channeled form of idealism that borrows the language of Christianity, Marianne Williamson, Hugh Prather.
- **Psychics and Occultists**—Astrology, Tarot cards, crystals, ESP, psychic powers, Nostradamus, Jeanne Dixon, Sylvia Browne, Llewellyn Press.
- **The Spiritualists** (Talking to the dead)—James Van Praagh, John Edward, Rosemary Altea, Allison DuBois.
- **The Integral Academics**—States and stages and levels and quadrants in a theory of "all of the above," Ken Wilber, Andrew Cohen, Dr. Don Beck and *Spiral Dynamics*.

If I was to get specific about my own personal beliefs, I'd have to toss in at least seven or eight of the categories above, though a few would come and go every year. Today, I'm a transcendental Advaita-leaning Buddhist with an integral orientation, who practices yoga, attends a Unitarian Universalist church, and lately feels a strong pull toward Christian mysticism that fosters a relationship to the divine on a more passionate, personal level. While no one in the New Age holds the exact same combination of beliefs (nor should they), many millions of us share the same basic idealism. We should all be able to support each other on our journey, and work together toward common goals.

The Perennial Philosophy

The philosophy of idealism has a long and rich history that stretches back into the mists of time. It was first primitively expressed in pagan and aboriginal religions, then elevated in Hindu sutras and Taoist poems and Plato's discourses on eternal Ideas (see *Chapter 9, The Philosophy of Idealism* for a full definition). Over the past few thousand years, the idealistic worldview has emerged again and again in many times, in many places, in many guises—Taoism, Buddhism, Zen, Neoplatonism, gnosticism, hermeticism, Rosicrucianism, transcendentalism, theosophy, New Thought, the counterculture.

In his 1945 book, Aldous Huxley called idealism *The Perennial Philosophy* and described it like this:

> *Philosophia Perennis*—the phrase was coined by Leibniz; but the thing—the metaphysic that recognizes a divine Reality substantial to the world of things and lives and minds; the psychology that finds in the soul something similar to, or even identical with, divine Reality; the ethic that places man's final end in the knowledge of the immanent and transcendent Ground of all being—the thing is immemorial and universal.

The modern New Age movement, which dates back to the 1970s, is merely the latest resurgence of the timeless *philosophia perennis*. As Ralph Waldo Emerson wrote of the "new views" of nineteenth century transcendentalism, New Age views are essentially "not new, but the very oldest of thoughts cast into the mold of these new times."

And these very oldest of thoughts tell us that in order to better serve our purpose, we must look deeply into the nature of our existence, and discover what is most real and most true. These oldest of thoughts tell us, as Henry David Thoreau did, that we must "settle ourselves, and work and wedge our feet downward through the mud and slush of opinion, and prejudice, and tradition, and delusion, and appearance... through poetry and philosophy and religion, till we come to a hard bottom and rocks in place, which we can call reality and say, This is, and no mistake."

The New Age seeker, like all other idealists throughout history, is ultimately trying to get to this "what is" place. Although, today's New Ager is more likely to call it a place of "higher" awareness than a "bottom" place. Yet, whether we look at the movement from the perspective of high up or hard bottom, it is clear we are talking about a something with a spatial element, something that holds a metaphorical *place*. As it turns out, the most interesting question about the New Age is not *what* is it?, but *where* is it? Where does the New Age sit on the map of spiritual territory?

Yes, it so happens there *is* a map of spiritual development. And taking a look at this map is the only way to get down to the nitty-gritty of what the New Age movement is, the purpose it once served, and why it could be so important to revive it. Beyond that, getting a good grasp of the map of spiritual development is undoubtedly one of the most life-changing, world-saving things you can do. Period.

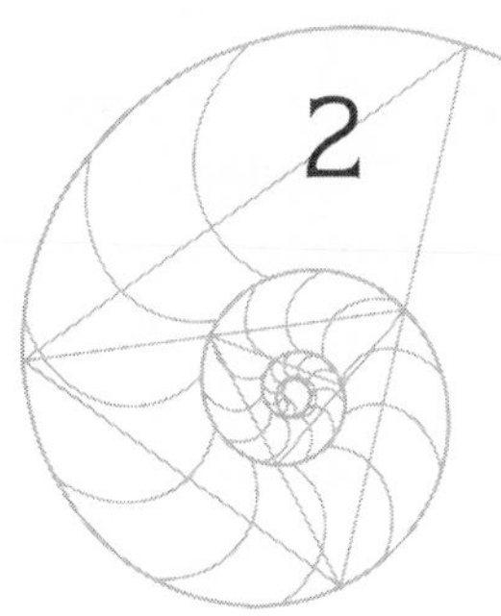

2 The Map of Spiritual Growth

By most accounts, there are three primary ways of looking at the world—the dualistic way (spirit and matter are both real but separate) represented by Western religions, the materialistic way (only matter is real) represented by science, and the idealistic way (spirit and matter are both real but the same thing) represented by the New Age and its many perennial philosophy predecessors. For the longest while I believed it was all a matter of choice—that we could pick whatever we liked—and that all points of view were equally valid.

Of course, one reason I believed that to be true is because idealism told me it was true. The intolerant dualist or arrogant materialist might try to reserve "the truth" all to themselves, but most idealists are adamantly pluralistic, and willing to let everyone have their own slice.

Today, I better understand that how we see the world is not exactly a matter of choice. I understand that each person's worldview is inevitably shaped by where that person is in the process of his or her spiritual development, which in turn is inevitably shaped by the genetic chemistry and the cultural wiring of that person's brain. This understanding was a huge revelation to me—a much-needed revelation that cleared up my confusion over how people can believe so differently, and how we get stuck in place.

It is the prolific Ken Wilber who is most responsible for introducing me—and a readership that stretches beyond the New Age—to the concept of spiritual stages through his many books on integral psychology and integral spirituality. Of course, if I had taken a philosophy class in college I might have run into discourses on the stages of knowledge which have been put forth since the time of Plato. Philosophers have long known that levels of knowing, or levels of spiritual wisdom, correspond to stages of *being*. From sensation, to knowledge, to understanding, to wisdom—philosophy teaches us we can only access higher modes of knowing by moving through the foundational modes.

This philosophical insight has lately been put to the scientific test through decades of rigorous research, and today, virtually all developmental psychologists agree that human beings advance from birth to death through various stages of spiritual and moral development. These stages are not merely a matter of theory, but based on hard data collected from hundreds of thousands of people who have described their inner processes to researchers. This data tells us that all of us move through these stages in a predictable order, although the rate at which we grow through them is not predictable, dependent as it is on environment and genetic influences, as well as one's own desire to grow.

Different researchers, including Abraham Maslow, Clare Graves, Jane Loevinger, Lawrence Kohlberg, William Torbert, Robert Kegan, Susan Cook-Greuter, and Carol Gilligan among others, delineate a different number of stages, depending on what criteria they decide to use, and give each stage a different name. But however many stages they identify, most agree they can be organized into at least three general categories: pre-conventional (the egocentric "me"), conventional (the ethnocentric "us"), and post-conventional (the worldcentric "all of us").

Now, if you haven't run across the concept of stages before, my introduction here may seem a little too academic, but really, the stages themselves are easy as pie to grasp. And if you are like me, discovering them will pretty much blow your mind, as well as completely transform your way of understanding people and events. Of course, if you are already familiar with the concept, then you know how quickly it illuminates human history and the challenges we face.

For our purposes, we will focus on six stages of spiritual evolution, grouped in the three general categories of growth, based on the criteria of "care." Spiritual maturity requires that one becomes less concerned with oneself and more concerned with others. The more we grow, the wider our circle of care and concern and the higher the spiritual stage from which we operate.

Back in the cosmic 1980s, many New Age writers vaguely described growth from one stage to the next in abstract terms of "ascension" toward higher awareness or higher consciousness. But thanks to developmental psychology, we now have a much better understanding of how we grow into new stages. It can be helpful to visualize the stages not as an ascending staircase, but rather as a spiral that widens and encompasses all the previous stages within it. This model of human development is called Spiral Dynamics, and was first introduced by psychologists Chris Cowan and Don Beck in their 1996 book.

As we are all born at Stage One, and we all have the potential for higher growth, describing these stages is not a way of ranking people, Wilber notes, but merely a way of describing a person's current capacity to include others in his or her circle of concern. We remain in each stage for however long it works for us—whether a few years, a few decades, or an entire lifetime. We usually work very hard to defend and justify where we are as the "right" place and will criticize others who are at different stages.

But once in a great while, if we're lucky, we run across new information or find ourselves in a new situation or experience something that our normal way of seeing the world cannot accommodate, and we grow, often in spite of ourselves.

THE PRE-CONVENTIONAL STAGE

Stage One: The chaotic/egocentric stage

This is the true egocentric stage of young children, damaged adults, and all of those whose development was slowed by growing up in chaotic or abusive situations. A person in this stage is motivated by the needs of the self and only the self. Care for others is generally lacking, an unaffordable luxury for those living in physical or emotional dire straits.

In Stage One, we find little sense of morality, and any difficulty the person faces is blamed on others. The getting and wielding of power over others is the primary focus of this stage, and aggressive showing off and violent lashing out is common here. A tendency toward superstition, magical thinking, or preoccupations with ghosts and aliens or any threatening "other" also shows up here. Far-out theories are often embraced without challenge. Rarely is any thought given to developing a rational point of view about life; meaning is all about what satisfies the self right now.

Those who habitually break the law are usually stuck here. Those who run giant corporations and embezzle money from shareholders and run off to a Caribbean island with the loot are also stuck here. Drug and alcohol addictions meant to numb the pain and isolation of this stage are also common.

In order to develop past this stage, the adult individual must be provided some measure of security or locate a source of structure, such as in a church setting or a therapy or rehabilitation situation or even a military or sports setting. Or, they may "hit bottom," get sick and tired of chaos, and look for a way out on their own.

Some, however, because of their brain chemistry or because they live in chaotic social situations, will never move beyond this stage, at least not without some kind of assistance. Giant chunks of the population of violence-ravaged and starving nations—as well as poverty-stricken and crime-ridden pockets here at home—stay trapped here, perpetuating chaos. While number estimates vary by researcher, in the U.S. it would be a safe bet to say that between 10 and 15 percent of the population linger in Stage One, and are in dire need of help to meet their basic needs—food and shelter, safety and security—and find a pathway to growth.

(For those who want to go a little deeper, this stage is also called the purple and red memes by Wilber, the Impulsive and Opportunistic stages by Torbert and Cook-Greuter, and the Magical-Animistic and Egocentric levels by Beck and Cowan in Spiral Dynamics.)

THE CONVENTIONAL STAGES

Stage Two: Faith and order/conformist stage

At some point, usually in childhood or adolescence, most of us will move past egocentric concerns to become aware of the needs of others. We begin to look for structure and meaning and a way to understand life. In the U.S., what we usually find is a religious system already in the home, or at least the neighborhood. (In other places or times, one might find a political system such as communism.)

After the chaos of Stage One, we have a high need for structure and certainty in Stage Two, and so our faith in the founding myths of a religious system is by necessity the blind and unquestioning sort. The world is unambiguously divided into good and evil, and our philosophy is often unabashedly dualistic: God above, the earth below. Our priorities are also unabashedly ethnocentric. It is us versus them, and all those who believe like us are "good" or saved, and all those who do not believe like us are "evil" or damned.

This is the stage of intolerant fundamentalism, whether of the Christian, Jewish, Muslim, or even the Buddhist variety, with each path declaring itself to be the only true path. All of us move through this stage, although without exposure to a religion to hold us tight to faith, our fundamentalism may be attached to science or a political group or to the military or AA or any other source of structure. According to Wilber, about 25 percent of Americans—and a much larger percentage of the Third World—will hunker down in this stage for life, soothed and satisfied by the absolutism they find here.

For the rest of us, often in later adolescence or young adulthood, we will meet enough different kinds of people, or see enough of life, to realize that blind faith really is blind and too often contrary to reason. We are likely to find ourselves filled with questions that faith refuses to confront, let alone answer. And so, ready or not, we grow out of Stage Two. For some, it is a painful process to let go of the structure of faith that once protected and sustained us. For others, it can be a welcome liberation.

(Stage Two is called the blue meme by Wilber, The Diplomat and Expert stages by Torbert and Cook-Greuter, and the Purposeful Absolutist by Beck and Cowan)

Stage Three: The skeptical "show me proof" stage

As we begin to ask more questions about life, we turn away from faith and spirit in general, believing only those ideas that can be proven or that make sense to our logic. For some, this stage is explicitly atheistic, but many retain a "who knows?" attitude that allows them to continue identifying with a religion, and perhaps show up in church once in awhile, while generally operating from a more modern, materialistic mindset.

This is the stage of spiritual growth which gave birth to the eighteenth-century Age of Enlightenment, in which human reason finally wrested free from its religious shackles and flourished in the light of science and the philosophy of materialism. This stage gives us a worldview that UC Berkley professor George Lakoff, author of *Moral Politics*, calls "Old Enlightenment,"—logical, literal, universal and unemotional.

From this stage, Wilber adds, the world is perceived as a "well-oiled machine with rules that can be learned, manipulated for one's own purposes." Widespread growth into this stage allowed Western civilization to make stunning leaps in industry and technology and created the elements of the good life we all enjoy today.

In this skeptical stage, our emotional need for structure and order remain high, and we see a great deal of "my way is the only right way" fundamentalism as well. However, ethnocentrism has softened up a bit and we see the growth of ideas like fairness and justice and universal rights for all. Unless, that is, we are coming from the economic side of the materialistic equation, in which case rights are trumped by the need for profit.

Although this stage efficiently banishes superstitions and myths that oppress, because it generally pushes against balancing spiritual ideals, it ends up tilting toward economic doctrines that are just as oppressive in their own way. I've run across a range of estimates on this stage in twenty-first-century America, but the consensus seems to be that somewhere between 30 and 40 percent of us live from this skeptical, moderate perspective.

(Stage Three is Wilber's orange meme, Torbert and Cook-Greuter's Achiever stage, and Beck and Cowan's Multiplistic/Individualistic level.)

These two conventional stages are, on the surface at least, wildly divergent in matters of belief, yet surprisingly compatible. Many Americans are able to master a daily shift between following the dictates of materialism at work and traditions of dualism at home and in church. Lakoff calls this talent "biconceptualism," and as we have seen over the past thirty years, both have joined forces to great effect in the political arena, with the alliance of social conservatives (dualists) and corporate conservatives (materialists) in the Republican Party.

The two conventional stages also make up the current ruling paradigm, a blend of social and economic rules which provide the order and structure that allows for spiritual growth. However, left unchecked, this paradigm also relentlessly oppresses and exploits, leading to pain and poverty and war and massive environmental damage.

Often, it is recognizing the damage being done by the destructive aspects of materialism that spurs one's growth toward the next stage. However, most who move on do so because Stage Three offers so little in the way of meaning fulfillment. Even with a casually religious gloss, materialism does not allow one to actually engage with spirit. Eventually, one's spirit may rise up in protest and urge us to the next stage.

POST-CONVENTIONAL STAGES

Stage Four: The sensitive individualist stage

As we grow into Stage Four, we expand our circle of care and finally abandon ethnocentric concerns for worldcentric hopes. Some continue holding to a materialistic philosophy and expand it with the higher callings of secular humanism. Most, however, turn away from the cold mechanisms of materialism and toward the stirrings of soul.

Stage Four is the natural home of idealism—spirit as essence of reality—as well the spiritual center of gravity for the New Age movement, which sprang up in the 1970s and 80s. From Stage Four, the universe is no longer perceived as a machine but comes alive with an animating spirit that encompasses all of us. We now feel upset by exploitation of natural resources and begin to put the health of environment above profit. We now feel connected to others in a way we never did before and begin to put people above profit. We begin to long for a new paradigm that values the whole and nurtures all its interrelated parts.

Although many in this stage set off on their own solitary spiritual seeking, some return to the religion of their youth, yet without the blind faith and literalism of Stage Two. Sacred texts are now understood as symbolic pointers to greater truths, and all religions are seen as equally legitimate paths toward a greater understanding of spirit.

Indeed, the insistence on the equal legitimacy of all views, no matter how far out or illogical, is a hallmark of this stage, and we see a lot of "you do your thing/I do my thing" thinking. This individualistic self-absorption opens the door to the dark side of this stage: narcissism. Like the other first-tier stages, Stage Four is also prey to some degree of fundamentalism and adamantly insists that it is the only "right" way of looking at the world. This either/or type of insistence can prevent one from embracing deeper spiritual paradoxes.

According to most estimates I've read, around 25 percent of the American population sees the world from this largely "spiritual but not religious" stage, overall a group of truly good people with holistic ideals and a sincere desire to create a better society. Unfortunately, this desire too often gets shoved aside by the demands of our own personal, ego-driven quests.

Stage Four is where we idealists often get intractably stuck, for reasons we will soon examine. And this is where we will remain stuck, in "flatland" idealism, until we figure out that there are higher stages of development waiting for us.

(Stage Four is Wilber's Mean Green Meme, Torbert and Cook-Greuter's Individualist stage, and Beck and Cowan's Personalistic/Relativistic level.)

Stage Five: The integral stage

Although the philosophy here is a more profound form of the same idealism that we see in the previous stage, it is such a radical leap from everything that comes before that Wilber calls the integral stage an entirely new tier of awareness. From this higher vantage point, one can see the "big picture" and the importance of *all* the stages of growth.

In Stage Five, we are able to integrate within ourselves all the other stages that came before. We no longer try to stamp out or marginalize the others, for we see that they are all correct on their own level. But neither do we protect points of view that are in error as we did in Stage Four. We become interested in the health of the entire spiral and try to help others feel less defensive and entrenched in their positions so they are more likely to grow to the next stage.

Most important, we are better able to detach from ego-driven concerns and no longer need to insist on the sanctity of our individuality. This freedom from egocentrism unlocks the needle of our moral compass and allows compassion for others to bloom wildly. Our priorities reorganize themselves toward the whole. Suddenly, it is no longer difficult to talk ourselves into stepping out into the world to work for change. On the contrary, it becomes painful to sit still when we can see so much that needs doing, and we fly out the door to engage in this work with a sense of joy and purpose.

In this stage, spirituality is no longer just one part of our lives, something separate from every day concerns; spirituality now inhabits and informs every part of our lives.

There are higher stages in the widening spiral of evolving consciousness toward enlightenment, but the jump to the new tier of Stage Five awareness might be the most important in the planet-rescuing sense. If a new paradigm becomes possible in Stage Four, it becomes real in Stage Five. At the dawn of the new millennium,

Wilber estimates that less than 5 percent of Americans live from this stage.

(Stage Five is Wilber's Yellow meme, Tobert and Cook-Greuter's Strategist stage, and Beck and Cowan's Integrative level.)

Stage Six: The unitive stage

This rare stage has been best described by the saints of old or longtime meditators like Zen monks and Hindu yogis. These sages tell us that it is possible to reach a stage in which freedom from ego is complete, and one no longer identifies with an individual self, but identifies instead with the universe as one Self. The border between self and world dissolves, and so does much of the struggle of the human condition. Radical acceptance of "what is" follows, as does radical action in service to others. Life flows—or so we hear from the less than one-tenth of one percent of Americans who may operate from this stage.

(Stage Six is Wilber's Turquoise meme, Torbert and Cook-Greuter's Magician stage, and Beck and Cowan's Harmonizing Contemplative level.)

NOVEMBER 10, 2008

The New Age, circa 2008

BLOG
Looking for the New Age

I spent a thrilling weekend at the "Celebrate Your Life" conference here in Phoenix, only days after Obama was elected. It took $440 to get me in, and as I pushed my way through walls of people filling up every nook and cranny of the Sheraton, it was obvious the New Age is alive and well. Although, of course, the term "New Age" was nowhere spoken (except at the end) or written in any of the literature I heaped into my tote printed with the words "At One Yoga."

This conference, which attracted several thousand people, seemed to me a perfect reflection of the many factions of the New Age movement today. The integral level of spirituality was represented by Marianne Williamson in her stirring keynote (oh it was marvelous!), in which she talked about Obama's election as an opportunity to get back to the work of creating a better society. She urged us all to take the next step and work on the healing of the world. (She called us "the higher consciousness community.") Wayne Dyer's keynote was also a wonderful meditation on leaving behind the shallow, desire-driven manifestation craze of the *The Secret*, and moving toward the more authentic "yielding to the moment" spirituality expressed by the Tao Te Ching.

I went to workshops with Dr. Joan Borysenko and Dr. Judith Orloff, who marry psychology to spirituality and intuition and gave me solid tools to use in my life. I was transported by Byron Katie and "The Work," the most simple cognitive therapy in the world—and I felt myself drop pain and anger over an unexamined belief I'd been carrying around for two years. I walked around the rest of the day feeling so light and free, simply loving what is.

I went to see Dr. Bruce Lipton give a mind-blowing science-oriented talk on "The Biology of Belief," and learned that DNA does not control cells, the environment does. I loved the funny, smart Lipton, and how he described his shift from materialism to idealism when he discovered how cells really work. He talked about the human body as a communication device for the divine.

Dr. Joe Dispenza also held me rapt, echoing a lot of what Lipton said about how our emotions "wire" thinking habits into our brains, and how we can literally rewire ourselves. He had me hanging on every word, my mind literally lay there still and quiet to absorb what felt like waves of truth. Then he started talking about how his daughter manifested an "unlimited shopping spree" for herself and I felt a thud of disappointment.

I accidentally found myself in a manifestation workshop—there were so many it was near impossible to avoid—and when I realized it, I wanted to bolt. But I was eventually won over by the lovely author, Alan Cohen, who turned on a little light for me about the ways manifestation efforts can help us get clear about what we really want, and can help us align with the universe. Yet I also did a little exercise with the woman sitting next to me who was clearly tortured by the fact that after years of trying to manifest good health for herself, she is still in constant pain. She blames herself for not doing it "right."

There was a lot of buzz about Gregg Braden and his talk about 2012 and the planetary disasters to come as the earth's magnetic something or other gets thrown out of whack by crossing the equator of the galaxy. I didn't go to his workshop, but a number of people were talking about it. It sounded to me like a holdover over the 1980s-style excesses of the New Age movement—a mixture of one part science and three parts imaginative nonsense—and clearly, it is still attractive to people in certain stages of growth. It is surely no coincidence that one of Braden's biggest fans, a sweet person I liked very much, told me she was "turned off" by Marianne Williamson and her call for us to get to work for the good of the planet. Instead, she is stockpiling food for the coming 2012 disasters which Braden convinced her cannot be avoided. Interestingly, the panel at the end of the conference, which included Borysenko, Cohen, Cheryl Richardson, and Neale Donald Walsch, made a point to distance themselves from the idea of 2012 as a significant date. In fact, Borysenko said the important date is now, and that its time for us to make a collective shift to a new state of mind that steers us away from disasters.

At the panel discussion, Richardson told the audience that she did know what comes after death, while Walsch claimed to have been "given" exact details of what the Afterlife is like. All in all, the conference seemed to me the perfect expression of the different stages of spiritual growth represented by the New Age today. Those in early stages who need to rely on authority, need to be sure, and those who have grown enough to be comfortable with the unknown, and are ready to let life and death unfold as it will. Those in the early stages want to take control and manifest, while those in later stages are ready to stop "arguing with reality," as Katie put it, and better learn to accept what is.

It was a glorious weekend for me—being uplifted and inspired by wonderful people, with wonderful people. I learned so much, and feel energized to keep orienting myself toward spirit, and away from ego. I am grateful, grateful. And more than ever, I love the New Age movement—or the higher consciousness movement, or whatever we want to call it. I love the bridge it builds for us, a bridge that leads to growth and a better life for us all. Now I just have to figure out how to throw a conference for people who don't have $440 to get in the door. Waves of truth should not be reserved only for the well-to-do.

Seeing the light

To understand the map of spiritual development is to understand so much more about the world and the people in it. We can see how any group of people who operate from Stage One egocentrism—whether in a struggling Third World nation or in a poverty-stricken inner city in the U.S.—gets stuck in a world of chaos and war and crime and violence. We can see how any group that operates from Stage Two fundamentalism is able to achieve more order, but will also quickly sacrifice the individual in fierce ethnocentric battles for dominance. We can see how any group that operates from Stage Three rationality has more concern for the individual, but is also destructive to the environment and often willing to sacrifice the individual to materialistic profit motives.

To understand the spiral also helps us see how one set of ideas can take on different shapes and tones. A religion experienced from Stage Two is more likely to present us with an unchanging and intolerant dictator-god, while the very same religion experienced through Stage Four allows us a more free-flowing, symbolic relationship with the divine. Or as Wilber puts it, there's a Stage Two version of Christ, a Stage Three version of Christ (the historical Jesus), a Stage Four version of Christ, and so on.

Likewise, New Age ideas interpreted from ego-based Stage One magical thinking allow Tarot card readers to make a good living catering to the self-absorbed, while the same ideas interpreted from Stage Five lead to an integral worldview that frees one from self-centered concerns and orients us toward the whole.

When we understand the spiral, we understand that our societal problems are not merely a battle between old paradigm and new paradigm, but a lack of knowledge of how each paradigm represents a different stage of growth. We understand why Marianne Williamson says, "Our biggest problems cannot be solved; our biggest problems must be outgrown." We understand why Barack Obama, in his 2009 inauguration speech, warned that if we want to create a government that works, and a country that fulfills its promise, we are going to have to "set aside childish things."

Bogged down on the spiral

With a basic grasp of spiritual development, it's easy to see that what many consider a spiritual crisis in the United States is actually a widespread lack of growth from one stage to the next. That includes not just those in the pre-conventional or conventional stages, but those of us lingering in post-conventional Stage Four as well. Too many of us have become entrenched where we are, unable to grow to the next stage and thereby lift the center of spiritual gravity for the whole.

That is why *an understanding of the spiral is absolutely key to any real transformation of society*. It must become common knowledge in the way it is common knowledge to know that once you are finished with grammar school, you will move on to high school, and then on to college if you so choose.

The only cure for the culture wars, and the paralyzing polarization of American society, is to make sure that more of us understand that all stages are valid and important stages in life, and that we are designed to evolve from one to the next. Stage Two religiosity is naturally supposed to give way to Stage Three skepticism, which is naturally supposed to develop into Stage Four idealism, which is naturally supposed to evolve into Stage Five integralism, and so forth. We need to make sure more of us understand that earlier stages are necessary preparation for later stages, and that being in one particular stage doesn't somehow make one better or smarter than someone in another stage. (Is a tenth-grader somehow better than a second-grader? No, they're simply at different stages in their learning.)

Furthermore, we have to make sure that the structures of each stage on the spiral remain sound, and that pathways to each stage remain open. If a Stage One young adult from the inner city being pressured to join a violent gang has no viable Stage Two alternative to help him make a different choice—a structured religion or school or sport or an institution like the military—then he's going to join the gang and stay stuck in Stage One.

In the same vein, if a Stage Three skeptic is ready to start exploring his spiritual side but finds no reasonable and clear-cut pathway to Stage Four, he is likely to just hunker down where he is and not understand why he feels so dissatisfied. This plight is actually so common that Wilber likens Stage Three (what he calls the orange meme) to the lid of a pressure cooker that keeps people trapped in lower stages.

Growing into Stage Four does seem to be a particular challenge of late. After all, the first widespread growth into Stage Four only recently started with the baby boomers in 1960s and 1970s, so we haven't had time to establish a lot of solid pathways to help us get there. The most popular and frequently used bridge from

Stage Three to Four was once the New Age movement in all its "do-it-yourself spirituality" permutations. But as we've seen, over the last few decades the structures of the New Age as a collective movement have crumbled from neglect.

True, the number of people languishing in Stage Three is, as Wilber says, due in large part to the pressure cooker lid of materialism that remains hostile to any hint of spirituality. But I am convinced that the disappearance of the New Age greatly exacerbates the problem. First, rather than being able to mount a coherent challenge to the assertions of materialism, the voices representing a new paradigm are so scattered that they can only take a few ineffectual potshots here and there. Second, without that wide and welcoming New Age bridge between stages—easy to find and access—people simply have a harder time figuring out how to get to Stage Four. Meanwhile, those who were left there after the bridge's collapse have no way to grow *out* of it, and into Stage Five.

For those of us who understand that we are running out of time to turn society around and give our children a viable future, this being stuck on the spiral is a monumental problem. For those of us who want to get ourselves unstuck, it's long past time to ask, "What happened to the New Age?"

Top Five Myths about the New Age

The first step in rescuing the New Age, and rescuing ourselves, is to insist on the true meaning of the movement. The mainstream circulates a number of myths about the New Age that have been repeated so often they are taken to be common knowledge about the movement. What they really are is common errors, and it's time to set the record straight.

Myth #1: The New Age is an occult revival

Go to any big chain bookstore, look on the shelf marked New Age, and you will find hundreds of books on how to develop your psychic powers, how to talk to the dead, how to cast Wiccan spells, how to divine the future, and all manner of esoteric subjects. This expediency of bookselling has somehow evolved into the cultural definition of the New Age as an occult revival. But in fact, one is only loosely related to the other.

Yes, a fair number of New Agers do have an interest in the occult or paranormal subjects, as do many non-New Agers. The idealism of the New Age gives us a picture of reality that allows for many possibilities ruled out by materialism and also provides a sense of philosophical freedom to explore and experiment with different ways of knowing. But just because the New Age accommodates the occult without demonizing it doesn't mean that it encourages belief in occult practices.

Genuine idealism actually discourages preoccupations with anything other than the here and now experience. Furthermore, it gives us a comprehensive set of rules of knowledge so that we may better recognize what is real and what is not (see *Chapter 10, Truth & Knowledge*). It also stresses the acceptance of reality even when it doesn't match our hopes and preconceptions.

The occult, like all esoteric subjects, focuses on mysteries and exclusive societies that pass on special "secrets." But New Age idealism does not come cloaked in secret. The New Age movement is an inclusive endeavor based on openness and transparency. Occult mysteries simply don't hold up very well under the light the New Age hopes to shine on reality.

There is indeed a thriving market for occult material today, as there always has been. But the cultural lumping together of the New Age and the occult has no foundation in reality. And there is no more reason to equate the New Age with the occult than with any other subject that is popular in the New Age. Certainly more New Agers have an interest in Buddhism than in the occult, and yet we don't see bookstores slapping "New Age" over the section on Eastern religions. Or the section on alternative health. Or the sections on physics, or humanistic psychology, or environmentalism or any of the other subjects that attract New Age interest.

It's time to take the New Age sign off the shelves of books on ghosts and divination and simply call them by their real name: The Occult.

Myth #2: The New Age teaches that "you create your own reality"

A number of subcultures flourish within the New Age movement—both lofty (integral theory academics) and not so lofty (channeling disciples). But the most visible subculture is undoubtedly the cottage industry that promotes "conscious creation," or prosperity consciousness. Indeed, it often appears that the New Age is *only* about disseminating prosperity consciousness, and with the recent runaway success of Rhonda Byrnes' DVD and book, *The Secret*, the year 2009 is one of those times.

The conscious creation concept is based on a much-touted Law of Attraction that first emerged with the New Thought Movement in the late nineteenth century. New Thought philosophy takes idealistic principles and then carries them to their most literal conclusion. Myrtle Fillmore with her Unity Church, Ernest Holmes with his Church of Religious Science, and Mary Baker Eddy with her Christian Science all claimed to have discovered an "ancient law" that says thoughts actually become real. The universe, says the law, inevitably mirrors your thoughts back to you in the form of concrete things and events, and by thinking correctly, you can produce any outcome you want.

The Law of Attraction is the basis of thousands of other "thoughts are things" style books that have appeared again and again over the last century. Every few years, the idea is repackaged and presented as a revolutionary new "secret" that will help us manifest our every desire—from money to jobs to houses to love to cures for disease.

These books sell very well because they help us feel empowered. And I do believe there are some hugely valuable ideas wrapped up in the "you create your own reality" philosophy. Idealism tells us that the material world is indeed a mental concept, and that our mental environment has great influence over how reality *appears* to us. Idealism also agrees that it behooves us to pay attention to our thoughts and intentions, and notice how much of what happens to us is a result of self-fulfilling prophecy. And certainly, when it comes to the human body, thoughts really are biochemical things that impact physical health and well-being.

Yet, an overly literal belief in conscious creation can also lead us astray. Genuine idealism, especially in its more Eastern forms, tells us that our thoughts are not real at all, but are, in fact, a bunch of meaningless noise churned up by the ego. Idealism tells us that the best tactic in dealing with thoughts is to stop identifying with them and let them go.

Of course, after putting conscious creation into practice for awhile, one stumbles over a number of problems with the supposed foolproof law. First, if everything that happens to me is a result of my own belief-injected thoughts, then why am I so often disappointed by expectations unmet and surprised by events unimagined? Then there is the truly offensive "blame the victim" ramifications of the law, which implies that we are responsible for attracting events like illnesses or natural disasters or criminal attacks.

But beyond the illogic of it all, most of us find that even after months of herding our thoughts around like sheepdogs, we pretty much receive from the universe what we want no more or no less often than anyone else. We discover most thoughts really are silly noise, and they hurt us or help us only to the extent we are able to stop attaching to them. So in the long run, the mix of successes and failures of the Law of Attraction actually does teach us a great deal about the true nature of our thoughts and their impact on our lives.

My only real problem with the Law of Attraction is that it so often represents a seeker's first exposure to supposed New Age ideas, and when that seeker finds herself disappointed in the law, she is likely to walk away from the movement believing all New Age ideas to be just as intellectually unsound and ineffective.

That is unfortunate, because even though prosperity consciousness has found wild success within the New Age market, it is not truly supported by New Age idealism. A true spiritual idealist is far more likely to be sitting in meditation and trying to detach from thoughts and outcomes than in trying to manifest them. Yes, there is much common ground between New Thought and New Age, but the Law of Attraction is its own assertive, stand-alone philosophy and should not be equated with the New Age. (For a more in-depth look at what idealism really means when it tells us we "create" our own reality, see *Chapter 14: Creating Reality*.)

Myth #3: The New Age promotes one-world religion

The New Age emphasis on the underlying unity of all of mankind in the context of spirit has often been interpreted to mean that the New Age wants nothing more than for all of us to cleave together in the one world religion so ominously prophesied in the Book of Revelations. This massive religion, some Christians fear, will then have unparalleled power to dominate the world.

This assumption is so far removed from what we actually see in the New Age that I cannot help but laugh whenever I stumble across it. The fact is, New Agers are so aggressively independent, and so determined to strike out on their own paths, that some social observers have wondered whether there is even such a thing as a New Age movement at all. Far from massing together into one-world religion, New Agers famously take the cafeteria approach to belief and drift about in a million different self-styled religions of one. Rather than grab for power, New Agers tend to toss their small share of power into the winds of individualism and watch it drift away.

True, I am arguing in this book that we New Agers should indeed start joining together in a common identity, but I advocate a symbolic identity meant to help us work together to realize our common hope of harmony. Neither I, nor any New Ager, would ever advocate an identity that demands specific belief or dogma.

The New Age is based in a philosophy that is open to question, not insistent on answers. It is not about starting a religion; it is about serving as a vehicle by which many people discover and explore many religions. From Eastern religions such as Buddhism and Zen and Taoism, to aboriginal and pagan religions and even different forms of Christianity, New Agers have proven remarkably open to embracing all types of religions.

However, just because we observe—and celebrate—the common religious feeling that exists at the heart of different traditions, doesn't mean we are trying to erase their individual distinctness. We do not want to "reduce the religious orchestra of the universe to mere monotones," as one Hindu teacher wrote. On the contrary, we believe each tradition gains greater relevance and meaning to be seen in the context of the whole.

We understand that in order to move billions of disparate people up the mountain, and up the spiral of development toward spirit, we need the use of many disparate paths. We understand Christianity to be a true and powerful path toward God. Indeed, many of the most liberal of spiritual explorers find that their journeys lead them back to Christianity, as we have seen with renowned religion scholar Huston Smith, and popular writers like Anne Lamott.

We New Agers respectfully honor the wisdom of all religions. And okay, I admit, I've hung a Celtic knot over the ceramic Buddha on my bathroom counter. But I don't want to mash the two traditions together or erase the uniqueness of each symbol. I just enjoy the sight of the two symbols sitting there in harmony, complementing each other.

The New Age recognizes that the world is vast and varied. It assures us there is enough room for all beliefs to coexist peacefully, "each verified in its own way, from hour to hour and from life to life," in the words of philosopher-psychologist William James, "each attitude being a syllable in human nature's total message." It takes the whole of us—and all our traditions and viewpoints—to spell out the meaning completely.

Myth #4: New Age beliefs are intellectually unsound

There is an entire cottage industry, spearheaded by the materialism-based magazine *The Skeptical Inquirer,* devoted to the debunking of silly ideas. The assumption of this industry—which has infected the culture at large—is that because many silly ideas like trance channeling or "you create your own reality" pop up in the New Age, the entire set of New Age ideas are silly. This blanket assumption gets tossed over all New Agers, who are then characterized as not-too-bright and sadly lacking in critical thinking skills.

It is true that the New Age movement has seen its share of crazy scams and schemes. It is also true that scamming and scheming goes on in all parts of society, targeting all types of audiences, be they religious or secular. Pyramid schemes, pills that melt your fat, Pat Robertson telling his followers that God wants them to send him money—scams and cons are common in all times, in all places, with people of all kinds of beliefs.

We cannot judge a philosophy solely by its lowest common denominator. Any set of beliefs is subject to the individual's abilities of discernment, and as individuals, we all live from different levels of spiritual development (see *Chapter 2: The Map of Spiritual Growth*). Thus we see materialism expressed at one end of the spectrum by common thievery, and at the other end by the noble ideals of secular humanism. Or we see Christianity expressed at one end of the spectrum by cults and snake-handling Pentecostals, and at the other end by the transformational ideology of Martin Luther King, Jr.

New Age idealism is likewise expressed at one end of the spectrum by phony psychics or channelers of alien messages, and at the other end by the spirit-filled poetry of Rumi or the meticulously constructed integral system of Ken Wilber. The gullibility and lack of discernment of those who hang out at the lower end of the New Age spectrum does not mean the whole spectrum is lacking.

We need to keep in mind that the New Age isn't really new at all, but the latest expression of the perennial philosophy that has been enlightening minds and uplifting souls for thousands of years. It is absurd to suggest that this time-tested philosophy is somehow lacking in intellectual rigor. The thinkers and philosophers who delineated this philosophy are prominent and many—Pythagoras and Plato, Spinoza and Hegel, Emerson and Thoreau. As William Irwin Thompson notes in *Reimagination of the World*, one can't dismiss the work of such men "without pulling apart the architecture of Western civilization."

Myth #5: The New Age is the work of Satan

The New Age movement puts forth many messages about unity, interdependence, love, compassion, hope, peace, and harmony. Never once have I heard a New Ager promote anything negative or evil. Never once have I heard a New Ager trash Jesus or the Bible or Christianity. In fact, countless New Age books pay homage to Jesus as the wisest of men. And yet…

Fundamentalist Christian literature is rife with books that characterize the New Age as evil, a plot hatched by the devil to lure good people away from God and onto the slippery slope to hell. Of course, fundamentalists believe *any* non-Christian idea or belief is a threat, yet a prominent number display a particular animosity toward New Age ideas. The New Age movement, says one professor of theology, "is the most dangerous enemy of Christianity in the world today."

This is the most odious and most destructive of all myths about the New Age. Here we live in a country celebrated for its diversity, a country founded on the principles of freedom and tolerance, yet we still have individuals using religion as an excuse to accuse those with different beliefs of being evil.

Of course, one reason Christians are so fearful of the movement is because of inaccurate myths like the ones above—the New Age promotes one world religion, the New Age promotes the occult. The irony is that it is Christian writers who did most of the work in building up these myths in the first place. They are basically crying out in alarm at a picture of the New Age they themselves have painted.

Although most Christians today are enlightened enough—and secure enough in their spirituality—to allow that there are many paths up the mountain, traditional Christianity is a religion that rests on claims of exclusivity. Fundamentalist Christians have every right to cleave to the scriptural assertion that their religion is the only path of salvation. They have every right to express their opinion that others may be wrong, or are lost. But to encourage the view that others are puppets of evil for their different understanding of God is in itself a most evil thing.

We New Agers tend to brush off such talk, rightly believing that it says far more about the fearful minds that put forth the accusation than it does about us. But if we let intolerance stand—whether it is directed at New Agers or those of other religions or sexual orientation—then we allow it to flourish. To accuse anyone of being "the enemy" or in cahoots with the devil is essentially hate speech, and should never be tolerated, in public or in private.

These myths about the New Age are misunderstandings based on a lack of complete information, but that doesn't mean they are harmless. Their steady circulation helps the mainstream push the movement, and its healing idealism, to the fringe of society, and ensures that it can never be a threat to the status quo.

But we New Agers very much want to challenge the status quo. We very much want to bring real change to our society. We therefore cannot passively cooperate with mainstream attempts to marginalize us. We cannot let these myths about the New Age stand. We have to replace them with the truth whenever we see an opportunity to do so.

When you hear a myth repeated about the New Age, take a moment to correct it. Tell the manager of the bookstore that New Age and the occult are not the same thing. If you run across an article that uses the term New Age to describe some whacky, intellectually unsound idea, shoot an e-mail to the writer and object to the misuse and degradation of the term. Most important, if you see or hear a religious attack against the New Age that suggests it is the work of Satan, do not allow such intolerance to pass unremarked.

The New Age might not be a religion in the usual definition of the word, but as a philosophy that serves to connect us with Spirit, New Agers should be accorded the respect allowed any other spiritual belief system. We have a right to be proud of the New Age. But if we don't start standing up for the true essence of the movement, we might as well get used to skulking around the edges of society, invisible and ineffective, without the rights or the respect to which we are entitled.

PART II

The Decline and Fall of the New Age

Something stronger than humanity—call it what you will, necessity, fate, God—has laid hold of humanity and will not lose its grasp. To be sure, even the leaders of the race have often been tempted to discouragement. Man has given them hemlock to drink, crucified them, burned them at the stake. But always the falling torch has been caught by another hand, and somehow the light has gone on.

— HARRY EMERSON FOSDICK —

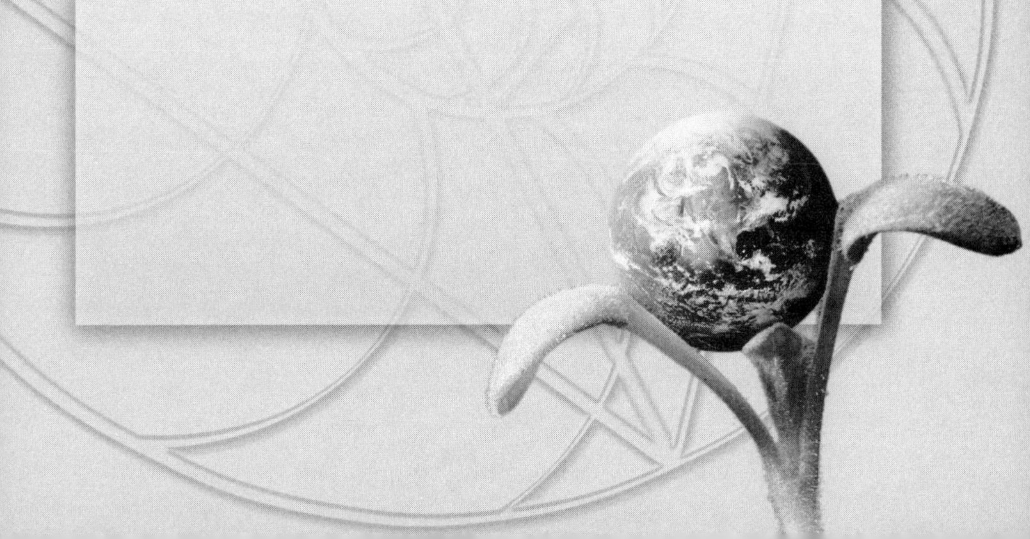

3 The New Age Under Attack

Back in the 1980s, most of us swept up by the New Age movement were certain the social phenomenon would continue to grow. It was, we believed, inevitable. The laws of evolution dictated that the human race would keep developing in awareness until we reached critical mass and tipped the whole of society into a new age of harmony.

It was, we believed, necessary for the survival of humankind. Nuclear proliferation and environmental damage had us poised on the brink of disaster, and the only way to save our future would be a paradigm shift arriving just in the nick of time. We felt this would be increasingly clear to all, and our numbers would swell, and swell some more...

Yet, over the next few decades, the term New Age began to fall from favor. Throughout the 1990s, even the most New Age-y people were actively distancing themselves from a label that had suddenly become pop culture shorthand for any kind of flaky, woo-woo idea. By 2002, the movement's most well-known publication, *New Age Journal*, changed its name to *Body + Soul*. Not long after, the popular reference Web site, About.com, dropped its New Age category altogether. It was official: the New Age was no more.

No one protested its disappearance, at least not publicly. Certainly no one seemed surprised to see it go. And now, today, almost no one identifies with the term New Age anymore.

Of course, from the number of holistic/idealistic sites on the Web, along with the $200 billion Americans spend in the alternative lifestyle market, we know the movement didn't really go anywhere, at least not as an individual spiritual pursuit. Most people would say it just shed an unhelpful and unrepresentative label. But in the interests of learning from history, it would be helpful to ask, what happened to the optimistic and revolutionary New Age-ness of it all? What happened to the collective social phenomenon poised to save the world?

Although a more important question might be: Now that global warming has pushed us *beyond* the brink of disaster and our survival is even more in doubt, is it really in our best interests to let the New Age stay lost?

Catching it from all sides

Two thousand years ago, when the Christian worldview first emerged to challenge the polytheistic status quo, the upstart Christians were gleefully fed to the lions. Four hundred years ago, when materialistic science first challenged the Christianity-dominated status quo, the upstart scientists like Galileo were hauled before the Holy Office of the Inquisition and tossed into prison.

I suppose we should count ourselves lucky that when the New Age brought the first large-scale wave of idealism to challenge the status quo, we upstart New Agers weren't devoured by wild beasts or locked up. However, following the venerable human tradition of hostility toward new ideas, the New Age was immediately set upon by both scientific materialism and religious dualism.

Many a science writer relished the role of "debunker," dismissing New Age beliefs in general and poking fun at New Age believers in particular. According to the science-minded, New Agers lacked critical thinking skills and lived in a fantasy land of their own making.

Yet, far more upsetting were the accusations leveled by Christian writers. An entire subgenre of books were issued from Christian publishers, which declared the New Age a plot of Satan to take over the world. Even today, if you type "New Age" into an Internet search engine, the first five pages of results are pretty much nothing but fundamentalist Web sites that accuse the evil New Age of trying to seduce good Christians away from their religion.

This reprehensible campaign had the intended effect of making the nice people of the New Age afraid to offend their neighbors and hesitant to identify with their own movement. When the majority opinion is that your beliefs make you a crackpot or the devil's handmaiden or both, it becomes ever more difficult to openly explore, let alone celebrate, those beliefs. Which, of course, is exactly why the status quo attacks in the first place. Attacks work.

History Lesson #1

If we don't do a better job of defining ourselves,
our detractors will be happy to do it for us.

An image problem; or the pre/post fallacy

Attacks on the New Age rarely originated from genuine knowledge of the movement and its intellectual underpinnings. Rather, the movement's critics usually responded to the superficial image of the movement created by a cynical media.

In a decade defined by Reagan-style religiosity and Wall Street-driven materialism, the mainstream media of the 1980s downplayed the New Age's legitimate ideas and their benefits, and shone an out-of-context spotlight on the more kooky practices happening under the New Age umbrella.

Reporters looking for a good story were understandably attracted to the entertainment value of the movement's colorful fringe—psychics, trance channelers, alternative healers. But in going for flash over substance, they created an indelible image of the New Age as a gathering of hucksters and clueless eccentrics. They then took the image they themselves created, and went on to heap ridicule upon it. For example, David Brooks, a pundit for PBS and the *New York Times*, called New Agers "vaporheads."

Considering the popular image of the movement the media presented to us, who could blame them for their opinions? After all, what sensible person would *want* to walk around with a pyramid perched on her head?

According to William Irwin Thompson, the media attention to the Harmonic Convergence in 1987 was the point at which the noise of mass media "overwhelmed the transcendental signal." Under the skewed glare of the media spotlight, the New Age *kairos*—its opportune moment—simply collapsed.

I do agree with Thompson; however, the image problem suffered by the New Age goes far beyond the media stampede toward mockery. The essence of the problem lies in a nearly universal lack of knowledge of spiritual stages and levels of growth.

With a map of spiritual development in hand, we can see that many products and claims coming from the New Age of the 1980s poured directly from pre-rational Stage One magical thinking. I don't think the media can be faulted for noticing this. But there was also a lot of profound post-rational Stage Four and Five growth and exploration going on as well that deserved the media's respect. Huge numbers of people used transpersonal psychology to put aside harmful habits of thinking and to break addictions, or used alternative medicine to heal their bodies of trauma or disease, or used insights from the great wisdom traditions to better connect with God and each other.

Unfortunately, the media assumes, as many do, that *all* spirituality—whether traditional religion or alternative New Age—is pre-rational, or *non-rational*. As Wilber notes, "Any transpersonal, nondual spirituality is unceremoniously lumped with, and dumped into, the pre-personal garbage pail."

All non-rational worldviews are treated as basically the same, even though pre-rational and post-rational spiritualities are poles apart. Wilber calls this "the pre/post fallacy," and believes that this common error is a huge obstacle in our collective evolution up the spiral of development.

"The means of our liberation are confused with the cause of most of our misery," Wilber concludes. "In running from what appears to be the cause of suffering, we are running from our salvation."

Those ready to grow beyond Stage Three rationality toward higher post-rational awareness are afraid to budge. Meanwhile, those in Stage Four and Five feel they must disown the New Age, or any other post-rational label, in order to avoid being tarred with the Stage One brush.

History Lesson #2

If a reporter asks you about the New Age,
don't send him to a psychic fair;
instead, hand him or her a map
of spiritual growth.

The New Age becomes a market – Part 1

One of the best things to happen to the movement was the discovery of an adventurous group of consumers known as the New Age market. This led to the first real attempts at organizing information about the movement and pinpointing its audience and their various interests.

Likewise, one of the worst things to happen to the movement was the discovery of the New Age as a market, especially in the book world. When an idealistic movement becomes subject to the materialistic goals of maximum financial gain, then the idealism gets trampled underfoot.

Mainstream publishers began in typically mainstream fashion by chopping the subject up into ever smaller niches for target audiences. Although the biggest-selling New Age books (*Celestine Prophecy, Conversations with God*) were broad and sweeping looks at idealistic principles—books that clearly satisfied a broad and sweeping hunger among seekers—publishers continued to chop and narrow until it was difficult to find anything on a New Age shelf except off-the-wall subjects like feng shui for the bathroom or the prophecies of Nostradamus.

This caused widespread category confusion; narrow, irrelevant niches made the entire New Age look narrow and irrelevant, and those truly curious about the larger New Age picture found little but crumbs to fuel their interest. Serious students looking for depth found little to study. (The exception: small presses like Shambhala or Hampton Roads.)

The publishers who pushed the New Age to the fringe then began to complain that they were losing mainstream consumers for their spiritual books. In an attempt to escape the problem they themselves had created, they scrapped the New Age category altogether, caring little that they were throwing the baby out with the bathwater.

Today, publishers trying to reach the holistic shopper use a new, broad category—Mind/Body/Sprit—a designation that means everything and nothing. Meanwhile, book stores still slap the phrase "New Age" over their shelves of occult, paranormal, and astrology books, as if that's all there is to it.

It's no wonder that Michael Grosso, author of *The Millenium Myth*, calls the New Age a "publishing artifact." It's also no wonder that even the most dedicated idealist now equates New Age with subjects that have nothing to do with real spiritual transformation, while authors of books on real spiritual transformation avoid the New Age label like the plague. "To be called New Age today," wrote David Spangler as early as 1989, "is the kiss of death intellectually, academically, and professionally."

Subjected to a market that operates by the rules of materialism, idealism is mercilessly trampled underfoot.

History Lesson #3
Fine chopping might be good for general reference, but the big ideas that lead to transformation can't be squeezed into a marketing niche.

The New Age becomes a market – Part 2

While publishers were confusing the New Age consumer, other companies were doing far more damage. Like the snake-oil salesmen of old, a wide range of companies peddled useless products and remedies to New Agers with minds more open, and expectations more grand, than the average consumer. Whether it was a pyramid on the head, or the advice of a so-called trance channeler, we with open minds and open wallets too often discovered that the main benefit of New Age products and therapies went to the seller in the form of cash.

Of course, New Agers themselves often contributed to the problem with gullibility and a propensity for magical thinking. But whether they deserved their disillusionment or not, many ended up feeling ripped off and fled the movement with the feeling of "this is a bunch of crap."

History Lesson #4
Transformation cannot be bought.

The New Age becomes a market – Part 3

The New Age movement began with the intention to free us from the old paradigm, but the seductive market beckoned to us with its entertainments and false promises. Principles meant to free us were instead put to use to help us succeed within the framework of the old paradigm. Instead of learning to live mindfully in the moment, we went to Tarot card readers to learn our futures.

Instead of aspiring to compassion and practicing loving-kindness, we aspired to prosperity and practiced *The Secret*.

In the saddest of ironies, the New Age as a market reinforced the old paradigm rather than dismantling it, and too often rendered genuine New Age impulses impotent.

History Lesson #5

The old paradigm has ways to keep us playing its games.

A political darkness descends

By the end of the 1990s, the New Age movement was clearly on the decline, although its most visible leaders—Marianne Williamson, Neale Donald Walsch, and Deepak Chopra among others—were still working to organize its adherents under a common identity with a noble project called the Global Renaissance Alliance, which inspired hundreds of positive-thinking "peace circles" nationwide.

Then events began unfolding on the world stage which tossed us all into turmoil.

The first blow was the 2000 election—some call it the stolen election—that put George W. Bush in the White House. Less than a year later, we were blindsided by the terrorist attacks of 9/11, the most shocking and soul-shaking event of our time. As if this were not horrific enough, we were then forced to watch as our own government manufactured reasons to declare war on Iraq.

Then came the final straw: The re-election of George W. Bush and the hard knowledge that the majority of Americans actually preferred the path of destruction over harmony.

Idealistic hopes for the future were dashed hard upon these rocks. During the long years of war and deficit and disaster, it often felt ridiculous—even insensitive—to prattle on about the possibilities for a more positive, harmonious future.

Under the shadow of our long political darkness, there was simply not enough light to help the ailing New Age movement gain new life.

History Lesson #6

Progress never unfolds in a straight line.

Clearly, the social pressures from the outside were immense and devastating to the movement. And although it is tempting to stop here and blame the collapse of the New Age entirely on outside pressures, the truth is, the movement ultimately fell prey to much more serious challenges from within.

4 Who Needs a Movement?

As soon as the New Age came to the attention of the mainstream, attacks from critics inflicted all kinds of damage on the fledgling movement. It was then undermined by the forces of the materialistic market. World events shook its foundations still further. However, if we New Agers had decided to rally together and stand up for our beliefs, pressures from the outside would not have had such destructive impact.

But that's not what we did. Instead of defending our movement and the ideals from which it was born, we surrendered it to the popular culture for mockery and mutation. Then we walked away, distancing ourselves from it as quickly as possible.

In the end, the New Age movement was undone by its own adherents.

Why did we walk away? Why did we abandon a movement that could have—should have—helped us transform society? Interestingly, the idealism of the New Age is itself largely to blame.

A pathless land

Idealism, especially its Eastern varieties, has always been quick to tell us that a particular spiritual path really isn't all that necessary. As Krishnamurti famously put it, "Truth is a pathless land and you cannot approach it by any path whatsoever."

The more we delve into the idealistic viewpoint, especially in its Zen and Advaita expressions, the more we are told that all religious and spiritual systems are merely thought constructs that are essentially meaningless. The more we are exposed to New Age philosophy and books and teachers, the more we are encouraged to stop identifying with New Age philosophy books and teachers.

"Real spirituality is about having no answers at all," writes Joan Tollifson in her marvelous book *Awake in the Heartland*. "It is about living without formulas, without conclusions, without beliefs, without comforting ideas, without saviors." Real spirituality, she adds, asks that we "drop all the labels, categories and frames that we use to contain experience," and simply "be present, without answers."

No wonder the *New Age Journal*, back in 1997 when it was still willing to call itself *New Age Journal* (it is now *Body + Soul*), called the New Age "the movement without name." And no wonder that Steven Sutcliffe, in his book on the movement's history, said that one reason the New Age appealed to so many was because it "was open to all, yet with no stigmatizing label or fussy membership criteria."

Indeed, for the path-avoiding idealist, labels are anathema, for a number of mostly good reasons:

♦ **Labels are anti-individual**

While other philosophies may be inflexible and absolute, New Age idealism is highly relativistic and encourages us all to blaze our own paths. We New Agers don't see ourselves as part of a faithful flock. We enjoy the role of intrepid explorer, trying on this tradition or that. And from the perspective of an unanchored explorer, no homogenizing label can be "right," no label can accurately describe the unique blend of practices of my religion of one.

And so we find that the mere mention of the phrase New Age

usually elicits little but patronizing, above-it-all smiles from those who most fit the profile. "No, not me," they say. "I'm a seeker, a wanderer, I can't be pinned down."

◆ **Labels are superficial**

Media images portray New Agers caught up in flighty nonsense, but a true New Ager is very concerned with depth and meaning. Most of us want to get past surface distractions in order to connect with the source of reality, and we have studied enough to know that "the Tao that can be named is not the real Tao," and that "the finger that points to the moon is not the moon." If we name our path, or otherwise get hung up on labels, then we feel we are headed away from reality rather than into it.

◆ **Labels are ego-driven**

Some games of the ego are hard to recognize, but labeling is not one of them. It is easy to see that the desire to be seen as a particular type of person, or qualify for this or that label, is usually the desire of the ego to be special. The ego wants to be different from others, wants to stand apart, stand out, and be named. American, Republican, Democrat, writer, doctor, lawyer, teacher, introvert, extrovert, jock, bookworm, gamer, computer geek, vegetarian, peacenik—there is no end to the ways we can make ourselves unique through a string of labels.

Of course, we know the soul cares nothing for categories and names. We know the soul is concerned only with the awareness of this moment. We know the soul is simple consciousness without adjective, emptiness without name. Thus, if I pin a label on myself, I cannot help but feel as if I am caving in to the dark side of ego.

Indeed, our own teachers openly scold those who might wish to align with a label. In a 2001 essay for *Re-Vision* magazine, Mariana Caplan complained that spirituality had become a fad. "It is a household term, a commodity that is bought and sold... an identity, a club to belong to." She made it clear that a truly spiritual person doesn't care about identity, and certainly doesn't need to belong to a group.

- **Labels are divisive**

Religious dualists depend on labels to keep themselves separate from others, whether it's Catholic or Christian or Muslim or Jewish. In the same vein, many use other types of labels to push others out of the mainstream, or mark them for attack, or as weapons to beat them into submission. Meanwhile, materialists are positively label-obsessed, chopping all experience up into the smallest possible slices in order to better control it.

Thus, if labels are incomplete at best, and harmful at worst, we figure it best to avoid them altogether.

This is merely a partial grocery list of an idealist's reasons to avoid labeling, reasons why, even in its heydey, only a minority of those who held New Age beliefs identified with the term. These are also some of the reasons why Sutcliffe says all New Age efforts to pin down a "stronger collective identity" are met with an "inbuilt resistance at the heart of the phenomenon."

Essentially, *the very beliefs that make me a New Ager all but require me to deny being a New Ager*!

So then what do New Age-y types call themselves? If pressed, they might say they are "sort of Buddhist" or "a little bit Zen," even if they've never entered a Buddhist temple or meditated more than once or twice. Or they might be "into yoga" or "reading about Taoism lately." Or, they might say they are "experimenting with Wicca" or "going through my Celtic phase" or "taking Kabbalah." Or, they could be Unitarian Universalist, or Religious Scientist, or even "Christian with an open mind."

Most, however, simply call themselves spiritual.

Spiritual but not religious

In September 2005, *Newsweek* ran a cover story about "Spirituality in America." The magazine printed poll results to the question, "Which best describes you?" Sixty-four percent of respondents identified themselves as one of the categories of "religious." Meanwhile, 24 percent identified themselves as "spiritual but not religious."

Do these 24 percent of spiritual Americans necessarily hold to New Age-style idealism? If we look at clues offered within the poll, it appears that a definite majority do.

When asked "What happens when we die?" a total of 18 percent gave answers that are explicitly idealistic, either saying the soul lives in a non-dualistic spiritual realm (13 percent), or is reincarnated (5 percent).

Another indication is found in the answers offered to the question, "How traditional are your religious practices?" Nineteen percent said "not traditional" and another 6 percent said, "On the cutting edge," for a total of 25 percent.

Other evidence that "spiritual" has become the innocuous codename for New Age beliefs can be found on the shelves of any bookstore. Peek inside most any book with the word spirituality in its title—say, for example, *Spirituality for Dummies*—and you will find a perfect description of the idealism once made popular by the New Age.

Not so coincidentally, the *Newsweek* number of "spiritual but not religious" nearly matches the percentage of Americans who are Cultural Creatives according to sociologists Paul Ray and Sherry Ruth Anderson. Their 2000 book, *The Cultural Creatives*, based on survey research studies on more than 100,000 Americans, concluded that 26 percent of adults in the U.S.—or fifty million people—have made a "shift in their worldview, values and way of life." Ray and Anderson go on to describe this "new" worldview, which again, is the same idealism that was declared new thirty years earlier when the New Age first hit the cultural scene.

So here we are, with a huge slice of the population sharing a similar spiritual idealism. Such numbers should give us an enormous impact on our culture, our institutions, our politics, our future. But even a cursory glance at society will tell you that while some of our ideas have trickled into the mainstream, real impact has been slight. Eight years after his book appeared, Paul Ray said he was still being faced with the question, "Why haven't we seen more evidence of cultural creative values in the public sphere?" (*What is Enlightenment?* Aug-Oct 2008)

His answer was that we are stuck in a "cultural identity crisis."

Clearly, our choice to avoid labels comes at a huge price.

We are isolated

I have been to Sedona, Arizona, and Ashland, Oregon, and found thriving alternative communities, where people openly share their spiritual ideals, and hopes, and dreams, and engage each other often. But those special places are few and far between in our largely center-right country.

For the rest of us living in more typical cities and towns, we spiritual idealists often feel stranded, trying to make ourselves at home in communities where we feel "no one is like me." Visit any New Age-style Web site with a community forum, and you will find the spiritual-but-not-religious contingent talking about how isolated they feel, how lonely.

Of course, they probably know quite a few people who share the same beliefs, but because spiritual idealists so strenuously avoid identity and labels, there is no easy way to recognize each other, no way to connect to each other on common ground. When you blaze your own trail, there simply is no common ground, there is only the haphazard crossing of paths.

We are invisible

How can we bring idealistic values into our collective way of life if we don't identify ourselves, don't identify who are and what we believe and what we want? How can we challenge the status quo, let alone transform it, if we are floating along in quiet ambiguity? The answer is: we can't.

Because we choose not to be counted as a particular something, we literally do not count. And by default, all our desires, our dreams, our hopes, our agenda for a better society—they do not count either. As Marianne Williamson acknowledged in an interview posted online, the "huge cultural revolution in this country...remains unnamed and therefore pretty much invisible to the old order."

Indeed, the 2005 *Newsweek* story on spirituality in America shone spotlights on Christians, Pentecostals, Jews, Muslims, and Buddhists, along with several other traditional expressions of religious feeling. But although their own poll showed that 24 percent of us are "spiritual but not religious," not once in the sixteen-page article did those 24 percent receive a mention. Only in the last paragraph, of the last sidebar, of the last page, is there a short description of the type of spiritual journey being undertaken by this huge slice of America.

We are ineffective

Unnamed, unidentified, and uncounted, is it any wonder we are so woefully ineffective?

For one thing, a group that does not accept that it is a group cannot communicate as a group, and certainly cannot reach a consensus about the goals worth collectively pursuing, let alone a strategy by which to pursue them. But even if we did have an agenda, we'd still be unable to access the power of our numbers.

Unlike religious dualists who proudly identify themselves and unify behind their conservative ideologies and organizations, we idealists haven't bothered to declare ourselves since the 1980s. We do not connect to each other, do not rally together; instead, we drift about on our own, dabbling here and there, for this cause or that, whenever the mood strikes.

In other words, we are completely lacking in what sociologists call social capital. Which is why, on too many election nights, we have sat stunned, wondering why our government and institutions do not reflect our ideals.

Our numbers cannot grow

Perhaps the most debilitating consequence of invisibility is that it prevents spiritual idealism from catching on. Every few years I make it a point to visit a local spiritual expo or conference, and each time I go I find a dwindling sea of graying women in attendance. There are a few older men here and there, even fewer younger women, and almost no younger men. One reason for the lack of diversity is that spiritual expos and conferences tend to be pricey and out of financial reach for younger people. Another reason is that formal gatherings don't necessarily appeal to the unanchored spiritual seeker. Yet I look around and cannot shake the feeling that this much-needed spirituality could possibly die out with the Baby Boom Generation. (Meanwhile, the new Christian mega-churches in my area have been assigned traffic cops to direct the flow of thousands of young people and families flocking in for multiple services each Sunday.)

Spirituality without a name, however vibrantly it lives in our own hearts, becomes anemic within the larger society and unable to sustain growth. Without a common identity we have no common ideas or vocabulary to express our convictions to others, and we cannot help others to grow in similar ways. We leave those who are dissatisfied with the old paradigm with nowhere to go except to sift through the hodgepodge of subjects that make up generic, noncommittal spirituality.

Case in point: I recently clicked on "Holistic Spirituality" on Beliefnet, which is the largest spirituality site on the Web. These are the options I was given: A lead article called, "Alarm Clocks are Bad for the Soul," links to astrology, numerology and Tarot sites, a treatise on how to get in touch with my angel guides, advice on how to keep a dream journal, and a photo gallery feature called, "The God Who Knits: A Spiritual Craft Gallery."

These are all interesting features, but nowhere did I find anything that helps me gain a workable understanding of an actual belief system, or spirit-based worldview. Click on almost any New Age page or directory, and you'll find the same thing, lists upon lists of esoteric subjects to explore, subjects that do not require us to examine our beliefs or develop a philosophy or become part of a community or make any kind of commitment to change.

Generic spirituality is a dead end. Real idealistic principles—the principles with the power to transform us—get lost in the shuffle. And so our numbers stay stagnant. We remain stuck at 24 percent of the population, an invisible and ineffectual minority, living in a society where the rules have been made by the *other* more visible and active minority—the religious conservatives who have worked tirelessly to build the social capital necessary for their regressive version of change.

The gravest obstacle

Many believe that the election of 2008 is a sign that the times they are a changin' again, and that idealistic values will now begin to hold sway in our society. But as Barack Obama himself said in his victory speech on election night, the outcome of the election didn't bring us change, it brought us "the *chance* for change." In 2008, the election gave us a way to unite under the common identity of "Obama supporter," and the social capital we created swept a progressive president into the White House.

But the election is over. How will we now build the social capital necessary to take advantage of this great opportunity to create a better world and to avert looming disasters such as global warming? Without a common identity to connect us, to unify us, to provide us with a clear purpose and guiding principles, creating change is profoundly more difficult.

Clearly Sutcliffe is right about the New Age—or holistic spirituality or whatever name we wish to call it—when he says our instinct to refuse identity is "the gravest obstacle to the lasting inroads on the primary institutions of the modern world that this spirituality would dearly like to make."

It is so important that we understand this. For at a time in history when the primary institutions of the modern world are *threatening the very survival of the planet*, our own blocking of progress is no mere annoyance.

In fact, it has become chillingly clear that our own blocking of progress is becoming the biggest threat of all.

5 Stuck on the Spiral

Spiritual development is not supposed to leave us lingering in a static condition. Idealism and developmental psychology both tell us we are meant to evolve through higher and higher stages of growth until we reach the nirvana of total unity with spirit.

Of course, true enlightenment is rare, but we're all familiar with examples of those who operate from Stage Five or Six—people like Mahatma Gandhi, Martin Luther King, Jr., Albert Schweitzer, Dag Hammarskjold, Elie Wiesel, Mother Theresa, the Dalai Lama, or any other number of selfless people who have been made famous on the world stage, or who have toiled quietly in our local communities. These people show us by example that with the right intention and a little effort, those of us living the abundant life of the twenty-first century should be able to grow into an integral worldview that will make possible the conditions for a new age of harmony.

But alas, we spiritual idealists have difficulty developing past Stage Four to the more mature, engaged spirituality of Stage Five. We've become stuck in place, and it's not in the profoundly deep "staying present and working our way down to reality" place. It's more of a flat "I should be able to do—or not do—whatever I want" ego-centered place.

We're stuck, and there's no getting around it, not when the evidence is all around us. Our technology has advanced by leaps and bounds, but our social systems, our institutions, our politics, along with our general approach to problems, are all still the same. Socially, not a lot has changed since the 1970s, despite our common acknowledgement that these systems have failed us. In his brilliant book *Community: The Structure of Belonging*, Peter Block calls us a "stuck community," trapped in a system that doesn't work despite a fervent desire for change.

We're stuck, and the reason, according to Wilber, has everything to do with how Stage Four idealism—which emerged in the West on a large scale for the first time with the Baby Boom Generation—has been flattened by the weight of our postmodern culture. We're stuck because of flatland idealism.

Trapped in flatland

When we first develop into Stage Four, or the individualist stage, we naturally experience a new sense of freedom from the confining absolutism of earlier stages. We finally understand that truth is relative to point of view, that no one person or tradition has a monopoly on truth, and that what we see depends on where we stand.

This is a big step that allows us to explore many different paths, which many of us are happy to do. Whether it's pagan nature worship or aboriginal shamanism or Celtic Christian mythology or the Jewish Kabbalah, we can dip into many traditions because we understand that all have a rightful place on the greater spectrum of truth. And they are all, in the Stage Four view, equally true and valid.

This pluralistic respect is all very well and good, not to mention a necessary step in our spiritual growth. The problem is that the New Age version of Stage Four became terribly attached to this view and took pluralistic respect to extremes, elevating what should have been a flexible relativism to hard and adamant dogma.

Instead of understanding that no one person has a monopoly on truth, we now believe *each* of us has a self-validated monopoly on truth. As no one else can see through my eyes, I am never wrong about what I see—nor how I interpret it. In the New Age, no matter what I believe, I am always right for me, my truth is always true, and no other idealist would dare point out my errors.

This is the positive Western all-men-are-created-equal expression of idealism, but the negative Eastern approach ends up in the same place. Buddhism and Advaita tell us that all views are illusory thought-constructs, and they are all equally valid because they are all equally *in*valid. We each dream up our own particular story of reality and no one story is any more real than any other.

Either way, because all views have equal validity, we cannot possibly claim that any one person's truth is higher or more developed than any other. The problem is, if all truths exist on the same flat plane, then stages of growth are ruled out by default. One cannot grow into a higher stage if one is required to deny that higher stages even exist. In the flatland of relativism there is literally nowhere to go, no progress to make. If our view changes, we assume we have merely switched to another spot that is ultimately no better or worse than the one we held before.

"Nothing is better, nothing is higher, nothing is deeper, all stances are equal in this egalitarian mush," writes Wilber.

This self-perpetuating, either/or Stage Four relativism has left us all in a state of arrested development. We cannot evolve up the spiral; in fact, we must reject the very idea of a spiral as an elitist hierarchy. Instead, we float around on currents of relative truth that go nowhere, and become sitting ducks for an epidemic that runs rampant through Stage Four. This epidemic is a virus of the ego, and it's called narcissism.

The New Age meets ego

A thousand years ago, Padmasambhava, the great Buddhist teacher who brought Buddhism from India to Tibet, predicted a long dark age in which "we could create myriad ways to keep ourselves entertained, becoming experts in how to spend free time," says the Tibetan teacher Sakyong Mipham Rinpoche, writing in *Shambhala Sun* (January 2009). Padmasambhava saw that "we would use our intellect not for betterment, but for hanging out in one form of distraction or another, constantly on holiday." And as we became more clever, "compassion would seem increasingly futile and we would forget how to bring meaning to our lives."

The great teacher's prescient words perfectly describe Western society today. So in talking about ego-run-amuck narcissism, we should probably first recognize that it is not uniquely a New Age problem, but is in fact, a problem widespread in Western culture, especially as it manifests in the United States. As Peter C. Whybrow notes in *American Mania*, our nation was built on "a foundation of unbridled self-interest and commercial freedom." Americans, he adds, are continually seduced by capitalism into unseemly "orgies of self-indulgence."

The irony is that New Age spirituality is meant to rescue us from the rampant self-interest of Western culture. Idealism, more than any other philosophy, attempts to shine a light on the ego's games. Idealism means to help us learn to see through them so that we may free ourselves of the ego's painful tightness and discover our true self, the soul. But in the New Age, our backwards understanding of relativism has become an ego inflater instead of the ego dissolver it was meant to be.

Now there's nothing wrong with a healthy ego. In fact, we cannot transcend an ego that is not strong and healthy, and an undeveloped and crippled ego can keep a person trapped in Stage One for a long and difficult lifetime.

However, an ego that protects and feeds itself with spiritual principles is truly a wonder to behold. The ego insinuates itself as spiritual advisor and does it so brilliantly that we never suspect what's really happened. The ego is then able to feast on its own whims and desires (now called spiritual "intuitions"), completely unhindered by the wide expanse of flatland idealism.

This is why, more than any other segment of society (with the exception of those caught in Stage One chaos), we Stage Four New Agers tend to do what we please, when we please, for ourselves and more often than not, only ourselves. Because our spiritual imperative is "I do my thing, and you do your thing," we feel little responsibility for others. And of course, no one can ever tell us we're wrong, because "I'm always right for me."

In the New Age, the ego is fat, happy and justified—and obviously in control. That is one reason we see a glut of "you create your own reality" material like the 2007 bestseller *The Secret*. The well-fed ego not only controls us, it's quite certain it can control reality itself. And so we see millions of manifestation books flying off the New Age shelves in bookstores across the nation. At a time we are desperately needed out in the larger world to work together for peace and economic justice and solutions to global warming, a New Ager is more likely to be sitting at home, trying to manipulate spiritual "laws" into manifesting a bigger house or a new car. This is New Age narcissism at its most blatant.

Sadly, an ego that is overdeveloped is just as confining as an underdeveloped one, and all but impossible to transcend.

The ego's brilliant maneuvers

I had a very tough time facing this truth. I'd heard the narcissism accusation flung at the New Age many times, but I was sure if it was deserved, then it was all those *other* people who were guilty of it, not me. I myself felt so well-intentioned and earnest and wanted only good for everyone—in addition, of course, to a bigger house.

Most of us can say the same about other idealists we know, basically good people all, with loving hearts and a heartfelt desire to see positive change in the world. But how often is this desire translated into concrete action to connect with others, or be of service to others? The amount of our efforts on behalf of others is the true test of independence from ego, and even the most seemingly spiritual people can fail this test.

Consider the words of one of my favorite authors in an otherwise lovely book on Eastern-style spirituality. She first recalls her unenlightened days as a "radical leftist, determined to save the world." Back then, watching the news was too painful for her. But after years of meditation and spiritual practice, she is happy to report she has "woke from the dream" and can now watch the news.

"I've noticed there is no impulse anymore to save the world. Watching the nightly horrors, I rarely get upset... There is a kind of equanimity now, an acceptance that didn't used to be here. The news seems like a movie, a conjuring act by the newscasters, with stories and emotions blowing past like wisps of cloud or smoke in the wind."

Happily unaffected by the suffering of others, she next describes herself as spending most of her time "doing nothing," sitting in her "bliss chair," gazing out the window, feeling "little ambition to do anything more than be quiet." She then suggests that the desire to be helpful to others is an effort to "fill the empty hole in the self." She is pleased that she has been able to switch her focus from what *should* be happening to what *is* happening.

Contrast this with Ken Wilber's description of the integral viewpoint of Stage Five spiritual growth:

> When you are alive with an integral vision, you will work your fingers to the bone, tread the earth until your feet are torn and tattered, shed lonely tears from dawn to solemn dusk, labor ceaselessly until all God's children are liberated into the vast expanse of freedom and fullness that is every being's birthright.

Idealism has long recognized the tension between the absolute and the relative, and tried to find a balance between surrendering to what is and taking responsibility for it. Wilber adds that it's not uncommon for well-meaning idealists to "confuse" the directives of the non-dual path—which teaches the wisdom of detachment—with the obligations of the relative path, which require us to work for the good of all. Detachment from outcome is wisdom; detachment from the world and other people is escapism.

This confusion pops up again and again for those in Stage Four trying to figure out how to accommodate relative truths. Cook-Greuter's individualist, feeling high on the freedom of relativity, is often content to let go of absolute truths, and simply "groove in the moment," as one observer put it. The individualist tends to be an "unproductive non-doer...indefinite and impossible to nail down." Which is fine for a time, but not as a permanent way of life. At least not at this point in history, when the viability of life on this planet literally depends on our continued growth up the spiral.

It is imperative that we free ourselves from the spell of relativity—and the gravity of flatland idealism—and allow ourselves to evolve toward the absolute. The ego will, of course, try to talk us out of this. The ego much prefers to stand alone and special, and will fight to keep us complacent in Stage Four, the narcissistic individualist stage that feeds the ego so well. And it will continue to try to win this fight by telling us "by working on ourselves, we are working on the world."

It's hard to recognize, even harder to admit, that one's ego has insinuated itself as one's spiritual advisor. But unless we are out there, sleeves rolled up, building community, and working to create the change we want to see, how can we in all honesty say that we are not suffering at least some degree of egoistic narcissism?

I believe it was our own narcissism, bred in part by the New Age movement itself, that finally rendered the New Age obsolete, once and for all.

People who believe themselves to be the center of the universe, people who believe "all I need is me," no longer care about being part of something bigger, and they certainly don't need a movement. And so, drunk on our own self-importance (or blissed out on the non-importance of anything), we New Agers abandoned ship, abandoned the vehicle we had once expected to help us create a better world. We leapt overboard into the warm waters of me-ness and struck off on our own, each of us in a different direction.

Sadly, in the process, we also abandoned each other, and more or less left society to rot. In a world where I do *my* thing and you do *your* thing, there are precious few doing *our* thing. Instead of working together for the growth and good of all, we have found ourselves completely isolated from each other, trapped inside our own heads, with no obligation to do anything but follow our own "truth."

Are You Stuck in Stage Four?

Once you get a good grasp of the stages of development, you begin to get a feel for why people think and feel the way they do, and what they are likely to say in response to certain questions. Or as Wilber writes, once you understand the particular level of the person you're dealing with, "almost everything he says is completely predictable... predictable value after predictable value."

Most of us don't notice that we are essentially mouthpieces for our particular stage of development. And those of us who hang out in Stage Four seem to be especially likely to respond in a telling way toward questions of spirituality. When asked, "What do you call your set of beliefs?" a Stage Four idealist will almost certainly say, "I don't feel the need to call it anything at all." Quickly followed by, "I'm not really into labels."

I have asked the question of the most New Age-y people I know from Oregon to Arizona to Massachusetts, and I almost always hear the same answer: "I'm a seeker." (Although "wanderer" and "explorer" are common substitutions.) Furthermore, although many admit to loneliness, many seem spectacularly unconcerned about their lack of connection to their fellow seekers and will say things like, "We each have to walk our own path," and "You have to be complete within yourself." They defend others' lack of commitment to any particular set of ideas by saying, "Different people are going to resonate to different things," and "To each his own; whatever other people are into is fine with me."

These sentiments are great improvements over the bullying and scary intolerance of Stage Two or the mockery and polite intolerance of Stage Three. But they're also a dead giveaway that one is sliding about the relative ground of what Wilber calls "the wasteland of whatever."

We all need to spend time in Stage Four, developing respect for others and learning the limits of individualism. But at some point, we also need to grow up into Stage Five and recognize our entwined destinies.

Hitting spiritual bottom

Back in the 1970s and 1980s, the burgeoning New Age movement promised to carry us to a new age of harmony for all, and millions climbed aboard. Even those idealists who didn't necessarily identify with the term New Age still shared in the dream of a better society and the belief we could make it happen together.

Unfortunately, the grandiose dream of the movement was undermined by the flatland idealism typical of Stage Four and the emergence of grandiose egos. Without a map of the spiral of development to point the way to higher stages, we got stuck on the spiral. Our egos gleefully decided we didn't need a movement and we quickly left it behind like any other embarrassing, over-the-top fashion leftover from the 1980s.

The problem is, spirituality practiced in self-centered isolation offers us no context—it offers no handholds to grab, no stages to master, and no reason to grow past our own needs. "Without a larger *raison d'etre* than the desire for self-satisfaction, we will only find narcissism—an endless hall of mirrors—at the end of our spiritual search," writes Elizabeth Debold in her eloquent essay on the "spiritual but not religious" trend (*What Is Enlightenment?* December 2005).

Here we are at narcissism again, the bane of the New Age and all around booby-trap for the solitary spiritual seeker. We set off on a path of radical freedom and end up in a closed-off and stagnant pool of radical self-absorption. And this is precisely where we individualistic idealists have been for the past decade or two, swimming about on our own, separated from our fellows, yet floating safely in the rings of our puffed up egos—trying to manifest our desires or following the vague directions of whatever feels right. Creatures of impulse rather than commitment, we have forgotten all about the vehicle that got us where we are. Although once in awhile, we do remember we were heading for the other shore...

Okay, so the other shore analogy is not perfect—the New Age is not about getting to some distant place or some future event. It's a process of learning to better inhabit the here and now, learning to better see reality, learning to better see ourselves, learning to better recognize ourselves in others. But we solitary seekers who avoided or abandoned the New Age—whether as a vehicle or emergent process—have yet to expand our circles of concern much beyond ourselves.

We are stuck, and worse, most of us have no idea we're stuck. I know I originally turned my nose up at such an insulting suggestion. I had worked too hard, for too many years, to become a more aware and moral human being. I had sacrificed my ego in a hundred different ways through work and motherhood. No one was going to tell me I was stuck.

And yet, when I took a good hard look at my habits, I had to admit they all revolved around me—my wants, needs, hungers, desires. After raising three kids spread far apart, and a grueling span of fifteen years with at least one child five or under, I finally got a little space to breathe and make some money, and my ego rose up with a demanding cry of "*My* turn!" I had assumed my greater sense of peace and contentment was a sign that I was finally growing wise in my old age. But really, I had just become good at rationalizing my subservience to the desires of my ego.

The older we are, the stronger our individualism, and the more likely we feel justified in the choice to abandon our collective ship. The older we are, the more we feel we have earned the right to do as we please (which of course we have) and the more difficult to rouse ourselves from the comfortable cocoon of narcissism in order to face the social consequences of our actions. This is true not only in an abstract sense, but in the concrete sense of how the brain is neurally imprinted with habits of thought over time. In older brains, the neural pathways of individualism are thick and strong, and difficult to rewire.

Younger idealists with neural pathways still forming are less likely to be hard stuck in their individualism. They are also more likely to notice that we are stranded, isolated, miles away from shore. But young or old, all of us are surely becoming more aware that the future is in jeopardy. And all of us long to get to a better place.

Getting in and out of our own way

I confess that in writing this argument, my point of view is subjective, my motivation is emotional, and as a result, I have often wondered if my conclusions are unfair. It could be that I am blaming my fellow idealists for self-centeredly abandoning the movement because I'm still self-centeredly aggrieved that the movement abandoned me. It could also be that I'm projecting my own guilt over my own considerable case of narcissism onto my fellows. And now, in my desperation to do *something* so that my children will have a future, I am becoming unhelpfully strident.

But whether or not I've accurately uncovered the reasons idealists abandoned the New Age, the fact remains, it was abandoned. And whatever my motivation, the question of whether we left behind something worth preserving is a valid one. Meanwhile, examining the costs of narcissism is an exercise even the most unemotional of observers would urge us to undertake.

Of course, we have no choice but to spend time in the individualistic Stage Four of our spiritual growth; however sticky it gets, it's the only way to get to higher stages, and we must learn to navigate its obstacles. And admittedly, with all the outside pressures bearing brutally down on the movement at the turn of the millennium—by religion and the media and the market—the New Age vehicle was not in good shape and was, in fact, listing badly.

So it could be that our collective jump from world-saving mission to our own individual concerns was inevitable, unavoidable. It could be that we actually needed to abandon the movement so it could be overhauled and rebuilt into something that better moves us, better helps us to grow.

But just because there were good reasons to leave the movement behind for a time doesn't mean that we are better off struggling along on our own indefinitely. Unless, of course, you have managed to reach Stage Five and your ego is well in check and you are fully engaged in compassionate work that uplifts others. There are many such integral individuals out there, working tirelessly to help others survive and thrive materially as well as evolve spiritually. We see them occasionally on the news or in the pages of our newspapers and magazines, branded as heroes for establishing charities or doing work that seems extraordinary to the rest of us, work *they* see as an ordinary part of life.

For those of us who aren't there yet, those of us mired in Stage Four self-absorption, it's long past time to ask ourselves: Is continuing along our own self-styled paths truly helping us evolve? Are we really developing the integral insights and capabilities that will improve our lives and allow us to create a better world? Or are we merely lulling ourselves into complacency while the world careens ever closer toward a cataclysmic end?

Recent history points to widespread complacency among us. For years, our government waged a war without reason, violated human rights around the world and at home, allowed corporations to pillage jobs and undermine the economy, refused to even acknowledge, let alone act, on global warming. Yet, despite a few sharp voices ranting and raving on the Internet or MSNBC, most of us idealists went about our lives without a peep. With heaviness in our hearts, yes, and a lot of fist-pounding at the dinner table, yes, but largely without any public objection whatsoever. (Naturally, the media and the government ignored what forms of public objection there were, but that's a different book.)

We are now so complacent that we actually complain when pricked by our own conscience to take responsibility. In his funny and insightful book, *The 99th Monkey*, Eliezer Sobel describes a lifetime devoted to New Age-style spiritual seeking from which he picked up "the potentially damaging notion that if I wasn't saving the world and being a Gandhi or a Martin Luther King...I wasn't truly living. The bar was placed so high that who among us would not constantly fall short?" He says he began to feel "ashamed" when life anywhere was not working, and objected to feeling personally responsible "for not having ended war, poverty, hunger, and starvation on the planet." Saving the world, he concludes, is just too much to take on.

I loved Sobel's honesty, because it made me feel better about my own similar narcissistic grumblings that unless I can be like Gandhi, why try at all? (This is the same petulant voice that tells me if I can't lose ten pounds in a week, why try to lose weight at all?) But I try to daily remind myself that there is a difference between moral *purity* and moral *clarity*. A spiritually mature person understands this difference, understands that we help create a better world in small but steady increments—by changing a few habits or donating a few hours or a few dollars to a worthy cause. It is the immature ego that places the bar impossibly high, allowing us to excuse ourselves from doing the spiritual work of stepping outside ourselves and our own interests. It is the ego that takes activities that are nice and easy and pleasantly centered on the self—yoga classes or retreats or trips to Machu Picchu—and calls *that* spiritual work.

A certain amount of self-absorption is a necessary step in spiritual growth; it helps free us from the conventional stages and allows us to work our way into the post-conventional stages. But once there, its usefulness ends, and rather than helping us along, self-absorption begins to numb us. And while the ego likes it this way, our souls eventually begin to feel a little desperate to break out.

I believe many of us are growing tired of our own numbness and complacency and stagnant growth. And many of us are waking up to the planet-endangering consequences of living only for ourselves. We are becoming more aware of what Wilber calls "the evolutionary drive within us" that seeks higher and more fully engaged ways of relating to the world and each other. We are now yearning to move beyond the vague pull of private whims to the urgent call of a shared vision with the power to change the world.

I believe we are yearning to leave our isolation and join together to create a new age. I also believe we'd best get to it, before it is too late.

APRIL 13, 2006

The Care and Feeding of Complacency

BLOG
Looking for the New Age

On the cover of *Time* this week (3 Apr 2006), is a special report on global warming, "Be Worried. Be VERY Worried," says the cover with the polar bear stranded on melting ice.

"Look on this picture and weep over it!" wrote Thomas Paine in the darkest days of the revolution. Is anyone today weeping? Is anyone really worried?

I am worried. I wring my hands, ask myself what I can do. The one thing I know how to do is write. I have spent months writing pages for the Web site and now feel foolish for overkill. I fear I'll numb people's minds with my slew of words.

But what else do you do in an emergency? You scream and yell for help. As Thomas Paine also wrote: "There are cases which cannot be overdone by language, and this is one."

I don't know how else to say it but in these stark words, Please help, please join me, please let's do something, please let's take the next step, please let's combine our strength, please let's move this crazily tilting planet toward sanity.

All my arguments, all my trying to come up with the "just right" combination of words... It's time wasted. There is no way to argue people into taking action. They must be moved from within.

On one hand, I am sure that we must all be painfully aware of complacency sticking to us like a suffocating gel, we must all be feeling equally desperate to get it off, get it off—and move and do something! But so many folks have banged the gong to get the attention of the townsfolk that no one pays attention anymore. The sky is falling, quite literally these days, warming and falling and flooding the earth—but we are too busy and too overwhelmed to stop and do anything.

I know I am busy to the point of weeping. Last night putting my son to bed, I felt caught in the relentless flow of daily activity, in which some work/parenting/family activity is required of me at nearly every moment of the day. Like being dragged around on a non-stop merry-go-round, it gives the impression that each day is the same as the last, that everything will continue indefinitely in this numbing rhythm. Thus complacency is fed and grows thick.

Even though each day feels the same for me, it is not the same day for the planet, not after absorbing another twenty-four hours worth of damage inflicted on it by me and my overflowing trash can and my water down the drain and my conspicuous consumption. The sands of the hourglass are running out, even faster than anyone could have predicted—or so says *Time* magazine.

Of course, as I learned from reading Michael Lerner the other day, it is not our self-interest or our will to survive that motivates selfless action. Self-interest usually only kicks in at the last hour, when the problem comes barreling through the front door in a flood or with a gun or an eviction notice, when it is too late to do anything about it. Any effort we make toward a better world rises only from internal values.

I've got the words from that *Les Misérables* song stuck in my head: "Will you join in our crusade? Who will be strong and stand with me? Beyond the barricade is there a world you long to see?" Such nice, stark words.

Conversation with my Sister-Friend: On Labels

As I wrote this book, I discussed my efforts with a number of friends and family members and the conversations usually seemed to go the same way. Most spiritual people have a fierce opposition to labels, and even the most recognizably New Age-y people I know would bristle at the idea of being called New Age. Here is the gist of how the conversation would go, much embellished by things I wish I would have remembered to say. (I am using a fictional stand-in for my friends and family, who I will call Gwen.)

Teena: I'm going to publish a book about the New Age. About the importance for New Age-y people like you and me to unify under a collective identity.

Gwen: What do you mean people like me? I don't consider myself New Age.

Teena: Okay, then what are you? What do you call your particular set of beliefs?

Gwen: Why do I have to call it anything at all? Why do you want to label me?

Teena: I don't want to label you. I am hoping to convince you, and spiritual idealists like you, to label yourself.

Gwen: Well, that's not gonna happen. All my life I've been fighting to get away from labels. People are always trying to pin me under labels, I don't like it.

Teena: Most New Age-y people don't, we very much want freedom from labels. But—

Gwen: I think we all just need to grow *up*, stop trying to be part of a herd, be responsible for ourselves.

Teena: I think that's what we've been doing for years now. We've been growing past the need for labels, taking responsibility for the health of our own souls, and that's good.

Gwen: Right, why get all tangled up in labels? Why can't we just *live* what we believe without naming it?

Teena: We can, and we do. But we've neglected to keep track of the price we've paid in—

Gwen: I don't see that. I love my freedom to follow my own path.

Teena: First of all, I don't think a label has to steal your freedom. A label can just as easily operate as an agreement that protects your freedom, such as U.S. citizen. Second of all, I wonder just how free you really are. Most New Age-y people practice their spirituality on the down low. Sure, there are brave souls like Shirley MacLaine who speak their truth and brush off the ridicule of the mainstream. And tons of people live in New Age-friendly places like San Francisco or Boulder or Sedona. But only a handful of communities are like that. The majority of us live in more middle America places. I live in Phoenix, not exactly the Bible Belt, but I don't talk about my spiritual viewpoint in the company of my friends and neighbors unless I know for certain they're sympathetic. Why? Because my views are seen as either exotic and threatening, or silly and irrelevant. So yes, we're free, just as anyone who drifts outside the boundaries of the status quo is free, but it's the freedom of a refugee or an outlaw. I don't think we can be truly free until we are able to openly declare who we are and what we believe and be respected for it within the bounds of the mainstream.

Gwen: I've never been compelled by what the mainstream thinks. I think the whole point of our spirituality is to leave the mainstream behind. That is, we need to move ahead of the mainstream, we need to lead the way, and eventually they'll catch up.

Teena: How can they catch up? They don't even know we're here! They can't even see us, let alone catch up to us, if we don't identify ourselves and tell them what we're up to and why. But we are so determined not to be branded as any particular thing that we have made sure we count as *no*-thing. Even though one in four Americans are spiritual idealists, our priorities rarely show up on the table when it comes time for debate. Invisible people do not get taken into account when it comes time to make decisions. Our public policy and our common resources are all controlled by the mainstream, and we need to be represented there. If we really want society to "catch up" and reflect our values, we need to have some influence in the context of the mainstream.

Gwen: But I think our ideas already are becoming mainstream—

Teena: The only reason you can say that is because you live in L.A. You work with Hollywood people.

Gwen: No, I can say that because Barack Obama is in the White House. He wouldn't be there if society wasn't starting to reflect our values—

Teena: I would absolutely love to believe that. But even if it's true, we can't expect Obama to single-handedly do the work of transforming society and saving the planet all on his own. He has to work within the context of the mainstream, and he's said over and over again, in many different ways, that it is up to *us*, we the people, to change the direction of the mainstream. It's up to *us* to organize ourselves into a collective force. If we spiritual idealists all agreed to take on a common label, we could go far in making our numbers a force to be reckoned with. We would be able to recognize each other and join our efforts. We would have a huge impact on society.

Gwen: Okay, maybe so. But I still don't see how you can lump everyone together under one label. We don't all have the same beliefs. If I call myself New Age, then will I have to believe in reincarnation? Where do you draw the line on what is New Age and what isn't? And who gets to draw that line?

Teena: The only thing that is essentially New Age is the basic premise that spirit is the ultimate ground of reality. That's the only line we have to draw. Many different beliefs can and do grow from that same premise.

Gwen: But why New Age? That label has never done anything for me. We've been there, done that. It's a joke now, it's embarrassing.

Teena: That's your ego talking. Only the ego can be embarrassed.

Gwen: That sounds insulting, as if you think my spirituality is shallow, when I know my spirituality has a lot of depth. In fact, to me New Age means a lack of depth.

Teena: Yes, that's a connotation it has been given by the media and competing philosophies as a way to marginalize the movement, scare people away. The New Age "brand" has definitely been tarnished. But we don't have to accept that connotation, we don't have to allow ourselves to be pushed into embarrassment.

Gwen: Nor do I have to allow myself to be pushed into accepting a label I don't relate to—

Teena: A lot of people say that New Age doesn't resonate with them. But what label is going to magically resonate with everyone? And why invest so much importance in the label anyway? Can you imagine refusing to vote for a progressive candidate that shares your values just because you don't resonate with the word Democrat? This preoccupation with the label (or non-label) is an ego-manufactured dilemma, a red herring that distracts us from the important work we need to do. I think you were right what you said before, we all need to grow up—and stop thinking we're too special for this label or that. I don't care if we all call ourselves Purple Potatoheads; all I care about is being able to unify under a common identity and build the social capital necessary to create a better world for my children and yours. The only reason we haven't done that yet is *not* because the phrase New Age isn't relatable enough, but because we've been too ego-bound to relate to any label at all.

Gwen: (long pause) All right. You win. I'll call myself a Purple Potatohead.

Teena: I'm not trying to win anything, you know.

Gwen: Well, whatever you're trying to do, you're not going to influence people by calling them a bunch of egotistic narcissists. You're only going to make people feel insulted, like I've felt during this conversation.

Teena: Maybe you're right, some egos will be insulted, as mine always is when I finally confront my own narcissistic crap. But our egos are our own worst enemy. They need to be confronted, they need to be insulted, they need to be pushed out of our way so we can get busy saving the world. I have kids, I want to see them thrive, I want grandkids. We don't have time to wait for the normal slow pace of evolution for everyone to catch up; we have a moral obligation to start helping evolution along, to create a better world now, today.

And I'm done sitting quietly in respectful silence while we all do our own thing. I'm done smiling and nodding when New Age-y people tell me that society is becoming more enlightened when nearly every news story, every day, tells us that the planet is in peril, and there is pain and darkness everywhere. So be insulted if you must, maybe that means I'm doing a good job. Or maybe it means I'm failing utterly.

Gwen: Have you ever thought that maybe the world is perfect as it is, even with all its pain and darkness, and maybe things are unfolding just as they should?

Teena: As a matter of fact, I believe that with my whole heart. Which is why I tell myself that this effort I'm making to re-brand the New Age is part of things unfolding, and my book will arrive at just at the moment it should.

Gwen: (laughs) Speaking of narcissism…

Teena: Oh I'm painfully aware.

PART III

The Case for Revival

I rest not from my great task!
To open the Eternal worlds, to open the immortal eyes
of man…
I see the Past, Present and Future existing all at once
Before me. O Divine Spirit! Sustain me on thy wings,
That I may awake Albion from his long and cold repose
Striving with Systems to deliver individuals from those
systems…

— WILLIAM BLAKE —

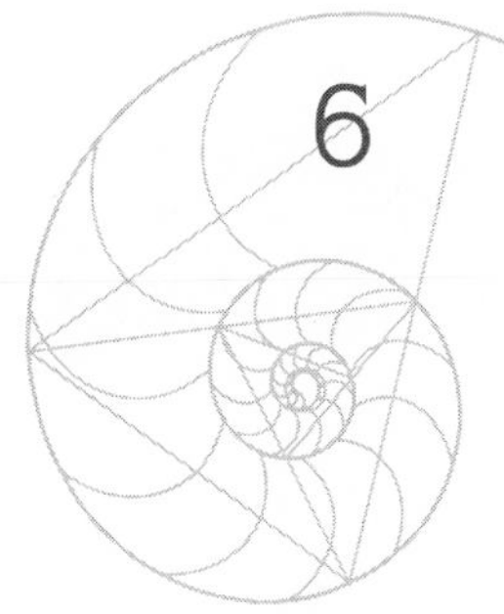

6 Turning the Tide of Too Late

Once upon a time, millions of idealists hopped onto the burgeoning New Age movement with the intention of saving the world. We saw that run-amuck materialism was a dire threat to our environment, as well as the driving force behind the disastrous economic disparity between nations. We recognized that the fear-based intolerance of fundamentalist dualism was destroying any chance of harmony among us and fueling all manner of war and terrorism. We realized that our only real hope for a sustainable future lay in inspiring greater numbers of people to look at the world through different eyes and approach our problems from a different angle.

Once upon a time, we idealists understood that we were on an important, lifesaving mission. We understood that because we were the ones that knew what needed to be done, we were the ones meant to make it happen. But not long after we began, the swell beneath us subsided, the movement foundered, and we simply hopped off. We went our own separate ways. We abandoned our mission, at least as an identifiable collective force, as if we had the perfect right to let it go.

It is surely no coincidence that at the same time as we Stage Four idealists (about 24 percent of the population, remember) were rebuffing the New Age and all other attempts to identify us as a group, the conservative movement and its fundamentalist contingent began gaining in power. Stage Two fundamentalists (also about a quarter of the population) had a mission of their own—conservative rule of the land—and they committed to it with true religious fervor, working hard to make it happen.

Lo and behold, their work paid off, handsomely. For nearly thirty years, the fundamentalist-dominated political party ruled the land, filled the courts and commanded the airwaves, and the consequences were worse than even the worst pessimist could have predicted. Just before the election of 2008, the government was bankrupt, our economy was in collapse, the country was still at war on two fronts, and it was (still is) a toss up between nuclear terrorism, economic collapse, or global warming as to which is going to finish us off first.

Even now, with new leadership in Washington, it looks like we could have plenty more destruction ahead of us. And maybe destruction is indeed our destiny, as seen in the fevered visions of the apocalyptic prophets of old. Maybe we are meant for chaos and whatever lessons it has to teach us. Maybe we do have to confront a string of disasters in order to trigger the kind of inner change that will allow us to create harmony.

But before the skies turn dark with smoke and ash from bombs, and before the rising oceans seep under our doors, we might do well to ask: Do we have another choice?

The millennium myth

Most all spiritual mythologies feature some kind of millennium myth, whether the Armageddon predicted in the Book of Revelations or the Mayan's famous 2012 end-of-time calendar or the Hindu *kalpas*—cycles of time in which the universe is continually destroyed and created anew.

Although these myths are often taken literally by those in Stage Two of spiritual growth, they are better understood as symbolic stories—cautionary tales meant both to warn us of the danger of staying in the dark of ego-based paradigms and to inspire us to reach for the light of a spirit-based worldview. If we read the end-of-the-world myths in this way, they can help us understand that change happens through continuous cycles of contraction and expansion, death and rebirth.

Indeed, if we look back through the short history of our nation, we see that in the United States cultural change has not been a steady march but more of a surging back-and-forth of three steps forward, two steps back, in what is often called "the dialectic of progress." The colonization of America was fraught with many dark episodes of starvation and violence and witch hunts, but at the end of a long and grueling war for independence, a new nation, inspired by the idealistic premises of The Enlightenment, rose from the ashes to become the world's first democratic nation.

This relatively golden period of new, heady freedoms lasted through the 1830s with the flowering of transcendentalism. But shortly thereafter, the country lurched back into the dark with the aggressive defense of slavery, the Civil War, the corporate exploitation of workers and land, and the tight social repression of the Victorian Era. The early twentieth century saw another spurt of idealistic advances with the labor movement and women's suffrage, followed again by dark years of The Great Depression, the rise of fascism, and devastating war across the globe.

Clearly, that deep, challenging darkness in mid-century created the conditions for idealism and conscience to once again flourish in America, allowing great leaders like Martin Luther King, Jr. and the Kennedy brothers to emerge and inspire us to care about the plight of the poor, and win the fight for civil rights.

Social change accelerated through the 1970s at such a rapid rate that there was surely no way to avoid a conservative backlash toward dualism and materialism. With so much change so fast, many Americans felt upset and off balance, and flocked to follow voices calling for a return to familiar old-fashioned values. And so, we have again endured decades of fierce resistance to progress and empathy, again suffered through dark years of fear and fundamentalism and war and corporate exploitation.

If we take history as a guide, it would seem safe to assume that the pendulum is about to swing back the other way. And now that the unabashedly idealistic Barack Obama has been elected president, we may soon find ourselves riding a new wave of idealism into a long period of growth and healing. I hope and pray this is so. But just because the conditions are ripe for expansion doesn't mean that it happens automatically.

Human beings, with all their potential for growth, are just as capable of sinking into mass apathy and helplessness, and history has shown us that dark ages can become entrenched and resistant to the light offered by even the brightest of leaders. We know that change in human society never happens merely at the call of a leader; change only happens when enough people stop accepting the status quo and step up to demand something better for themselves, and for their children.

But unlike the dark ages of the past, our window of opportunity for redirecting the course of progress is closing with alarming swiftness. Each successive dark age has done ever more damage to the planet and now, with global warming and peak oil, our very survival is threatened. If we sit and wait for the pendulum to swing toward idealism all on its own, it will certainly be too late. The apocalyptic stories meant to be instructive myths will become horrific reality.

Changing direction

In their book, *Presence: An Exploration of Profound Change in People, Organizations and Society*, the authors point out that when people "start to see themselves as the source of their problems, they invariably discover a new capacity to create results they truly desire."

In other words, we will remain powerless to effect change until we ask the critical question, "What have we done to ourselves?"

We know that the only way to transform society is to usher in a wave of spiritual growth up the spiral of development toward idealism and beyond to integralism. But if all the idealists are stuck in flatland and refusing on principle to join any wave at all, then we instead form the wall that blocks this necessary wave from forming.

We idealists are literally standing in the way of progress, which cannot flow through us, closed off as we are in our individual universes, practicing our unnamed religions of one. And every day we wake up and continue on our own little solitary paths, and neglect to reach out to connect to each other or give aid or insist on peace and justice, we are thickening the wall that is blocking progress and further sealing our own doom.

Either we figure out how to get over ourselves, writes Wilber, or we will continue to "actively contribute to the fragmentation and devastation that everywhere threaten tomorrow."

It is difficult—and painful—to accept that we idealists, full of love and good intentions and goodwill toward all, can be the source of the problem. It seems much more logical to blame the state of the world on *them*, the unaware hordes with all their unenlightened policies. But we cannot force others to see differently or make them grow any faster than they can grow. And if we shift the responsibility of generating change to *them*, then we make ourselves helpless.

"Without the capacity to see ourselves as the cause, our efforts become either coercive or wishfully dependent on the transformation of others," writes Peter Block. "Taking responsibility for one's own part in creating the present situation is the critical act of courage and engagement, which is the axis around which the future rotates."

We are the ones who have to change, *we* are the ones that have to choose differently, *we* are the ones that have to construct the new paradigm. The future has always depended on *us*, not on them.

Yes, it is difficult—and painful—to accept that we are the source of the problem. But is also wonderful, joyous news. Because if we are responsible for what's broken, then we have the power to fix it. We don't have to wait for everyone else to somehow "get it" or change their ways.

Whether you were ever part of the New Age or not, if you are an idealist, it is your mission to save the world. And I don't mean that in the egocentric, grandiose "we're the chosen people" sense; I mean it in the unglamorous "we're the ones sitting in the emergency exit row" sense. There's no one else, no saintly folk with extra time on their hands waiting to swoop in and save us from ourselves. As we have heard again and again, "we are the ones we have been waiting for."

Some idealists may beg to differ. So much of spiritual practice is designed to teach us detachment and to drop judgment and to see events as neither good or bad, to see that all is perfect, just as it is. Eastern philosophies especially tell us that everything is a state of mutual arising, beyond our control, and no one thing is any more important than any other thing. And often, the more we can detach, the more spiritually evolved we feel.

Yet idealism also tells us that our purpose in being born into the world is not simply to recognize the world as *maya*, or illusion, but to engage the *maya*—live it, struggle with it, hate it, love it, experience it fully—and thereby help God increase his knowledge of his own infinitely complex existence.

True, one way to experience the *maya* is to sit on a cushion, completely unaffected. But as Andrew Cohen points out, "The evolving cosmos is in desperate need of our conscious participation in order for its creative potential to continue to develop." If we're not careful, he adds, the spiritual pursuit of peace can end up "taking us out of the game," the game we were born to play.

We are ultimately creatures of the earth, set down on a relative path and made responsible for each other. It is your responsibility, and mine, to get up each day and do what we can to create order out of the chaos of the *maya*. It is my responsibility, and yours, to revitalize the New Age community, by whatever name we wish to call it, and help build a strong spiral for the spiritual development of all.

It is your responsibility, and mine, to rescue our planet and heal our world.

The difficult leap from words to action

In writing words like these—The world is at risk!—I realize I'm taking on the role of Chicken Little, lamenting the falling sky to people who have heard it all a thousand times. We have been exposed to similar words of alarm over and over and over again since the dawn of the atomic age. News of our impending extinction is now positively dull and mundane, with no power to move us.

Even if we do understand the dire nature of the situation, it is still near impossible to rouse ourselves to action. The usual analogy to insert here is of those idiot frogs, slowly being cooked to death in that pan of heating water, when they are perfectly capable of jumping out. But that analogy has become mundane, too.

We are all faced with this yawning gap between what we know we should do and what we actually do. It is part of what sociologist Robert Putnam calls the "dilemma of collective action." It goes something like this:

People know that we all have to start doing things differently, and we know we'll be better off if everyone does their share. However, the individual benefits by shirking responsibility in the hope others will do the work for her. Even if she's wrong, and no one else picks up the slack, at least she's not the only sucker. In the end, even though we know we have to change, nothing ever really changes because no one wants to go first. Putnam also calls this "the tragedy of the commons."

The motivation to shake off habit and apathy will not come from outside warnings or logical arguments. The decision to leap across the chasm between words and action comes from within, and is most often an emotional realization that hits out of nowhere.

Here is how the realization hit me. A few years ago, my youngest son and I were walking the dog around our neighborhood on our regular evening stroll. It was unseasonably warm for October, even by Arizona standards, and I said something about global warming.

"What's global warming?" my then ten-year-old son asked.

The feelings of dismay that rushed through me at that moment literally knocked the breath out of me. I had no idea he didn't know about global warming—hadn't discussed it at school or absorbed it from conversations at the dinner table or from television. My older children knew, without any explanation from me, and had long since learned how to make gallows humor cracks about it.

But my youngest boy, my baby boy, he somehow didn't know, and I was overwhelmed at the thought of explaining to him the facts: that his future is in peril, that the world in which he feels so safe and so eager to grow up may soon be unlivable because of our own inability to live differently.

I could barely get out my short, matter-of-fact explanation because I was so caught in the throes of realizing, right there on the dark street two blocks from my house, that I may someday have to watch my children and grandchildren die in some terrible environmental cataclysm.

As we continued our walk, I felt the weight of this possibility settle in, and all I wanted to do was weep and wail in regret, tell my son how sorry I was that I haven't done more to stop it. Because it seemed unavoidably clear to me that I have shirked my responsibility to him—to all my children. From the moment each child was born, it became my responsibility to create a future for that child, and what have I done? Not enough. Not nearly enough.

I am now working hard to move from words to action. To understand that it is my mission to reach out to my fellow idealists and help create a community with the power to change things. I don't feel I have the right to refuse this mission. I don't feel I have the right to be concerned with just myself and my own comfort anymore. If I continue to sit idly by while the planet is made unlivable by a failing paradigm, then I will have to bear the responsibility, and the blame, for it.

I am working hard to move myself, to become what Peter Block calls "someone who produces the future, someone who does not wait, beg, or dream of the future." I am working to become an active member of different communities—online groups, political groups, service groups, spiritual groups. I am donating more money to worthy causes, volunteering more time to organizations that build community and help others. I am speaking up more frequently, and standing up publicly for idealistic values like peace and love and unity.

I am working hard to practice what I preach, in big ways and small, and I am learning that waking up to reality, while painful, is not a bad thing. I am learning that in saying the world is at risk, I am not necessarily spreading bad news. After all, if this reality actually gains our attention and motivates us to change, it could be the best possible news.

"We should not fear this challenge," says Al Gore of global warming. "We should welcome it."

The challenge of a world at risk gives us the chance to step outside our own small selves with our own small concerns and become bigger people, better people. This challenge offers us a golden opportunity to grow and expand and move up the spiral of development, and evolve into a true global community. This challenge offers us the chance to tap into the power of a spiritual identity and, at last, create a new age that fulfills its promise of ushering in a better world for us all.

Is it too late for the Baby Boom generation?

In the early days of working on this project—a call for a New Age revival—I assumed that I'd be addressing the demographic group that makes up the New Age market, which is comprised largely of women of a certain age and income level who are interested in spirituality and a holistic lifestyle.

But as I talked to different spiritual people of the Baby Boom Generation, I discovered that most of them wanted nothing to do with any kind of movement or the creation of a community. Even those who most fit the New Age profile would literally make faces at the mention of the term New Age. They would then reaffirm their commitment to their own path, their own needs. It seemed clear to me that baby boomers have been operating on the individualistic terms of uncommitted seeker for so long, and this role has become so well rationalized in their minds, that I would find no receptive audience there.

To be frank, I felt some anger after such conversations, not to mention a sense of betrayal. After all, I was raised by one of the first baby boomers—my mother was born in 1945 and she was an open-hearted, peace-loving flower child. I absorbed the communal values of the young boomers and strongly believed in their call to create a better world. When the most hopeful of them forged the New Age community in the 1970s and 80s, I eagerly hopped on board. And I was absolutely bereft when the movement seemed to dissolve away to nothing but a consumer category a few decades later.

To find such clear evidence in my conversations that those who once inspired me had not merely been accidentally lost on the way to community but had decisively turned their back on it was painful. And in that pain, I decided it was too late for the Baby Boom Generation. I decided that so many of them had chosen interminable mirror-gazing and self-soothing as their spiritual path that it was useless to talk to them anymore. I began thinking of them as the "dead weight" generation, well-intentioned but completely unable to get out of their own way, and ours.

I also began to understand why Ken Wilber half-jokingly wrote in *Boomeritis* that "the knowledge quest proceeds funeral by funeral," and that baby boomers might have to die before the widespread narcissism that blocks the spiral of development can be breached. And I began to address all my writing to newer generations who—with futures threatened by the many catastrophes of rampant individualism—would be better able to grasp the need for spirit-based community.

It was Marianne Williamson who changed my mind and changed it big. She spoke in Phoenix in November 2008 about the new mid-life and the opportunity those of a certain age now have to "get it right." I listened with tears streaming down my face as she convinced me it is never too late for any of us, no matter how old we are, to finally get to work on the vital business of saving the world.

In her book, *The Age of Miracles,* Williamson describes an "epiphany" now pressing in on baby boomers "that in many ways we wasted our youth—not in that we lived it frivolously, but in that, in far too many cases, we lived it only for ourselves." She then goes on to say:

> We haven't lived through what we've lived through, bled the way we've bled, and been humbled the way we've been humbled to have it just be *over* now. In fact, we owe too much to the world to get off that easily. We were all born carrying a promise—a promise to make the world better—and there's a yearning to

> make good on that promise that none of us can suppress forever. There's a silent question blaring loudly in our hearts: What will I do with the time I have left?

Even Wilber, the world's most outspoken critic of the Baby Boom Generation, agrees that "profound transformation often occurs in the second half of life." As they age, the boomers increasingly face their own mortality, "which marvelously concentrates the mind and releases it from things of this world. The finite self becomes more and more transparent, more easily let go of, and a certain spiritual perfume fills the air."

Our so-called prime adult years, Wilber adds, keep us so preoccupied with the demands of career and family that growth into higher stages is rare. (Looking back at my own life, I can certainly say that's been true for me.) But once we pass through mid-life, and reach our 50s and 60s, we may suddenly find ourselves "ready to pop." And we may feel ourselves becoming "deeply, deeply open" to transformation from Stage Four individualism to a Stage Five integralism that deeply, deeply understands the value of community.

I read Wilber's words years ago, but did not much believe them until I heard Williamson give her speech on that warm November night in Phoenix. She said the year 1968, with the assassinations of King and Kennedy, was the symbolic point at which the idealistic dream of a new age of harmony began to die, and now, forty years later, the election of Barack Obama has served as the symbolic point at which it is time to resurrect the dream. On that warm night, she called specifically to the baby boomers to take their hard won wisdom and "align with the creative pulse of the universe," and "prepare the ground for a glorious future."

It is time, she said, "to accomplish what we came here

to do." And on that night, two thousand people jumped to their feet and applauded wildly.

"Each of us has gone through our own private dramas," she adds in her book, "taken our own individual journeys; now we meet as though at a predestined point, to pool our resources of talent and intelligence, faith and hope. Ultimately, we are individually glorified as we find our place within a collective heartbeat. We have journeyed alone, and now we'll journey together...It is time for us to become elders and caretakers of this precious planet, not just in name but in passionate practice."

Amen.

7 The Power of Spiritual Identity

We idealists may have unintentionally wandered off toward irrelevance, but we can turn around and head back to the empowering fold of community and take up our important world-saving mission at any time.

Yes, it is important to understand the drawbacks of labels, how they can limit and reduce, and how the ego often craves them for its own purposes. And it is certainly true that the need to belong to a group is often based in ego. But far more egoic is the idea that we are too unique to belong to any group at all.

The decision to reject the New Age emblem—an emblem with the potential to unify and galvanize us as a community and move us up the spiral of development—has proven to be terribly shortsighted. The further we have drifted away from a common identity, the greater we have drifted into fragmentation and narcissism.

Of course, this step away from identity may have been a necessary step in our collective evolution. Spiritual development often happens through differentiation and integration: we start from a thesis, create an antithesis, and then integrate the two into a synthesis. It is possible, maybe even probable, that abandoning an organized movement in order to discover the limits of individualism was exactly what we were supposed to do.

But we've been hanging out in differentiation and antithesis for a long while. And as we have seen, the costs are disastrously high: spiritual stagnancy, isolation, invisibility, and ineffectiveness within the culture at large. Clearly, it's time for synthesis between individual and community.

It's time to establish a spiritual identity.

The magic of knowing who you are

Idealism is based on the principle that everything that exists, including ourselves, is a manifestation of a greater spiritual reality. From the idealistic perspective, salvation quite literally lies in the recognition of who you are.

This essential truth has been repeated throughout history by Hindu sages, Taoist monks, Zen masters, Greek idealists, mystics, and storytellers. (Remember Hans Christian Andersen's story of *The Ugly Duckling*?) We have been taught over and over that learning who we are—and owning who we are—is the path to salvation, the path to authenticity, the path to power.

According to idealism, we learn who we are by learning to see through the ego to the soul, the true self, which is one with Spirit. In other words, we learn to identify with the soul instead of the ego (see *Chapter 15, The Riddle of the Self*). This *sounds* like it should be a simple switch in perspective, but it is actually fraught with great difficulty.

After all, the ego that escorts us into the world is quite certain *it* is the true self—and it works very hard to maintain that illusion and keep us identified with it. And as we've seen, our attempts to deflate the ego by banishing identity have inadvertently had the opposite effect. Our aggressive individuality has only left us more in thrall to the ego, and stalled on the spiral of development.

If we want to get unstuck, if we honestly want to discover our true selves, our souls, we are going to have to learn to transcend the egotism that has trapped us in place. We are going to have to basically start from the beginning and move again through the stages of spiritual growth—from egocentric to ethnocentric to worldcentric.

A spiritual identity is key

In the effort to transcend the ego, it would at first glance seem counterintuitive to feed the ego with a particular identity. It would seem we should follow the example of those Buddhist hermits of old who dropped all identities and retired to their solitary cave to meditate non-stop.

I've always wondered how many monks actually achieved enlightenment by abandoning community, or how many just went crazy like so many of the hermits we see here in the West, muttering to bushes, lost in a world of their own creation. I don't know the answer, but it would appear that solitary cave-sitting for enlightenment is not all that popular anymore—or at least not as popular as communal cave-sitting.

Today, when the spiritually hungry are serious about transcending ego, they usually don't head off to be alone, they join a meditative school or monastic order of some sort. They accept an identity and join a group that provides a context for their search for self. Whatever boost their egos may get from the identity is more than offset by the ego-humbling dynamic of being just one among many. Meanwhile, the discipline imposed by the group, with all its schedules and rituals and mundane activities, helps dissolve the ego far more effectively than any activity one could undertake on his or her own.

The soul, of course, doesn't really need the identity. The soul is a simple moment of consciousness that exists beyond identity. But in order to be able to connect with the soul, we have to get the ego out of the way. By subsuming the ego, the false self, in an identity that explicitly reduces its importance, we help make it more permeable and increase our ability to see through it to the real self, the soul.

I got my first inkling of this as a newly-baptized Christian. By taking on the identity of Christian, I surrendered my sense of self, my ego, up to God, for the first time in my life. Being able to set aside the oppressive ego worked like a bellows on the tiny flicker of my soul, which I felt expanding within me. I was able to burn brightly with peace and acceptance for quite some time.

Yet however much I enjoyed the release from ego that Christianity provided, I eventually grew out of my ability to hold to the blind faith in dogma that just didn't feel true to me, dogma I (mistakenly) believed was required to stay a Christian. I left my church, and for a long confused time, I worried I would never feel that closeness to spirit again.

Fortunately, I found books that taught me that the ego can be dissolved by any number of paths and identities. Which is not to say that the particular identity we choose isn't important. As I learned from unsuccessfully trying to talk myself into holding to a fundamentalist version of Christianity, it does no good to adopt an identity that doesn't ring true to you or requires you to take positions you recognize are not good and loving. If the identity is not the right fit, you will simply wander away from it, ego still fat and unthreatened.

To open up to the awareness of the true self, we cannot leave the ego unthreatened. We have to work at dissolving it, and joining a group that speaks truths you understand—and encourages contemplative practice—has proven over many centuries to be the most reliable way to do that. Perhaps it *is* possible for some people to sit alone in a cave long enough to be able to skip identity. But any sense that I am so special that I can get to worldcentric without the ego-dissolving help of an identity seems to me a sure sign that one is still languishing in egocentrism. And still stuck.

The right identity

We are fortunate to live in a time when all the great wisdom traditions of history are available to us simply by heading down to the bookstore or clicking onto the Internet. When searching for a path that feels right, we have a great many expressions of spirituality available to us.

However, this plentitude of paths also makes it difficult to find one path more right than the other. On one day I might feel most attracted to seasonal pagan rituals that take me closer to the rhythms of nature. On another day I might prefer the simple silence of Zen. Still yet another day I might feel in need of the Christian symbols of my childhood as expressed by the great Christian mystics.

This is another reason why New Agers tend to refuse labels and prefer to describe themselves in terms of being seekers. Yet we rarely stop to think about how playing the role of seeker devastates community and undermines all our hopes for an alternative future. After all, a seeker is basically a tourist, just passing through, picking up knick knacks and souvenirs along the way. Playing the seeker conveniently absolves us of accountability, makes it easy to avoid responsibility for anything going on. It allows us to move unresisting through the gears of the old paradigm and leaves us unchallenged to help create something new and better. And, of course, it leaves the ego untouched.

If we truly want to get our egos out of our way and be able to work together to create a better world, we have to move beyond seeking, and start finding. "The New Age is about self-discovery," writes David Spangler. "But it is also about self-definition and incarnation. It is about making choices, setting boundaries, defining limits."

If we truly want to help create a new age of harmony, we need to surrender the individual ego to a collective identity—an identity that encourages accountability even as it remains open to possibility. An identity specific enough to serve as a cohesive force for community, yet flexible enough to accommodate different beliefs and practices. An identity that soothes the isolation of individuality without stealing away its freedoms. An identity that allows us to find a balance between solitude and society, self and other, ego and soul.

The only identity I know that meets all these needs is the New Age identity. It takes the best from old wisdom traditions and from new scientific insights and combines them in a spirit-based philosophy that fully addresses all aspects of the self—body, mind, spirit.

It also offers the most integrated philosophy, and most inclusive identity, to be found on the planet. It is the only identity I know that allows one to be a Zen Pagan Christian or a Kabbalah-studying Taoist or a yoga-practicing bohemian and makes it possible for all of them to relate to each other. Like a masterpiece of music that allows all manner of instruments to play a wide range of notes in harmony, the New Age identity supports the great range of beliefs that rise from the core principles of the perennial philosophy.

This inclusiveness is important, for we Stage Four individualists are in dire need of the common ground of a common identity. More than anything, we need common ground on which to engage each other, speak to each other, listen to each other, serve each other. More than anything, we need common ground on which to form a community—and build the social capital necessary for the transformation of self and society.

So...

For argument's sake, let's say this is exactly what we decide to do. Let's say we are all good and tired of being invisible and ineffective. Let's say we feel ready to join with our fellow idealists into an identifiable collective that will allow us to set common goals and work together to bring about a real transformation of our society. Why on earth should we call ourselves New Age? The term has been maligned and misused and misunderstood for decades now. So why not let it die? Why not find a better emblem?

Why New Age is still the right emblem

The term New Age is said to have originated with Alice Bailey, the most prominent promoter of Theosophy after Helena Blavatsky. Bailey published a book entitled *Discipleship in the New Age* in 1944, the same year the American artist and mystic Walter Russell spoke about "this New Age philosophy of the spiritual reawakening of man."

But it wasn't until the mid-1970s that the term was first widely applied to the most recent movement to coalesce around the resurgence of spiritual idealism. And it wasn't until the 1980s, when I myself first adopted the term and the ideas that it represented, that the emblem became widely recognized.

No doubt my view of the New Age label is unique to my own particular age. I was a teenager when the movement was most popular, and because I embraced the emblem so enthusiastically at such a young age, it became part of my spiritual identity.

I realize that just because the term holds special meaning for me doesn't mean everyone else feels the same. Older idealists are likely to have experimented with different belief systems before the New Age became popular. If the term appealed to them at all, they probably tried it on for a time, then discarded it with relative ease. Younger idealists didn't encounter the term New Age until it was regarded as passé, and so have likely never identified with it at all.

Yet, even those who never identified with it still know the term and have a general idea of what it means. Certainly no other term introduced in the past twenty-five years to describe spiritual idealism is nearly as recognizable—or memorable.

The stickiness factor

The Tipping Point, Malcolm Gladwell's 2002 book on trends and social epidemics, became such a huge bestseller that his ideas are now more or less common knowledge. One of the terms he coined in that book was the "stickiness factor," which describes an idea or phrase that not only sticks in people's mind, but is easy to pass along.

Visionary writers, along with progressive organizers, want very much to find a term that will stick with their idealistic audience. They try hard to find the just right words that unify a group and motivate it to action. But, being visionaries, they rarely employ terms already used by someone else. After all, a visionary is by definition a trailblazer, an innovator. So most New Age writers tend to reinvent the wheel, and come up with something new and different.

Yet all substitutes to the term New Age have failed to stick. Remember the Global Renaissance Alliance introduced in 2000 with much fanfare? It's long gone. The holistic movement has fans, but is more particular to alternative health and food products. Body/Mind/Sprit is an unwieldy publishing category. Radical Spirit, New Consciousness, Translucent Revolution, Self-Actualization—all these terms have made brief appearances before getting lost in the shuffle.

In June 2006, *Newsweek* magazine and Beliefnet.com began calling New Agers Lohasians, derived from the marketing acronym LOHAS (Lifestyles of Health and Sustainability). The Beliefnet message board filled up with posts from people who thought the term referred to a Lindsay Lohan celebrity cult. I haven't heard the term used as an identity again.

Today, if you go to New Age-style expos or seminars, you will likely hear speakers refer to the "higher consciousness movement." I like the term because it has an evolutionary character which suggests the need for growth into the higher stages. But there really isn't a way to translate that phrase into a self-descriptive moniker. ("Hi, I'm Teena, and I'm a Higher Consciousness-er.")

Of course, there is still Cultural Creatives, which pops up now and again. And in 2008, Paul Ray and Jim Garrison announced a new effort to try to unify the movement under this emblem, which gave me a little thrill. I was happy to discover someone else pointing out the devastating dearth of social capital that accompanies the lack of a unifying emblem. (*What is Enlightenment?* August, 2008)

Ray and Garrison recognize that a common cultural identity will serve as a vital rallying point for the scattered idealistic population they call Cultural Creatives and help us work together toward our dearly held goals. And if they succeed in getting the fifty million spiritual idealists across the nation to get behind the Cultural Creative label, we will all have good reason to celebrate and be grateful. I wholeheartedly support their effort, or any effort made to unify us all under any emblem that will stick.

But it seems to me that the term Cultural Creative is more adjective than noun, more descriptive of a range of values than a specific philosophy with a specific aim. And in the nine years since the term was introduced, it has not yet gained traction within the movement or in the wider culture. Neither does it produce a visceral jolt to the system the way New Age does.

It seems to me counterproductive to keep trying out different names for the New Age movement—names that do not fit, do not stick, do not inspire. In my opinion, we need to step up and reclaim the name that everyone already knows. We need to rescue the term New Age, and insist on its true meaning as a philosophy of oneness and spirit and hope.

APRIL 6, 2009

Rebranding the New Age

"There is a shiny commercial skin that covers everything American," writes Joe Bageant in a wonderful essay featured on Alternet.org today. He decries the "glossy branding of every item and experience," especially spiritual experience. The New Age movement has always done the same—criticized the commercial commodification of spirituality, while lambasting labels and branding. (Of course, this lambasting is usually done in a book that costs $24.95 hardcover, or during a four-hour workshop that costs $195.)

Now here I am trying to push the branding of our spiritual ideals. Or more accurately, push the rebranding of them. The definition of a brand is this: "A collection of experiences and associations connected with a particular entity." New Age beliefs and ideals have already been branded by the culture. Today, it is a widely misunderstood, widely mocked brand that has become a liability whenever we communicate our beliefs in the context of the mainstream.

Case in point: My one guilty TV pleasure, shared with my daughter, is watching *The Bachelor* on Monday nights. In this last season, airing between January and March 2009 (the infamous Jason/Melissa/Molly triangle), several New Age-y people were featured on the show. The first, one of the contenders, an attractive and intelligent-seeming woman, let the Bachelor know that she had a "vision board" to help her manifest the things she wanted in her life. Cut to: Bachelor Jason, smirking for the camera, "I don't get it." She was portrayed as ridiculous and, of course, was sent home the first night.

Later, another contender's mother had a little ceremony to send off the spirit of the dead bird she hit with her car, then later sat down with Bachelor Jason to talk about reincarnation and past lives. Cue the kooky music. Cut to: Jason's frozen smile. With a nutjob mom like that, there was no doubt why that girl was sent home packing sixteen minutes later.

Now the producers of *The Bachelor* were not being unusually insensitive. This kind of portrayal of New Age-style beliefs is *de rigeur*, socially obligatory, and reflects the cultural brand connected with the New Age. While neither person identified themselves as New Age, they were stamped with the brand nonetheless, and then publicly mocked for it.

Most spiritual idealists today try to distance themselves from the New Age brand, as if it has nothing to do with them. But the reality is, popular culture is a perpetual motion machine that labels and brands us regardless of our approval or disapproval. Instead of trying to run away from an inevitable branding process, why not turn around and embrace it and do something positive with it?

A good brand is an asset, not a liability, and can open the doors to untold opportunities. Instead of abandoning the creation of the New Age brand to those who don't understand it, we should take ownership of it and create a brand that better communicates, better inspires, and better transforms.

The "I have a dream" factor

No doubt some would say it is unrealistic to openly embrace a term with as much baggage as New Age, as unrealistic as many believe it is to envision a utopian New Age in the first place.

But as Rabbi Michael Lerner writes in *The Left Hand of God*, if you are a spiritual idealist, "the strategy of realism is a huge mistake. When you stop asking, 'What do I really believe in?' and substitute instead a focus on asking, 'What is realistic?' you are on a slippery slope toward the values of materialism and selfishness that receive much clearer statement" by others.

If we are going to change the world, Lerner continues, we have to stop worrying about being realistic and turn instead to our values, our ideals, our visionary hopefulness—"the kind of hopefulness that makes you willing to fight for your highest ideals and take risks to make them happen."

The fact is, in spite of all efforts to sweep the New Age under the rug—or ridicule and demonize it out of existence—the term has remained stubbornly sticky, still hanging on, more than a decade after the supposed death of the movement.

Perhaps that is why even the pessimistic Sutcliffe says that the term New Age remains the idealistic/holistic/spiritual contingent's "one potentially explosive emblem"—a potential thus far unrealized.

I propose that we help the emblem explode.

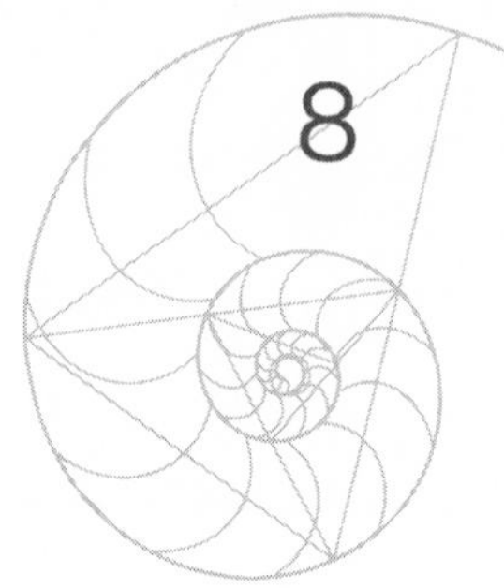

8 Community and Social Capital

In the New Age of the 1980s, author after author grandly announced that the evolution of human consciousness would make a societal transformation to a new paradigm all but inevitable. We were told that all we had to do was develop our own consciousness, and then *voila*! By some hundredth-monkey osmosis, the rest of humanity would follow in a massive wave of awakening into harmony.

Yet decades later, the rest of humanity still languishes in its slumber. Mass awakening is not, by any means, inevitable. Not that a number of important things haven't improved (i.e., the election of Barack Obama). But overall, working on ourselves, and only ourselves, has pretty much left the world undisturbed and plenty of important things in worse shape than ever (i.e., the environment and the growing gap between rich and poor). Clearly, we are missing a vital element in the philosophy of "changing oneself as a way to change the world."

Or, perhaps we are not missing something so much as we are looking at it from the wrong direction. We have been assuming that if we change ourselves for ourselves—free ourselves from ignorance and suffering and secure our own happiness—a corresponding change in society will appear as a by-product. But I believe it actually works in reverse. We need to change ourselves for the world, for the benefit of others, and a corresponding change in our own happiness will then appear as a by-product. Working on ourselves benefits the whole only when we anchor it in the context of the whole and our connections to each other.

"To be fully ourselves," wrote Tielhard de Chardin, we must move "in the opposite direction, in the direction of convergence with all the rest. [We] must advance towards 'the other.' The peak of ourselves, the acme of our originality, is not our individuality, but our person; and according to the evolutionary structure of the world, we can only find our person by uniting together."

Or in the words of Joseph Campbell, "The fullness of man is not in the separate member, but in the body of society as a whole... If he presumes to break himself off, either in deed or thought and feeling, he only breaks connection with the source of his existence." And if a man presumes to break himself off in his spiritual evolution, he doesn't evolve very far, nor does the world evolve with him.

Individual transformation is ultimately the result of *communal* efforts. The personal shift is intimately tied up with a collective shift. If we truly want to change ourselves, then we need to anchor ourselves in the context of the whole and build what Peter Block calls "a communal structure of belonging that produces the foundation for the whole system to move."

Social capital, social fields

It was sociologist Robert Putnam, in his 1998 bestseller *Bowling Alone: The Collapse and Revival of American Community,* who introduced many of us to the concept of "social capital"—the value of social connections and networks, and their impact on our lives. He presented study after study that reveals how American lives have suffered over these last decades of increased fragmentation.

Everything from the effectiveness of our government and public education to our own personal levels of health and happiness have fallen sharply since the 1960s.

It is nearly impossible to succeed at any endeavor without social capital. A person's ability to find a job often depends on social capital. Any advocate's ability to get a law on the books depends on social capital. A church's ability to convert souls depends on social capital. A candidate's ability to be elected president certainly depends on social capital. Indeed, Barack Obama's presidential victory was largely due to the effectiveness of his social network of donors on the Internet and a vast social network of volunteers on the ground.

"Social capital turns out to have a forceful, even quantifiable effect on many different aspects of our lives," Putnam says. It "greases the wheel of society" by establishing social norms of reciprocity, establishing trust between citizens, serving as a conduit for the flow of information and learning, and most important, by widening our awareness of how our fates are linked.

Putnam calls social capital both a "private good" and "public good," benefiting those individuals directly invested, but also those bystanders who have nothing to do with a particular network.

The New Age has long recognized the value of social networks of like minds and has often described such networks in terms of "fields." In physics, a field is a measurable quantity of force or energy associated to each point of space-time. A social field can be similarly understood as a cohering force within the energy of consciousness.

Different writers from different disciplines have called this field by different names. The biologist Rupert Sheldrake, for example, talks about a "morphic field," an organizing intelligence within organisms or systems. Or, from the discipline of physics, we find David Bohm theorizing an "implicate order," which he described as a language that arises from reality, allowing different parts of the universe to communicate with each other. Looking from within the discipline of psychology, Carl Jung identified the "collective unconscious," which connects all individuals and explains shared instincts and common experiences such as particular dreams.

What these disparate thinkers are telling us is that a collectivity creates a special dynamic. Whenever we join with others in a shared identity and mutually agree to operate using the same set of ideals or language, we create a social field that becomes a generative source for everyone within it. This field gathers us up, invisibly connecting us. And within this growing network of connections, we are empowered by the law of increasing returns through an ever-growing series of positive feedback loops.

Look at how traffic works, how a multitude of people are able to move together at high speeds down a highway in a feat of remarkable trust and cooperation among strangers. We each, at separate times and places, agreed to take on specific rules of the road because those rules allow us all to get where we are going without careening into each other. Strangers who have never met each other are able to travel together in perfect accord in order to get to different locations. This social field creates a positive feedback loop: The more we use the system of roads, the more roads are built, and the more places we can go.

This is an example of the private good, helpful to individuals (in this case, drivers), and is the result of what Putnam calls "bonding" social capital. A similar dynamic can be created by any community joined by a common identity. Just as drivers on the road don't have to know each other in order to move together and confer benefit on each other, we don't have to personally know the people in our network in order to enjoy the benefits of bonding social capital. We simply have to operate on the same understanding of reality.

Imagine if all of us who consider ourselves "spiritual but not religious" were to take on a New Age identity and create a social field with other like-minded idealists. We would continue to move along toward our own individual goals, but our shared understanding of the rules of the road would allow us to move more quickly. And in pursuing kindred interests, more relevant information would flow toward us, more new doors would open, and helpers would pop up more often in a synergistic multiplier effect.

This would be an amazing thing, and an extraordinary start. I say start because bonding social capital in and of itself doesn't address the public good, and as idealists, we are particularly concerned with the public good. In order to impact the public good, we need what Putnam calls "bridging" social capital.

Whereas bonding social networks are inward-looking, bridging networks are outward-looking. They purposefully reach out to make connections with others. Bridging social capital is built through personal interactions that allow us to enter into dialogue with each other and create shared meaning. And shared meaning, David Bohm adds, creates the vital "coherence" necessary to affect social change. He uses the concept of light to explain:

> Ordinary light is "incoherent", which means that it is going in all sorts of directions, and the light waves are not in phase with each other, so they don't build up. But a laser produces a very intense beam which is coherent. The light waves build up strength because they are all going the same direction. This beam can do all sorts of things that ordinary light cannot.

Bohm goes on to say that ordinary thought in our society is obviously incoherent, "going in all sorts of directions, with thoughts conflicting and canceling each other out." But if people were to sit down together and talk to each other and "think together in a coherent way, it would have tremendous power."

Imagine seeing coherent New Age principles expressed often in the media, on television, and in public discussions of all sorts. Imagine if political candidates had to take into account a coherent New Age vote. Imagine if the entire fifty million of us who espouse idealistic values worked together on a coherent New Age agenda of progressive goals. What couldn't we accomplish?

While bonding social capital allows us to form a community in the abstract, it is bridging social capital that allows us to create a living, breathing community with truly miraculous powers to transform the world for all of us.

If we want to save the world, we first need to bond with a common identity. Then we can get down to the real work of transformation: building social bridges that will connect us with each other.

The Stages of Community

All communities form according to a predictable pattern, said M. Scott Peck in *The Different Drum*, his analysis of how communities work. He outlined four general stages of community, and the first is pseudo-community, in which all members are nice to each other, no one challenges each other, no one goes very deep. This is certainly an apt description of the New Age in the 1980s.

Next, there is a stage of chaos and blatant resistance to community in which people defend their positions and their place. Clearly, most New Age idealists spent the 1990s in resistance and refusal to identify themselves as anything at all.

The third stage, which I believe has been unfolding these past few years, Peck calls emptiness. In this stage, people begin to release their expectations, preconceptions, and judgments, which prevent the formation of community, and start understanding their need for each other.

This brings us to the final stage, or true community, in which the members of the community finally begin relating to each other with true empathy, and together discover

> a new ability to reach their common goals. It would appear the New Age has reached that threshold now. The movement has evolved through all the stages of preparation and is poised for the development of a true New Age community.

The structure of belonging

I am about as liberal and New Age-y as a person can be, yet I live in a conservative Christian-y area in the conservative state of Arizona. In most any social situation, I hear my neighbors speak in ways that let me know my opinions would not be welcome. I love Arizona, and enjoy my neighbors, but I often hear myself thinking, "I don't belong here."

A few years after I moved here, Marianne Williamson, an author revered by New Age audiences, came to visit Phoenix on a speaking tour. I was happy to buy a ticket, and as I joined the flow of people heading toward the auditorium, I remember feeling almost giddy with relief to be surrounded by people like me. I felt genuinely connected to Williamson's audience and was able to enjoy a satisfying few hours of feeling like I belonged. More than anything Williamson actually said that night, that is what I remember most.

A sense of belonging is at the core of community, and to create a *structure* of belonging is to create a community. The way to do this, according to Peter Block, is deceptively simple: We sit down together in small groups and we talk to each other. Or rather, we ask each other questions and we listen to each other. In other words, we begin a conversation, a dialogue.

The approach to our conversation makes all the difference. If we convene a typical action-oriented meeting centered on problem-solving and information dissemination, then we preserve the status quo and reinforce feelings of alienation. We get the same result in "discussions" in which we try to persuade others to our point of view or win an argument that the other person must necessarily lose.

But if we convene a gathering centered on the rhythm dialogue—the rhythm of posing questions and sharing our hearts without judgment or analysis—then we build relatedness, awareness, empathy. We build the structure of belonging. (And frankly, we go-it-alone idealists are in dire need of a sense of belonging to anchor us and help us feel accountable for each other.) Furthermore, we start creating a common culture of collectively shared meaning. (And frankly, we go-it-alone idealists drift about in an incoherent culture in which we have almost no shared meaning at all.)

The questions we ask each other are all-important. We need to pose questions that, when answered, lead us to accept the role of investor, owner, and creator of our world. Questions such as: what do we want to create together? To answer this question inevitably leads us to declare new possibilities in the presence of others.

"The key phrase is in the presence of others," Block adds. "A possibility, when declared publicly, heard and witnessed by others with whom we have a common interest, at a moment when something is at stake, is a critical element of communal transformation."

This is why Block says most everything necessary to building community—and bringing a fresh future into being—happens in a small group. Genuine community requires "that all voices need to be heard, but not necessarily all at one time or by everybody." The small group allows the process to become personal, allows all voices to be heard. The small group therefore serves as the "unit of transformation."

The New Age has long extolled the importance of gathering together in small groups to effect a larger transformation. We like to call them circles.

The Circle

In the early days of the movement, the workshop and seminar was undoubtedly the most common type gathering for the New Age seeker. But over the decades, the emphasis moved from passive learning to active connecting and relating in small circles. In the late 1990s, books such as Robin Deen Carnes and Sally Craig's *Sacred Circles*, Christina Baldwin's *Calling the Circle*, and Jean Shinoda Bolen's *The Millionth Circle* all encouraged us to begin gathering and engaging each other. Meanwhile, the Global Renaissance Alliance headed by the movement's biggest names (Marianne Williamson, Deepak Chopra, Neale Donald Walsch, Wayne Dyer, and more), spearheaded an effort to organize peace circles throughout the country.

Today, a quick Internet search shows that a great many peace circles and meditation circles and wisdom circles and healing circles and pagan circles are convened here and there, now and again. And also thanks to the Internet, we can join any number of virtual circles that cater to our preferred brand of spirituality.

But overall, most spiritual idealists remain largely unconnected to any kind of group of live human beings, and we are missing out on this crucial component of spiritual growth and community. We are also missing out on the *only* real means of bringing the change to our society that most of us so fervently want.

"Large scale transformation occurs when enough small group shifts lead to the larger change," Block writes. We know this because the small gathering is a microcosm of the larger community. Each circle is a center with an intensity granted by the whole. Conversely, as each circle unfolds, "slowly and with great consciousness," these individual circles become whole centers in and of themselves, which then begin to combine with other centers to achieve some scale.

Or in the words of Jean Shinoda Bolen, "It's like throwing

pebbles in a pond; each one has an impact and an effect, with concentric rings of change rippling out and affecting others."

Of course, this is all dependent on enough people making the decision to throw a pebble and start a circle. An alternative future cannot be compelled into being by a few visionaries or leaders stretching their arms out over the land. An alternative future comes into being only through the choices made by individuals and the conversations that unfold between them in their own living rooms.

"Sustainable changes in community occur locally, on a small scale, happen slowly, and are initiated at a grassroots level," writes Block. As the leaders of the faded Global Renaissance Alliance would likely attest, a vibrant circle cannot be organized or directed from the top down, it must grow organically from ground made fertile by the convictions of individuals who are ready to own up to their accountability for the whole.

Neither can the agenda and content of the circle be dictated from afar, but must be developed by each group's own internal wisdom. If we can get people together in a room "in the right context and with a few simple ground rules," says Block, "the wisdom to create a future or solve a problem is almost always in the room."

OCTOBER 13, 2008

The Risks

BLOG

Looking for the New Age

After talking myself into believing I was getting a sign from the universe to move ahead on the Web site, I decided to make a YouTube video for the home page. Oh, it was going to be so cute and funny, talking to people about the New Age. So I drove up to Flagstaff and Sedona where all the liberals and New Agers are, and struck out terrible. The two owners of the New Age stores in Flagstaff refused me, and the wind died in my sails right then and there.

I have been stuck ever since on how to approach people,

whether to approach people to invite them to contribute to my little endeavor. I am "live and let live" to a fault, terrible sales person, no hardcharging promoter, so what do I think I'm doing? My next step was to try to contact different authors and invite them to add their two cents, but it is hard, hard, to bring myself to it. Then tonight I run across this in Peter Block's book on Community (oh, what a book, profound book, beautiful book), in a little section called "The Risk of Invitation:"

"The anxiety of the invitation is that they might not show up. I do not want to face the reality of their absence, caution, reservations, passivity, or indifference. I do not want to have to face the prospect that I or a few of us may be alone in the future we want to pursue.

"And I do not want to face the same truth about myself, for my fear that they will not come is the caution I feel myself about showing up, even for the possibility that I am committed to. My fear is that what I long for is not possible, that what I invite them to is not realistic, that the world I seek cannot exist. And so I imagine myself as a misplaced person, an exile. It is today's version of an old story that I am wrong and I will soon be found out. The fear that no one will show up is a projection of my own doubt, my loss of faith."

It is equal parts unnerving and comforting to see one's fears and anxieties laid bare by a stranger. Now what to do with this diagnosis? The few invitations I've offered thus far regarding this project have indeed resulted in no one showing up. I keep wanting to make this a sign from the universe as well, to let myself off the hook, and go back to life as normal, and think about what restaurant I'd like to take my kids to tonight, what movie to grab at Blockbuster.

But I can't, I can't, I believe the words I have written. I have to go forward. But at least I have the understanding of one Peter Block of Cincinnati, Ohio.

Declaring a new possibility

The ground rules that will create a new age of harmony for all are indeed simple. We sit together in a circle and ask questions that lead to accountability (see Chapter 23 for more on how to start a circle and ask the right questions). We must also be willing to declare the possibility of a New Age.

"A possibility is brought into being by the act of declaring it," Block writes.

The New Age, or what Block calls "restoration," becomes a reality as soon as we declare it a possibility. Once we have made our declaration, "a declaration of the future we choose to live into... and done so with a sense of belonging and in the presence of others, that possibility has been brought into the room." In essence, that possibility is brought into being there in that room, in that gathering, in that community.

"This room, today, becomes an example of the future we want to create. There is no need to wait for the future," Block continues.

When we gather together and declare the possibility of a New Age, then the New Age is right here, and right now, in the room with us.

So I am hereby publicly declaring to you, reading these words now, in whichever room these words find you, the possibility of the New Age for all of us. I am accepting my accountability for the whole and choosing to live into the possibility of a better world today.

And now I will ask *you*: what do we want to create together?

Essential Reading for the New Age

A number of New Age classics have reached the bestseller lists, but below are the authors that have been essential reading in my own New Age experience. They each write with such scope and depth and skill, one could probably gain a complete understanding of idealism through any one of them alone. They have all been my favorite at one time or another, so rather than rank them in any kind of order, I present them here chronologically, by date of birth.

Ralph Waldo Emerson (1803–1882)

The nineteenth century version of the New Age was transcendentalism, and its premier spokesperson was the widely respected Emerson. Indeed, he was such a prolific speaker and highly quotable writer that his name still pops up in speeches and books of the present day. After running across his name again and again, it is a great literary surprise to finally read Emerson and have him describe your own idealism to you in what is probably the most beautiful language ever put on paper. Emerson thought deeply about the nature of reality and his essays are rich with imagery and sweeping arguments that carry one into the true nature of things. The formal style takes a little getting used to, but with patient reading, Emerson will show you the true majesty of idealistic thought.

Henry David Thoreau (1816–1862)

Another brilliant transcendentalist, Thoreau's *Walden* remains the quintessential exploration of the authentic life. But unlike Emerson's lofty and soaring prose, Thoreau writes in a spare, incisive style, revealing the beauty and joys of the mundane. "Sometimes as I drift on Walden Pond, I cease to live and begin to be," he says simply, and with the deftly drawn details of his account, we are there with him. While *Walden* is his most famous work, his journals and essays are also gold mines of insight.

Walt Whitman (1819–1892)

Idealism in its purest and most eloquent form found its voice in Walt Whitman. His *Leaves of Grass* does not read like mere poetry but like the utterings of exuberant Spirit itself.

Rabindranath Tagore (1861–1941)

The winner of the Nobel Prize in Literature (1913), Tagore was an astonishingly prolific writer of poems, stories, and plays, as well as an artist and science enthusiast. But it is his philosophic writings that make me frequently stop in awe to absorb yet another wondrous insight into life and reality. I have quotes from his work scribbled in notebooks all over my house.

Henri Bergson (1859–1941)

Another Nobel Prize winner for literature (1927), Bergson was perhaps the foremost philosopher of conscious evolution. He began with the ages-old philosophy of idealism and interpreted it through the lens of Darwin's recently published theory of evolution, and came up with a brilliant synthesis of logic and intuition, mind and heart.

Pierre Tielhard de Chardin (1881–1955)

A unique combination of Jesuit priest and respected paleontologist, Teilhard stretched himself between the worlds of religion and science and discovered the mysticism in the middle. His philosophical writings were repressed by the Catholic church during his lifetime, but luckily were published after his death. He believed humans were evolving toward a conscious network, a "noosphere," that would one day circle the globe, all but predicting the Internet. His writing shimmers with wisdom, heart, and hope.

Jiddu Krishnamurti (1895–1986)

Raised to be a "World Teacher" by the leaders of the Theosophical Society, Krishnamurti eventually rejected the role thrust upon him, and declared that "truth is a pathless land." He spent the rest of his life giving talks on the nature of reality and how to discover it on one's own. Reading his words is like sitting next to a gentle stream that gradually calms the mind.

Joseph Campbell (1904–1987)

Well-known as the world's foremost mythology expert, Campbell's writings are much more than an exploration of mythology. He deftly takes up strands of religion, philosophy and psychology and weaves them together into a dazzling whole, then shows us how this whole is personally significant to each of us. His gift for discerning what is beneath universal symbols is joined with a talent for translating abstract insights into concrete words. Campbell reveals to us to all the hidden aspects of our mental lives.

Alan Watts (1915–1973)

Along with D.T. Suzuki, Watts was one of the first interpreters of Eastern philosophy for a Western audience. Beginning in the 1930s with *The Spirit of Zen*, through his death in 1973, Watts wrote dozens of books and essays that made the formerly inscrutable thought of the East almost easy for a novice to grasp. His writing shines with profound understanding, humor and uncommon talent with a metaphor. A few hours with Watts can make you feel as if a hundred little lights have been turned on inside your mind. In my opinion, he was the most extraordinary spiritual teacher of the 20th century. And if you have the chance to listen to any of his recorded lectures, avail yourself of the treat.

Huston Smith (1919–)

A philosophy professor that became fascinated by the different religions of the world, Smith is another multi-faceted writer of remarkable knowledge and talent with words. He helps us to recognize the universal truths that are shared by every wisdom tradition, and how we may more fully live them. A generous, compassionate soul shines from every page.

Chogyam Trungpa (1940–1987)

A Tibetan Buddhist teacher that often scandalized the Buddhist community with his very American ways and questionable method of "crazy wisdom," Trungpa nonetheless writes brilliantly, cutting to the heart of the matter in direct, no nonsense language. Perhaps because the man himself was unabashedly flawed and prey to ego, he intimately describes our own weaknesses to us, and how we trap ourselves in illusion. I find his work bracing and honest.

Ken Wilber (1949–)

More than any other writer, Ken Wilber is the compelling voice of sanity and reason speaking from the heart of a movement that has too often slid about in excesses of illogic. There is no silly stuff in the voluminous works of Wilber, just basic truths organized into an integral system that take all areas of human knowledge into account, from religion and spirituality to psychology and science. Beginning with his first popular book written when he was just twenty-three years old, *The Spectrum of Consciousness*, all the way to his thickly dense *Sex, Ecology & Spirituality*, Wilber sees directly into the heart of reality and generously translates his vision into mental concepts for those of us trying to understand it all with more clunky brains.

Marianne Williamson (1952–)

If Ken Wilber is the cool, logical analyst of New Age idealism, then Marianne Williamson speaks from its warm, feeling heart. All her work nudges us gently, compassionately, toward seeing the world—along with ourselves and each other—through the eyes of love. Whenever I feel lost in fear, Marianne Williamson helps me reorient myself and feel found.

New Age Classics

These are the books that have been widely embraced by New Agers and idealists of all kinds. These are the books that sparked the movement and kept it burning with optimism for decades. These are the books that made our lives make sense. Many of these books sold millions of copies, or have been in print for decades. A few even broke records to become phenomenons in the publishing industry. Most all are fascinating books, and well worth your time. Listed alphabetically, by title:

The Alchemist, by Paulo Coehlo (1995)

Publisher's Weekly says, "This inspirational fable…the tale of Santiago, a shepherd boy, who dreams of seeing the world, is compelling in its own right, but gains resonance through the many lessons Santiago learns during his adventures. He journeys from Spain to Morocco in search of worldly success, and eventually to Egypt, where a fateful encounter with an alchemist brings him at last to self-understanding and spiritual enlightenment. The story has the comic charm, dramatic tension, and psychological intensity of a fairy tale, but it's full of specific wisdom as well, about becoming self-empowered, overcoming depression, and believing in dreams. The cumulative effect is like hearing a wonderful bedtime story from an inspirational psychiatrist. Comparisons to *The Little Prince* are appropriate; this is a sweetly exotic tale for young and old alike."

The Aquarian Conspiracy: Personal and Social Transformation in Our Time, by Marilyn Ferguson (1980)

This was the first and best book to describe the then-burgeoning New Age movement. Ferguson was able to identify the impetus and substance of the movement in clear, convincing language. She persuades us that it is in our power to choose what kind of society we want to live in. A remarkable and inspiring read that feels fresh all these years later, this book deservedly remains what many have called the New Age bible. A must read.

Be Here Now, by Ram Dass (1971)

A trippy, psychedelic, poetic book by the New Age's very first celebrity wise man, Ram Dass. Both a work of retro '60s art and a groovy crash course in Hindu thought, the book has just as much power to blow your mind as it ever did. And after your mind is blown, you'll kick back and finally enjoy that everything that happens "is all part of the drama."

The Celestine Prophecy, by James Redfield (1995)

One of the bestselling books of the 1990s, *Publisher's Weekly* calls this "a fast-paced adventure in New Age territory that plays like a cross between Raiders of the Lost Ark and Moses' trek up Mt. Sinai. Originally self-published, the book sold phenomenally, sparked by word of mouth. The saga begins when the unnamed middle-aged male narrator whimsically quits his nondescript life to track down an ancient Peruvian manuscript (pretentiously called the Manuscript) containing nine Insights that supposedly prophesy the modern emergence of New Age spirituality...Redfield has a real talent for page-turning action, and his lightweight quest employs auras, energy transfers, and other psychic phenomena. But several of the Insights are incredibly vacuous and politically correct, and long stretches of dialogue are banal and cliched."

Conversations with God, by Neale Donald Walsch (1996)

Another book that caught fire in New Age circles and sold so well that it launched an entire industry known as CWG. Amazon.com describes the book this way: "Blasphemy! Heresy! Who does this man think he is, claiming to speak directly to God?! Jesus did it, Muhammad did it, the Jewish prophets did it, but none of their Gods had the sardonic wit or raw verve of Prophet Walsch's God. Neale Donald Walsch isn't claiming to be the Messiah of a new religion, just a frustrated man who sat down one day with pen in his hand and some tough questions in his heart. As he wrote his questions to God, he realized that God was answering them...directly... through Walsch's pen. The result, far from the apocalyptic predictions or cultic eccentricities you might expect, turns out to be matter-fact, in-your-face wisdom on how to get by in life while remaining true to yourself and your spirituality."

The Cultural Creatives: How 50 Million People Are Changing the World, by Paul H. Ray, Ph.D and Sherry Ruth Anderson, Ph.D. (2000)

A book that got a lot of attention when it came out, it is a basic updating of Ferguson's *Aquarian Conspiracy*. Unfortunately, it came out just as George W. Bush made his questionable entrance into the White House, carrying with him a new resurgence of conservatism. Yet despite becoming somewhat lost in the wake of events, the book made a convincing and well-detailed case for the continued existence of a movement that by the year 2000 had stopped calling itself New Age. It also identified many of our most important concerns in our personal and collective lives at the beginning of the twenty-first century.

Jonathan Livingston Seagull, by Richard Bach (1970)

I remember fiercely loving this short and sweet allegory about a gull who lives to fly when I first read it. With a constant refrain that freedom lies in our thoughts about reality, Bach's sweet story is an expression of pure idealism. Amazon.com says, "Flight is the metaphor that makes the story soar. Ultimately this is a fable about the importance of seeking a higher purpose in life, even if your flock, tribe, or neighborhood finds your ambition threatening. (At one point our beloved gull is even banished from his flock.) By not compromising his higher vision, Jonathan gets the ultimate payoff: transcendence. Ultimately, he learns the meaning of love and kindness… This is a spirituality classic, and an especially engaging parable for adolescents."

Out on a Limb, by Shirley MacLaine (1983)

I hold this brave, outrageous, you've-got-to-be-kidding-me book in the highest affection. Because of this book—or rather because of its no holds barred account of MacLaine's journey through the movement when it was all brand new—many people publicly wondered if MacLaine was off her rocker. She visits psychics and channelers and tries on every idea, silly or not, that was floating around at the time. The result is a book that is original, groundbreaking, and deeply moving. And for those millions of us who first discovered the New Age because of it, it was a life-changing experience. In my opinion, whether Shirley is off her rocker or not, idealism is forever in her debt.

The Perennial Philosophy, by Aldous Huxley (1945)

While probably not the first book to point out that many of our longstanding religions share the same mystical foundation and idealistic principles, it is certainly the most influential book to do so. Huxley's philosophical masterpiece is a compilation of other writers' works organized according to theme such as "Truth," and "Good and Evil" and "Faith." This gives the book a scattered, incohesive feel, but patient reading is rewarded with many thought-provoking gems.

***The Power of Now*, by Eckhart Tolle (1999)**

This runaway bestseller is surprisingly well-written, and as long as it is in your hands, you feel as if enlightenment is pooling just beneath your feet and all you have to do is step in. If it is not really that simple, Tolle still convinces me that it should be, and certainly is about to be. His writing is warm and supportive and I am sure if I just read the book a few more times, then I will start living in the now for more nows than not... After reading his book, you may also want to write him a note and thank him for the encouragement. Unlike some of those mean teachers who tell you that you have to work hard for years and years, Tolle pats you on the back and says, you can do it! And while I'm reading his book, I believe.

***The Prophet*, by Kahlil Gibran (1923)**

This book of poetic prose was given to me as a teenager and it left me breathless with its beauty. It also left me full of longing to connect with the divine. I can't say it any better than Amazon.com: "On the most basic topics—marriage, children, friendship, work, pleasure—Gibran's words have a power and lucidity that in another era would surely have provoked the description 'divinely inspired.' Free of dogma, free of power structures and metaphysics, consider these poetic, moving aphorisms a 20th-century supplement to all sacred traditions—as millions of other readers already have."

***A Return to Love*, by Marianne Williamson (1994)**

What a pleasure to discover the straightforward opinions of Marianne Williamson in this, her first book. Inspired by her experience with the idealistic principles of *A Course in Miracles*, Williamson writes with honesty, wit, and humor in describing her own struggle to let go of fear and choose to look through the eyes of love. Even though I am not a devotee of the Course, I completely related to, and was inspired by, her journey.

The Road Less Traveled, by M. Scott Peck (1978)

The mega-selling book about psychological health and growth was hugely influential on me as a young woman, maybe because it covers a much wider scope than mere psychology. As *Publisher's Weekly* notes, Peck takes "a mystical, Jungian tone more compatible with New Age spirituality," and "writes of psychotherapy as an exercise in 'love' and 'spiritual growth,' asserts that 'our unconscious is God' and affirms his belief in miracles, reincarnation, and telepathy. Peck's synthesis of such clashing elements (he even throws in a little thermodynamics) is held together by a warm and lucid discussion of psychiatric principles and moving accounts of his own patients' struggles and breakthroughs. Harmonizing psychoanalysis and spirituality, Christ and Buddha, Calvinist work ethic and interminable talking cures, this book is a touchstone of our contemporary religio-therapeutic culture." Peck's later books took a hard turn toward dualism and Christianity, but *Road Less Traveled* remains one of my all-time, eye-opening books.

The Tao of Physics, by Fritjof Capra (1975)

This is a Wow!-book that delights and sweeps one up in Capra's enthusiasm for his subject. An illuminating and convincing look at how the relatively recent findings of quantum physics are in surprising sync with the ancient tenets of Eastern philosophy. The dissonant gap between science and religion is narrowed and becomes resonant harmony in Capra's capable hands. There are many books that explore the very same theme, but this was one of the first, and certainly the most well-known in the New Age.

The Seat of the Soul, by Gary Zukav (1999)

Catapulted into bestsellerdom by a blessing from Oprah Winfrey, this book is an "insightful, lucid synthesis of modern psychology and new-age principles" according to Amazon.com. Zukav's goal is to help you evolve into a "multi-sensory" being, one who "values love more than the physical world," and one with a life filled with more compassion, trust and understanding. While I personally have never been able to get past the first twenty pages, my sister swears it rocked her world.

Siddhartha, by Herman Hesse (1922)

A lyrical novel written by the German Nobel Prize winner, I discovered it in my twenties and throughout the reading, it induced in me a kind of pleasant trance. Amazon.com says of the main character: "Born the son of a Brahmin, Siddhartha was blessed in appearance, intelligence, and charisma. In order to find meaning in life, he discarded his promising future for the life of a wandering ascetic. Still, true happiness evaded him. Then a life of pleasure and titillation merely eroded away his spiritual gains until he was just like all the other "child people," dragged around by his desires. Like Hermann Hesse's other creations of struggling young men, *Siddhartha* has a good dose of European angst and stubborn individualism. His final epiphany challenges both the Buddhist and the Hindu ideals of enlightenment. Neither a practitioner nor a devotee, neither meditating nor reciting, Siddhartha comes to blend in with the world, resonating with the rhythms of nature, bending the reader's ear down to hear answers from the river."

The Varieties of Religious Experience, By William James (1903)

Still in print over a hundred years after its first publication, this book by the famous psychologist/philosopher has been revered by readers from many disciplines, but is especially valuable to idealists and New Agers with an interest in spirituality and religion. A Harvard professor and the father of pragmatism, James was a practical man and able to look at his subject in a fair and logical manner. The result is a clear explanation of mysticism and idealistic philosophy that helps us understand it as the most reasonable of choices available to us when deciding on our own philosophy.

Zen and the Art of Motorcycle Maintenance, by Robert Pirsig (1974)

A story that wanders between a gentle meditation of profound philosophical insight and harrowing psychological thriller, Amazon.com says it is "arguably one of the most profoundly important essays ever written on the nature and significance of 'quality'...[It is] definitely a necessary anodyne to the consequences of a modern world pathologically obsessed with quantity. Although set as a story of a cross-country trip on a motorcycle by a father and son, it is more nearly a journey through two thousand years of Western philosophy. For some people, this has been a truly life-changing book."

PART IV

New Age Philosophy

Let no one delay
to study philosophy
while he is young,
and when he is old,
let him not become
weary of the study;
for no man can ever find
the time unsuitable or too late
to study the health of his soul.

— EPICURUS —

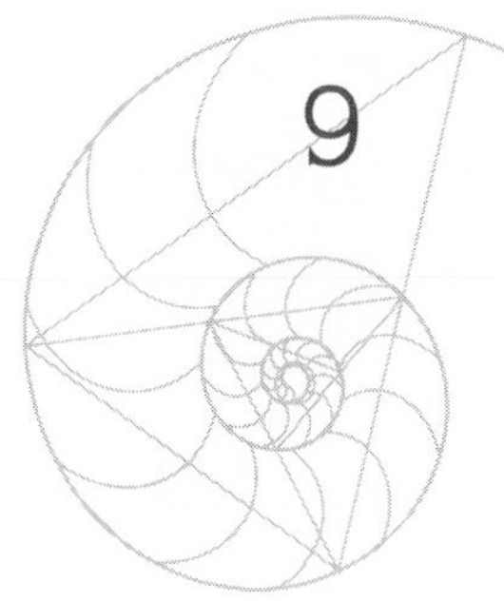

9 The Philosophy of Idealism

Stars may burn out and continents may drift, but the experience of being human eternally presents us with the same intractable problems. We wonder where we came from and how we got here. We wonder about the world around us and how it got here. We wonder why the environment that sustains us can so suddenly forsake us.

Philosophy takes our wonder and turns it into a number of questions known as the "problems" of philosophy. How do we know what is most true? What is the nature of reality? Is there a God? What is the nature of man? Why are we here? Do we have free will? Do we come into the world with moral obligations?

We all have some kind of answer to these questions, even if the answer is "I don't know." This means we all hold a philosophy. Even if we're not quite sure how to put it in words, we all look at the world from a particular direction, through a certain window, with a certain set of assumptions about reality.

Many of us, perhaps even most of us, don't give our philosophy much thought, let alone identify it with a name. Our beliefs about reality are one of these things that lie beneath the surface of awareness, like childhood memories or our own heartbeat.

Yet, just because we don't often focus our attention on it doesn't mean our philosophy is incidental. On the contrary, our philosophy quite literally determines the meaning we give our lives. It determines how we interpret the events that happen to us, it determines the actions we choose to undertake, it even determines how we feel about our own thoughts.

It is no exaggeration to say that the philosophy we hold is the most important element of our mental lives.

Windows on the world

There are generally three ways of looking at the world, and all philosophies are embellished varieties of these basic three. One's worldview is formed by many things, including one's childhood environment, cultural environment, and one's unique neurobiology. These factors greatly influence how far we have grown on the spiral of spiritual development and what we are most likely to believe about the nature of reality.

The map of spiritual growth (see Chapter 2) tells us that after first leaving the chaotic anything-goes stage of egocentrism, we enter the more orderly "mythic faith" stage. From this stage, we are usually attracted to the philosophy of dualism. This worldview perceives two very separate realities—God (Spirit) above and the world (matter) below. Dualism further says that the only correct way of looking at the world is through the window provided by holy scripture and religion. The dualistic moral order is thus very strict and paternalistic, and very much dependent on obedience to authority.

If we continue to grow, we will enter the "skeptical stage," and will most likely hold to the worldview of materialism, which is based on the certainty that matter is all there is. This philosophy insists that the only way of looking at the world is through the window provided by the scientific method of empirical proof. The materialistic moral order is still largely authoritarian, but it adds a new element of fairness and logic and calculations of the greatest good.

Here in the Western hemisphere, we learn dualism in church and materialism at school, and although they may be miles apart in their approach, they manage to co-exist very well. While fundamentalists may stay firmly entrenched in one view or the other, most Westerners learn to switch back and forth and accept both dualism and materialism to varying degrees, depending on whether they are at work or at school, or what's going on in their lives at the time.

Both worldviews are also in accord in their distrust of the self, the small slippery self caught up in its own experience. Both remove the self from the quest for knowledge and direct us instead to defer to others, whether it be long-dead prophets raving in the desert or a group of physicists in white lab coats.

Eventually, some will find the narrow focus of materialism inadequate and will grow into the next stage, where the spiritual self re-emerges without the trappings of fundamentalism and blind faith. This is most often the way of idealism, the philosophy of Eastern religions and the New Age, and it is based on the understanding that Spirit is all there is. The idealistic moral order is grounded in the idea that we are all One within the context of Spirit, and so it operates from a moral order based not on authority but on deep empathy and concern for others.

Idealism says that in order to truly see the world, one must look through many windows and learn to understand how each impacts what we see. It also says that since all seeing is dependent upon a self who sees, there can be no knowledge of the world without knowledge of the self. It says we must not blindly follow paths forged by others but must follow the path that pushes up beneath our own two feet.

The perfect idea

In the chicken or egg debate of what comes first in reality—matter or consciousness—the perennial philosophy asserts that consciousness, or spirit, gives birth to matter, and not the other way around. Hence, a saying one hears often in the New Age: We are not human beings having a spiritual experience, but spiritual beings having a human experience. Materialists who assume that matter gives birth to consciousness are simply looking at it from the wrong direction.

The word idealism comes from Plato's theory of eternal Ideas, the changeless entities he believed to give form to all matter. According to Plato, everything we experience, from truth or beauty to a bed or a horse, is an inferior copy of a perfect Idea that exists independent of reality.

The world we experience, said Plato, is but a pale reflection of the greater spiritual reality of Ideas.

Today, philosophers use more sophisticated terms to describe the concept. Buckminster Fuller, for example, called the Idea a "pattern integrity." He was reportedly fond of lifting a hand during his lectures and asking students what they were seeing. He would then point out that because all the cells of his hand would be dead in a year or so, replaced by new cells, then his hand could not be an actual thing with any permanence.

"My hand is actually a 'pattern integrity,'" he would say, "the universe's capability to create hands."

A pattern integrity, or Idea, is clearly a mental abstraction, something intangible, yet also completely real. From the idealistic perspective, every part of the universe—whether a hand, a tree, a car, or an ocean—is the manifestation of an abstract pattern, a phenomenon of Mind or Consciousness or Spirit. (In the German language, Mind and Spirit are the same word, *Geist,*)

This doesn't mean that matter does not exist; rather, it means that matter exists as an expression of Spirit. In other words, Spirit is the essence of matter, and the physical objects that make up the universe are literally made up of the immaterial substance of spiritual energy.

Spirit is reality, and no matter how you slice it, reality is Spirit.

Seeing the light

Unless you grew up in a Buddhist household, or had baby boomer parents who spent a few years in India to find enlightenment, then, like me, you may have never been exposed to the idealistic worldview in childhood.

But whether exposed to idealism or not, many of us who come of age in Western culture with its dominating philosophies of materialism and dualism, develop a nagging feeling of something "not quite right" about what we are generally told about reality.

Maybe you find yourself holding an opinion with no logical basis in the traditional worldviews. Or maybe you feel or see something that the traditional worldviews say you're not supposed to feel or see. Or maybe you have a conversation with an open-minded teacher or see a movie based in a different reality or run across an eye-opening book in a library.

But no matter how it happens, if you are ready, that first moment of crossing paths with idealism hits like an epiphany. The proverbial Aha! All at once, that nagging feeling of things not making sense falls away, and the new view of reality you see finally matches what you have intuitively felt all along.

Indeed, once that window shade snaps open, once you "see the light" from the idealistic point of view, you can't turn back. Once you glimpse the possibility that reality might be other than what it appears to be, you can never deny that sense of possibility again. As the great idealist Ralph Waldo Emerson put it, "Every materialist will be an idealist; but an idealist can never go backward to be a materialist."

I'm sure that if Emerson had had access to modern research

in developmental psychology, he would have added that idealists don't go backward to materialism because idealism is most often the philosophy held by those who are in Stage Four or Five of their spiritual development. And once we have attained a certain stage, we rarely regress back to previous stages. However, any philosophy or set of beliefs can be adopted by anyone at any stage, and that philosophy will be shaped accordingly.

The stages of philosophy

All our ideas about reality are inevitably molded by the perspective of where we sit on the spiral of development. Christianity, interpreted literally from Stage Two of spiritual growth, looks to be a widely divided dualism, with God high up on his throne and we sinners down here on a mucky, spirit-less Earth. But Christianity seen through the eyes of someone at Stage Four is no longer strictly dualistic. A Stage Four perspective allows for a greater grasp of symbolism, allows one to recognize Christianity's powerful metaphors as doorways to greater spiritual truths, and thus allows Jesus to become a symbol of the divine that lives in all of us. In the fourth stage, Christianity becomes idealistic.

Indeed, liberal Christians have much more in common ideologically with the New Age than they do with fundamentalist Christians. That is why a number of books exploring the deeper meanings of Christianity—books by authors such as Thomas Keating, Matthew Fox, Anne Lamott, or Huston Smith—are popular with New Age readers as well.

In the same vein, scientists coming from a Stage Four perspective may also transcend literal materialism to become idealists, too, as we see with renowned physicists like Erwin Schrodinger, Max Planck, or David Bohm. It was Planck who wrote, "Consciousness I regard as fundamental. I regard matter as derivative from consciousness."

It also works in the opposite direction. Even the most advanced, higher-stage New Age beliefs, interpreted from a Stage One perspective, can translate into the lowest magical thinking or fearful obsessions about alien "others." Meanwhile, idealistic principles interpreted from Stage Two thinking can be very fundamentalist and ethnocentric, as we see with the Hindu caste system that has thrived for thousands of years.

No set of beliefs is immune from the narrow and overly literal interpretations of the early stages of spiritual growth. And no matter how far we think we have advanced, we still carry these inner stages within us, and in response to certain pressures they can rise up to influence us at any time.

Yet, generally speaking, we can see that certain philosophies are a more natural fit with particular stages. We can also see that one stage is not somehow better than the other, and that the health and well-being of all the stages of the spiral are essential for spiritual growth. Stage Four idealism is built upon the structures of Stage Three skepticism, which is built upon the structures of Stage Two fundamentalism and so on.

For those of us who hope to grow into Stage Four, or who hope to grow *from* Stage Four into the higher stages, we need to make sure our idealism is structurally sound and provides a solid foundation for our evolution. In other words, we need to wrestle with the problems of philosophy.

The problems of philosophy

How do we know what is most true? What is the nature of reality? Is there a God? What is the nature of man? Why are we here? Do we have free will?

The following pages take up these problems, one by one, and delve into the answers suggested by idealism in general and by New Age philosophy in particular.

Not every sage and philosopher quoted here would necessarily agree with the New Age context in which, to me, they seem to belong. Nor will every idealist agree with my interpretation of these principles. One of the primary tenets of New Age idealism is that we must stay true to our own experience and what we see from our own unique vantage point.

Still, while interpretations of idealism vary according to time and place and circumstance, its basic principles have remained constant. And its basic lessons have not changed all that much since Plato established his academy, the very first Western school of idealism.

After exploring these ideas, and reading the words of many great idealists sprinkled throughout, you may be tempted to say of the New Age as Emerson said of the New England transcendentalists, "Whoso knows these seething brains, these admirable radicals, these unsocial worshippers, these talkers who talk the sun and moon away, will believe this heresy cannot pass away without leaving its mark."

10 Truth and Knowledge

"Man has a profound need to believe that the truth he perceives is rooted in the unchanging depths of the universe," writes Huston Smith, "for were it not so, could truth be really important? Yet how can he so believe when others see truth so differently?"

We live in a world with billions of others, and as we move together through a shared history, we all experience the sky as blue, babies as precious, and broken bones as painful. We can all agree on these details, yet our view of the big picture can be very different, depending where we are on the spiral of spiritual development. Many believe reality to be created by a personal God (dualism), some believe it to be an arbitrary accident (materialism), and others believe it to be the manifestation of impersonal Spirit (idealism).

When we search for answers about the nature of reality, we are likely to pick from answers generated by one of these philosophies or perhaps make up some mixture of our own. And although many undertake this task with a careless attitude and lack of thought, most of us approach it with a serious desire to find "the truth." We don't want to walk around dependent on unstable and unproven opinions, we want to have real and accurate truth in our possession. And not just because it is satisfying to be right. As William James observed, "The possession of true thoughts means everywhere the possession of invaluable instruments of action."

In other words, truth is power. If you don't have all the facts about a situation—whether it's the speed limit on the road you're driving or the purpose of the life you're living—then you can't make sound judgments or decisions. You cannot even act in your own best interests. Only in understanding the reality of a situation can you effectively deal with it. The more truth you are able to grasp, the more power you possess.

Truth is powerful, without a doubt, but for us humans, it also tends to be slippery, changeable, relative. What we see inevitably changes according to point of view. As much as we would like to be able to get hold of the truth and nothing but the truth, the fact is, in choosing which worldview we look through, or refuse to look through, we greatly influence what we will see.

Thus, no matter which philosophy we follow, before we can answer questions about reality, we must first answer questions of epistemology, or how we attain knowledge.

Approaching truth

According to my high school chemistry teacher, the right way of knowing is called the scientific method. One must state the problem, then form a hypothesis that answers the problem, then test the hypothesis through experiment. Not all my high school teachers were quite as strict as Mr. Chemistry, but most insisted that one should observe the world through the window of reason and logic. This is the materialistic approach.

Meanwhile, my Sunday School teacher was equally adamant that the right source of knowledge is the Bible. Indeed, I was told repeatedly that my very soul depended on my acceptance of the knowledge revealed to the authors of the Bible and interpreted by my church. Any information that clashed with biblical dictates was not to be trusted and most likely instigated by the devil to blind me to the truth. This is the dualistic approach.

Interestingly, both scientific and religious approaches, so often in conflict, are in perfect accord in their distrust of the self. Religion goes so far as to say that relying on the self to attain knowledge is sinful. Meanwhile, because science insists that the correct method of inquiry is paramount, the self is actually immaterial to the outcome and should thus be ignored.

Of course, the scientific rules of knowledge have been a marvelous boon to us, giving us a great grasp of truth about outer, physical processes—and granting us great power in manipulating the exterior world for our benefit. But when it comes to the interior world of human experience, we usually discover that over-reliance on scientific rules can sabotage our grasp of truth.

The scientific rules do not allow that the best way to calculate the distance to the sun might not be the best way to calculate the attributes of one's soul. Indeed, science does not recognize the validity of any inner experience that doesn't have a measurable biochemical basis, and so it must discard the existence of the soul altogether.

When the rules *about* truth supersede the truth we actually experience, then truth is lost.

Dualistic religion does recognize the existence of the soul. However, religion's list of rules regarding truth is even more restrictive and stubbornly blind to the aspects of life that exist outside its ancient documents. Religion puts forth a completely predetermined picture of reality that does not allow for new information.

Once again, the rules about truth supersede the truth in front of us. And once again, truth is lost.

Because the traditional rules on the attainment of knowledge so often throw up roadblocks to truth, the New Age asks, is there a better approach? What rules for the discovery of truth may we adopt that will not become more important than truth? How may we learn the nature of reality without being forced to turn a blind eye to what we may already know?

In other words, how may we discover truth that is whole and complete, balanced between what is without and what is within?

Rule 1. Trust yourself

After our lifelong inculcation in ways of knowing in which a self is a liability, the New Age comes along with the outrageous declaration that the only real authority is you. You are the only one qualified to determine the truth of your experience, using your observations, your reasoning, and your intuitions.

It is a shocking idea at first. But if you think about it, everything in the world of our experience—whether it is the color of the sky or the idea of god—is knowable only by way of a self. Our only contact with reality is a self's perception of reality. The sky cannot possibly be blue until a pair of eyes sees, and a mind identifies, its blueness.

It is impossible to separate an experience from its experiencer, and all truth flows from this indivisibility. Which is not to say that the self creates truth; rather, we connect with truth through the self. We are not the source of knowledge, but we are the conduits of knowledge.

Evidence of our deep connection to knowing is carried within our very bodies. Each of us is full of rivers of intelligence, home to an internal ocean of knowledge that grows our bodies and beats our hearts and digests our food. We do not consciously know how we do these miraculous, complicated things, but this knowledge is part of each self. And it is this self that can be trusted to discern the truth of its experience.

Idealism reminds us that all prophets are self-proclaimed voices of God, all experts self-proclaimed voices of knowing, and any legitimacy they have for me is granted by myself and my agreement with them. Even when we pretend we are bowing to a greater power, a small human self inevitably remains the source of authority.

As Emerson most elegantly phrased it, "Man does not stand in awe of man, nor is his genius admonished to stay at home, to put itself in communication with the internal ocean, but it goes abroad to beg a cup of water from the urns of other men. We must go alone."

In the New Age, we realize that the jig is up, so to speak. We stop giving away our power, stop begging "a cup of water from the urns of other men," and start communicating with our own internal ocean.

Rule 2. Question authority

Both materialism and dualism are bound to the dictates of authority, and very often, authority is reliable. But then again, quite often it is not.

History has proven again and again that authority is as great a source of error as it is of knowledge. The sun does not revolve around the earth, slavery is not morally acceptable, and attaching leeches to a sick man will not make him well. Our churches and governments must continually issue apologies to make up for past mistakes, some of which have gone beyond mere ignorance to cause great harm.

Appealing to authority is an exercise in memory, not intelligence. Instead of figuring out what we think, we merely remember what we've been told. We become like animals tethered to a post, able to move only as far as the rope allows. Meanwhile, the truth fades away beyond our reach.

This doesn't mean we should toss aside the hard-earned knowledge of those who came before us. We can, and should, learn from the men and women who have searched diligently and sincerely for truth within both secular and religious institutions. Indeed, the New Age has become infamous for mining a wide range of disciplines for insights and freely incorporating them into the New Age worldview.

Again, we have to remember, all authority is granted legitimacy by the self. We choose our authorities depending on whether they confirm what we already hold to be true. Especially here in twenty-first century America, with so many choices of authority available to us, we are able to choose whichever church or school or teacher or book or politician or TV station that agrees with our preconceptions.

Of course, in other places and times, authority has compelled us to obedience through threats of death or imprisonment or social censure—as the Catholic Church did in the Dark Ages or the dictatorship of China might do today. However, the plentitude of heretics and dissidents in both cases prove that the choice of authority is always open. No matter how much we'd like to think we are deferring to the power of a higher authority, the truth is, we are always submitting to our own minds.

In forming a worldview, it is clearly unwise to depend solely on authority. M. Scott Peck, in *The Road Less Traveled*, warns that there is no such thing as a good hand-me-down philosophy. To be vital, our philosophy "must be a wholly personal one, forged entirely through the fire of our questioning and doubting in the crucible of our own experience of reality."

Rule 3. Know the limits of sense perception

Information about the world comes to us through a number of sources besides authority. Reason is but one mode of perception, intuition still another.

Yet our most basic method of gathering information is through our senses. Authority might be fallible, but surely seeing is believing, right? Well, not exactly.

When we look at an object, all we actually see is the colorless light waves that strike the object and are reflected back to us. These light reflections stimulate the cones and retinas in our eyes and it is the brain that interprets them as colors.

Likewise, waves trembling through the air strike our eardrums, and our brains turn the vibrations into sound. Different molecular structures in food slide over our tongues, different taste buds respond, and our brains turn the information into sweet, salty, or sour.

The sight, the sound, and the taste of things are literally experiences of the mind, and different minds can, and do, create different sensory experiences of the very same object.

There is also a vast amount of information our senses are not equipped to discern. For example, our ears will hear sound waves of a certain range but are deaf to the higher wavelengths of radio waves. Our eyes easily perceive large objects yet cannot discern the small organisms such as the bacteria and germs that share our lives. What human beings can hear, smell, touch, taste, and see is but a small fraction of reality.

Of course, we have no choice but to rely on our senses to provide us with information about the world. But idealism asks us to consider that sense-information about reality is not the same thing as reality itself. Not only that, but this sense information must then be processed by our emotional, prejudicial minds.

Rule 4. Know the limits of reason

Reason is the most respected mode of attaining knowledge and is commonly held to be our only trustworthy tool for weighing truth. Certainly, we would not be able to arrive at any truth at all without the use of reason.

Yet, it is important to remember that reason doesn't work in a vacuum. It needs material to work with—namely, sense material. But, as we've already seen, the senses don't provide complete information about reality.

Reason, already hampered at the outset, is then further limited by what Carl Jung called "ego-consciousness."

The mind is not an indifferent receptacle. The ego and its swirl of desires causes one's reason to select and interpret information according to its own needs and interests. It is a very efficient screening system that brings our attention to facts and data which support its preconceptions, and discards facts and data that clash with its preconceptions.

Our hallowed reason is thus reduced to helpless slave—slave to our passions and preconceptions—and will support any view one's emotions wish to impose on it. That's how reason is able to create arguments for either of two contradictory views with equal plausibility, as we see every day in political fights and courtroom battles in which scientific experts come up with different findings from the same set of "facts."

Reason then, can be a powerful defense against recognition of truth and often perpetuates illusion with elaborate rationalization. Witch hunts, slavery, Nazism—all these were defended compellingly by reason in their day, which is why Jung called our confidence in reason "our greatest and most tragic illusion."

The New Age cautions us to beware the limits of reason and our over-reliance on the rationality of our minds. Reason is surely one of our most valuable tools in the determination of truth, but it cannot do the job alone.

Rule 5. Learn to use your intuition

Anyone who's taken an algebra class can remember the frustration of trying to solve a problem beyond one's mental reach, and the surprise of the moment when the mind leapt beyond the logical steps of formula and got the answer. Yet, when the teacher pushed us to show our work, we had no answer, for there was no way to explain how one got there in a single step when everyone else took the long way.

There is never a logical way to explain intuition, an inner skill that not only shortcuts reason, but reaches into places that reason cannot go.

Unlike rational processes that advance in linear fashion and leave a clear path of incremental steps, intuition is a direct leap into the heart of things. This leap is hidden, mysterious, yet often uncannily accurate.

With intuition, subject and object merge together and produce a calm sense of certainty, or telltale bodily response, like a pleasant electric charge. Nabakov spoke of the *frisson*, the telling shiver of truth. Intuition often comes with a shiver-like feeling, a sense of knowing that is palpable, immediate, unshakable.

Intuition is closely related to the mystic insights from which most of our religions were born. In mysticism, the subject (self) and object (reality or God) quite literally merge together, producing an ecstatic, trance-like state. When mystics lose themselves in this state, deeper truths flow from them in the fiery poetry of symbol that the logical mind does not always understand.

Yet, just because intuition is non-rational doesn't mean it is irrational or contrary to reason. As Aristotle first observed, the highest form of reason (theoria) is a type of disciplined intuition.

The nineteenth-century transcendentalists would later speak of this higher form of knowing as "transcendental reason," a lightning-fast process superior to the slow and clunky steps typical of logic. Today, many researchers talk about "whole-brain" knowing, which employs the intuitive left hemisphere of the brain as well as the logic-focused right hemisphere.

Intuition is absolutely vital in gaining complete knowledge. Great thinkers often describe their revolutionary ideas as coming from intuitive flashes that are only later corroborated by hard evidence. As Einstein noted of his discovery of the theory of relativity, "I did not arrive at an understanding of these fundamental laws of the universe through my rational mind."

Of course, as with the other modes of perception, it is possible to give too much weight to intuition. Like reason, our sense of intuition can be influenced by emotions and ego desires, and so is not infallible. If we accept whatever "feels right" as the only criterion of truth, then we are vulnerable to getting caught up in the realm of the ridiculous and constructing fantastic theories that clearly have no relationship to reality as experienced by the other modes of perception. This is a trap that has plagued many a New Ager.

"Intuition is not a sufficient foundation for any philosophy," wrote Harvard professor of philosophy William Ernest Hocking. "But we are not likely to achieve any true philosophy without it."

Rule 6. Use all modes of perception

Truth is not a one-dimensional matter. Life unfolds simultaneously as a physical experience, a mental experience, an emotional experience, and a social experience. A complete truth must incorporate all these aspects.

Our best chance of reaching a true and complete philosophy "rooted in the unchanging depths of the universe" is to glean our knowledge from all sources available to us, whether it be from the East or West, whether ancient scripture or yesterday's latest scientific discovery. We need to confirm what our intuition tells us with our senses. We need to take what authority proclaims and corroborate it with our reason.

When all modes of perception work together, each verifying the others, we move as close to truth as humanly possible.

Rule 7. Truth is (mostly) relative

Okay, so if we all follow these new rules of truth—trusting ourselves, observing our own experience, getting in touch with our intuition—does that mean we will someday all arrive at one common truth? Not a chance.

A quick look at the variety of beliefs held by New Agers shows that even when looking through the same idealistic window, the world still looks different through different eyes. And although this can bother those who are looking for the comfort of an absolute—to a New Ager, this is exactly as it should be.

After all, a poor farmer in sixteenth-century China lived a life vastly different than that of a wealthy stockbroker in twenty-first-century Manhattan, and it would be absurd to expect them to arrive at the same version of truth. Not only would it be absurd, it would be contrary to the entire purpose we humans are on this earth to fulfill: to explore different facets of experience and discover fresh truths unique to our own time and place (see *Chapter 11, The Story of Creation*).

Ken Wilber describes how different versions of truth all can be relatively "true" in his book, *The Spectrum of Consciousness*. He describes all consciousness as a spectrum of vibratory levels, much like levels of electromagnetic radiation express themselves in various wavelengths. Just as we become aware of a specific radio wave only when we tune in to that particular wavelength, so too we become aware of those levels of truth that our consciousness tunes into.

And, just as a radio wave that seems different from a light wave can still be part of the same spectrum of electromagnetic radiation, so too a religion in China that seems different from a religion in America can still be part of the same spectrum of truth. Each point of view is the result of our being tuned in to a different vibratory level.

From this vantage point, writes Wilber, "no approach, be it Eastern or Western, has anything to lose—rather, they all gain a universal context."

Safeguarding the universal context of relative truth is a primary goal of New Age philosophy. Rather than feeling discouraged that people see truth so differently, the New Age understands that each person's fragment of truth is an important piece of a larger puzzle. From the materialist with her hard lines of numbers and facts to the idealist with his blurry, relative lines—each new piece of truth adds another dimension, another shade of meaning to the whole.

Rule 8. Truth isn't *only* relative

In the New Age, each person's fragment of truth is respected as an integral part of the whole. But this doesn't mean that we do not recognize that some fragments are clearly more in line with reality than others.

"The fact that all perspectives are relative does not mean that no perspective has any advantage at all," Wilber continues. "That all perspectives are relative does not prevent some from being relatively better."

In the New Age, we regard every fixed belief as relative, not because there is nothing absolute, but *because there is*.

Plato, the architect of idealism, said the only way to explain our ability to understand math or logic or other true things is because they are innate within us, and we recall them from a previous acquaintance before our birth. Likewise, the Spanish philosopher Ortegy y Gassett noted the "double condition" of truth. He said that although subject knowledge of truth is "transitory and fugitive" reality, there is also an eternal reality which exists "without alteration and modification."

The mystics and sages who have glimpsed the heart of reality tell us that truth is not relative at all—but burns through all the rules and divisions and compartments we construct for it, complete and whole and all-encompassing.

The relative *appearance* of things does not take away from their absolute reality. Idealism advises us to rely on the stability of the Absolute while we experiment with its relative attributes. After all, in order to bring my truth closer to the truth, I must be free to try out new ideas, explore them, test them.

Of course, I am going to make errors. And if I neglect to use all modes of perception, I'm likely to make many errors. But in the end, it is not my job, or yours, to determine the truth for all time, for all people. It's not my job, or yours, to determine any greater truths at all. We merely have to decide what is true for ourselves, and only ourselves, at this particular moment. When we do this consistently, we may find our own small truth growing, expanding and opening in an ever widening spiral toward the absolute source of all truth.

Living the truth

New Age rules of knowing can have a stunning impact on truth and one's view of reality. By incorporating a wider range of knowledge sources—from East and West, science and religion, psychology and myth—we end up with a more complete picture of reality. By incorporating intuition, we develop a much more detailed and accurate picture of reality, as well as a picture more balanced between our inner and outer worlds. And by trusting ourselves to evaluate our own experience, we see a picture of reality more relevant to our own lives.

Yet, the most profound impact these rules have is on the personal level—in our relationship with ourselves and with others. From the beginning, we are empowered to rely on ourselves, believe in ourselves, trust ourselves and the guidance of our inner voice. We are allowed to mature beyond children who parrot what others tell us and become grown-ups able to think critically, and independently, for ourselves.

In learning that we are trustworthy, we come to realize that others are trustworthy as well. And because we don't have to be right all the time, we can afford to let others express their own points of view without feeling threatened. We may even begin to listen, truly listen, to what others think, and to honor what they have discovered on their own unique journeys.

This greater respect for oneself and others expands out to a greater respect for the world around us and its entirely mysterious depths. The more we learn, the more we know we have yet to learn. And in becoming more comfortable with our uncertainty, or what the Buddhists call "not-knowing," we may find ourselves walking lightly, almost playfully through new ideas. Our lives open up to a wonderful new sense of adventure.

When anything is possible, how can we not lead richer and fuller lives?

11 The Story of Creation

In the beginning...Never were more arresting words spoken than these. We cannot help but wait for what comes next. We cannot help but want to solve the most ancient of all mysteries, the mystery of how it all began. This teeming and wonder-strewn world—how did it come to be? And we who struggle upon it—why are we here?

In the beginning, said the wisest of men, and the people listened well. To know what happened in the beginning was to know everything, the how, the why, and the reason for it all. Our ancestors told stories of a dark void of nothingness, shattered by the light of creation. They told stories of passionate young gods, giving birth to the world and to us, their children. And it was on the foundation of these stories that the people built their lives.

Today, the past has lost its veil of mystery and the story of creation is no longer a story. It is a science. Instead of passing on old poetic myths about the origin of the universe, we look through microscopes and telescopes. Yet, the story of our creation is still a vital tale to tell because it reminds us that we are all one people, united in a common history.

Even more important, our creation story informs us of our purpose in being alive. In the words of Thomas Aquinas, "As the end of a thing corresponds to its beginning, so it is not possible to be ignorant of the end of things if we know their beginning."

Bangs and ripples

Since somewhere in the twentieth century, scientists have been fairly certain that the universe came into being through an enormous explosion of energy known as the Big Bang. Before the bang, it is theorized that the entire universe was squeezed into an unimaginably dense state, with the anomaly we call the bang releasing this material in a fantastic explosion and throwing it outward to create an expanding universe.

Everything that has happened after the bang is pretty much an open book. Scientists can describe the further unfolding of the universe in scrupulous detail. But describing the exact moment of the bang is more a matter of scientific creativity than scientific certainty.

The physicist Alan Guth described the first expansion of the universe as a phase change—like the change of hot water into steam—in which energy transformed itself into matter. Still another physicist, David Bohm, suggested that creation was less a Big Bang and more of a little ripple on a vast sea of pre-existing energy.

As scientists like Guth and Bohm try to describe the origin of the universe, they sound much like the storytellers of old, spinning myths of a primordial watery substance from which the gods emerged. But even the more poetic interpretations of the bang cannot completely satisfy our curiosity. We still want to know what came *before* the Bang.

Mainstream science, and the philosophy of materialism, sidesteps the issue when it asserts the birth of the universe was also the birth of time and declares it meaningless to ask what came before the beginning. If there was no time, then there was no "before."

But idealism is not allowed such a pat solution. Idealism must question whether the birth of the universe in time was the birth of all being. Are there levels of existence outside of time and materiality? After all, *something* must have triggered the Big Bang. And whether science is ever able to penetrate this mystery or not, idealism is full of wonder about what that something might be.

The first cause

It was Aristotle who first observed that there are several ways of explaining the cause of an event. One he named the *efficient* cause, which describes the actual physical relationship between events. This physical cause/effect relationship forms the causal chain on which science is built, and it works in an orderly, incremental fashion.

In fact, it is so wonderfully orderly that scientists have been able to follow it all the way back to the smallest fraction of a second after the Big Bang, the moment in which their extraordinary investigation ends.

But Aristotle also identified another type of cause. He called it the *formal* cause, which is the relationship between an event and its purpose, or *telos*. All things, said Aristotle, happen for the "sake" of something else. "The reason (telos) forms the starting point." In a teleological—and idealistic—view of the universe, the beginning of things is inextricably tied to the end of things.

In both definitions of cause, all things happen for a reason. The important question is this: At what point does the reason exert its influence? For example, did man learn to use tools because he developed opposable thumbs (efficient cause)? Or did he develop opposable thumbs in order to better use his tools (formal cause)?

Anthropologists say tools and hands developed together. This example and countless others tell us that as life evolves, reason and result evolve together, mutually creating each other. Life is synonymous with purpose, or *telos*, and just as Aquinas observed, to know the end is to know the beginning.

Some might object that we can't possibly know what the future end will be. But the end does not exist in the future. The end of things is always now. A future time, no matter how near or how distant, becomes real only when it becomes now. The future is an abstract idea that exists only in our minds. Time, and its ends, exists nowhere but now.

Thus, a teleological understanding of creation tells us that the first cause is inextricably connected to this very moment. Life has evolved, and continues to evolve, in order to bring about everything that is happening now. And now. And now.

Creative evolution

According to Darwin, evolution is the systematic organization of life based on a chain of efficient causes. Although Darwin's theory sent shock waves around the globe when first introduced, it is not an especially revealing myth. Even if it is correct about efficient causes, the theory of evolution neglects to address formal causes and so doesn't answer the heart's question of *why* human beings exist. Nor does it give us any clue to our function other than survival.

To answer these questions, we need to look deeper into the myth and discover the *telos* secluded within.

Darwin's theory of evolution is explained as the work of "natural selection." Life chooses to retain and refine those random mutations that best lead to the survival of the organism. But what, asks Ken Wilber, drives an organism toward "random" mutations? The basic forms of life survive just fine without mutations. In fact, the simpler forms survive much better than the more complex forms, so survival is clearly not the point of natural selection.

In his masterpiece, *Creative Evolution*, the French Nobel Prize-winner Henri Bergson insisted that evolution is not compelled through outer conditions, but grows into being from an inner intelligence and purposeful design. Life, he said, reflects an *elan vital*, the vital urge of purpose that gropes gradually toward knowledge and consciousness and "more light."

When we look back at the sweep of evolution, we see that life has indeed become ever more conscious of itself. The higher and more complex the form, the greater its level of consciousness. As life forms evolve, Wilber adds, they transcend themselves in creative leaps in order to develop new capacities toward consciousness.

It is this end that leads us back to the first cause. If the universe is developing toward consciousness of itself, then its purpose must be self-consciousness. And a universe that is conscious of itself must, of course, be a "self." Aristotle envisioned a Prime Mover, a first cause that he described as "pure thought, thinking about itself."

This mysterious Prime Mover, this conscious universe-self, is called many things—Mind, Consciousness, Intelligence, Spirit. It is also called the Tao, Brahman, Allah, Jehovah, and God.

A new myth

In the beginning, there was the void. Empty, timeless nothingness, this void nonetheless held the potential for being. This potential rippled and contracted, yearning for reality, gathering its will... then bang!

Being—desiring to experience itself, become more conscious of itself—exploded from the void, flinging its creative energy into physical being.

In Eastern Orthodoxy, creation is called God's kenosis, or God's self-emptying. In creating the physical universe, God created the physical dimension of himself in order to encounter himself.

"Evolution," Wilber writes, "is best thought of as Spirit-in-action, or God in-the-making, where Spirit unfolds itself... manifesting more of itself at every unfolding... an infinite process that is completely present at every finite stage."

And why did God use his own essence instead of creating something new? If God's purpose is to experience himself, then creating something other than himself would not allow him that experience. He would be able to observe the universe, but not be able to see it, hear it, touch it, taste it. The only way for God to experience life is to be inside life.

God therefore unfolds into space-time, dividing his essence into fragments that are then able to serve as mirrors for each other. All parts of the universe reflect God back to God in a never-ending process of separation and reunion.

What if God was one of us?

Many object to the idealistic story of creation on the grounds that God is too good, too pure to wallow in the muck of ordinary life with us. But the New Age asks, why shouldn't God want to experience the world he created?

Why shouldn't God want to feel the pleasure of holding a newborn baby after the pain of giving him birth? Why shouldn't she want to know the satisfaction of hard work and the disappointment of dreams lost? Why shouldn't she want to laugh and cry and scream along with us? Most of us eagerly pass the gift of life on to our children, which means we think that life is worth living in spite of its moments of ugliness. So why shouldn't God find life worth living also?

And what better way for God to experience himself than to unfold into space-time, dividing his essence into fragments that are then able to serve as mirrors for each other? In this never-ending process of separation and reunion, all parts of the universe are able to reflect God back to God.

This New Age story of creation is a myth, one part educated guess, two parts intuition. But like all creation myths, its value does not rest in its exact degree of conformity to actual events, but in the degree that it illuminates for us the deeper meaning of our existence. And as tiny humans floating along in an inconceivably vast universe, we very much need to know why we are here.

The *telos* of being

From the smallest atom to the largest galaxies, all parts of the universe have conspired together for the purpose of creating self-conscious life. Yet this purposeful universe is also inconceivably vast, and we who inhabit this small corner of it can feel lost and insignificant. Many times I have wondered how I, one person out of billions, living on one planet out of billions, can be important.

But I have also read the words of the wisest of men, and I have listened well. In the beginning, God stretched himself across fiery new space so that I might have life. How do I know this to be true? Because I am here. The telos of being is always here in this moment, and all that exists in this moment is the purpose of all that has ever existed. Each of us is backed by all of creation.

My life, your life, all life, was brought forth from within God for the purpose of his own self-discovery. I live to learn who I am so that God may know who he is. I live to experience the infinite possibilities of existence so that God may experience his own existence. I am here to learn, to experience being, and everything I think and feel and do adds another brushstroke of color to God's self-portrait.

And because I am a one-of-a-kind instrument of God's self-awareness, my one small life is immeasurably significant. "Even if this were only the relationship of a drop of water to the sea," wrote Carl Jung, "that sea would not exist but for the multitude of drops."

Yet the wisest of men will also ask of this myth, who can tell for sure? Even if the myth came straight from the mouths of the gods themselves, perhaps the gods have lived so long that they themselves have forgotten where they come from.

Or perhaps, as the wise man named Buddha said, it doesn't matter what happened in the beginning, for life always begins anew, right here, and right now. If we look away toward the past for too long, we might miss it.

12 God, the One That Is Many

As a child who weekly attended Sunday school, I saw many pictures of God. He was old, wise-looking, and had a glowing white beard.

God looked kind in pictures, yet I was afraid of him. Although I was told He loved me, He wasn't easy to please. He had a long list of rules, some of which were common sense, some of which made no sense at all. He also held a fearsome grudge and I worried that no matter how good I was, I'd still end up listening to my skin crackle in the fires of hell.

Later, when my Sunday School faith in God faded, I still felt the presence of something, some kind of greater power. I wasn't sure if it was in me, around me, or above me, but it was somewhere. To call that something God seemed impossible without going back to the list of rules and the threat of hell. And so, without adequate words to describe what I felt, I supposed myself to be an atheist by default.

Today I know that my beliefs were never close to those of atheism, but my confusion brought home to me the importance of the symbols we use in describing the nature of God.

For many of us born into the science-dominated twentieth century, the religious symbols that represent God are too limited, and too dated, to sustain mature belief. Yet without a viable symbol to help connect us to the divine, we can feel literally cut off from God.

Something missing

Separated from God is not a comfortable place to be. We end up feeling terribly lost, then scolding ourselves for feeling that way. After all, science has mapped out the entire universe in minute detail, so we should know exactly where we are. Yet, we don't. And because we don't, we often feel restless, dissatisfied, out of place. We squirm about and try to settle ourselves with going to school, getting jobs, getting married, having babies, buying houses, and filling them up with as many things as our credit card limits will allow.

Through continual grasping, we distract ourselves from the knowledge that to be cut off from God is to be cut off from our source, our context, our meaning, our peace. Some people keep grasping their entire lives. Others figure out that grasping is never going to make them feel better, and they become determined to find what's really missing from their lives.

Many of those others have found their way into the "spiritual but not religious" New Age. One might even say that the search for our lost God has been the driving force behind the New Age. The movement aims to heal the rift between self and God—a rift opened by science and the razing of our religious symbols—by rebuilding the symbolic bridges that connect us with our source.

The New Age begins this task by asking us to once again consider the symbols of divinity revered by human beings throughout the ages. It asks to look again, closely, and discover what these symbols have to tell us.

The masks of God

Glancing through a book on world mythology, one can see that the God of Christianity is not the only one with a white beard.

The great Greek god Zeus, too, had a white beard, and a quiver full of thunderbolts that he hurled at wayward humans. He also had a grandmother, Gaia, the divine Earth itself, and a remarkable number of aunts and uncles, brothers and sisters, who were also embodiments of specific divine qualities. Some were virginal women, others were lusty men or a wicked combination of man and animal. Some were serious, some were tricky, some laughed, some cried, some were wise, others foolish.

Hindu gods are even more numerous. Some are female like Kali, the mother god, slayer of demons; some are male like the playful Shiva, who continually creates the world through his dance.

Other pantheons have arisen from Europe, Africa, North and South America—gods that are earth and sky, human and animal, visible and invisible. Meanwhile, in China, the Taoists looked to the Tao, the faceless universal life force.

In exploring these symbols, one learns, as Krishnamurti noted, that when we approach God, our "thought can project anything it likes. It can create and deny God. Each person can invent or destroy God according to his inclinations, pleasures, and pains."

We also learn that despite the multiplicity of images we humans have created, we are singularly compelled to create them. Symbols of the divine have spontaneously arisen within all people, in all places, in all times. The mythologies of virtually every culture known to us, observed Joseph Campbell, are based on the same "universal doctrine" of divinity, which asserts that all the visible parts of the world are the result of an all-encompassing power, or mysterious ground of being.

The various images of deities, he concluded, are like "footprints left, as it were, by local passages of a Universal Self." This

Universal Self travels through the imagination in many forms and, in Campbell's words, wears many masks. And the ubiquity of these footprints tells us that this Universal Self most assuredly exists.

Thou art that

Although we may love and feel devotion to one particular mask, the universal doctrine of humanity teaches us that there is more to divinity than any one image can carry. It teaches us that although God is our father, she is also our mother. It teaches us that although God looks like us, she also looks like animals, trees, oceans, mountains, suns, and moons. God is in heaven, but he is also in the world. God is transcendent, but she is also immanent.

In the New Age, God is understood to be all things, everywhere, both within the world as ground of being, and beyond the world as unimaginable possibility.

This concept, in which all reality in all its forms and non-forms is recognized as a manifestation of the divine, is called panentheism. One is All, All is One; or in the words of the Hindus, *tat tvam asi*, thou art that.

But let's set aside symbols and abstractions for a moment and consider reality through the lens of science. If we were to take up a microscope and look closely at things, we would find that the whole universe is made of the same basic substance or stuff, subatomic bits which spin together to create atoms, which create molecules, which create cells.

Of course, we can all agree this is the case, but why should we also agree to call this stuff by the name of God?

At play in the fields of the Lord

When Bendictus de Spinoza, the seventeenth century idealist, undertook his investigation of reality, he followed a system of rigorous logic in examining the substances that make up our universe. He concluded that by the definition of substance, there can be only one substance, the infinite substance of God. According to Spinoza, "God is in the indwelling and not the transient cause of things." And, "Besides God, no substance can be granted or conceived."

Today, physicists tell us that the universe is indeed made of one basic substance—and that substance is called energy. Matter broken down to its smallest subatomic particles appears to be tiny units of energy vibrating at different speeds (called string theory).

Just as a steadily sounding note or a steady color is the outcome of vibrations, said Alfred North Whitehead, the primordial element is "an organized system of vibratory streaming energy," which manifests itself during a period of time, and forms the physical universe.

This streaming energy is often described as a field that exists everywhere and produces all things. Herman Weyl, a philosopher of science, suggested that each particle of matter is actually a highly-charged value in this field of energy. "Such an energy knot, which is by no means clearly delineated against the remaining field, propagates through empty space like a water wave against a lake."

Life, against all odds

The fact that energy behaves this way, "knotting" itself into clumps of matter, is an astonishing, extraordinary thing. One of the basic laws of physics (the second law of thermodynamics) is based on the observation that energy flows toward entropy, or chaos. By its very nature, energy is supposed to flow toward disorganization. Yet against astronomical odds, energy gathers together in certain places of the universe and organizes itself into incredibly complex patterns.

This increase of order in our solar system does not violate the law of entropy because it is balanced by an increasing disorder in other parts of the universe (think black hole). Physicists will say that's just the way it happens, and they don't know why. But many of us would say the why is obvious. Energy that organizes itself into purposeful intelligence clearly possesses purposeful intelligence.

Thinkers from many different disciplines have noted again and again the extreme improbability that life as we know it could have evolved by fortuitous chance. "Darwin's theory of natural selection based on 'random' mutations is no longer supported," wrote Campbell. "As legions of scientists and science observers have pointed out, the selection of mutations by pure chance would have taken much longer than the known age of our planet allows."

Furthermore, physics maintains that the total energy of the universe stays at a constant value (zero), no matter how far apart different phenomena occur. The universe, which stretches across untold billions of light years, necessarily keeps track of every event, big and small, in order to maintain the balance of energy expenditures within the whole. The universe clearly, amazingly, exists as a unity of one.

The energy that forms our universe does not merely exist; it also strives, learns, adapts, and evolves. It does not follow physical laws in blind submission, it uses physical laws to organize itself, form itself, express itself.

Energy that creates life is alive, energy that creates consciousness is conscious. What other name would be better suited to describe such miraculous, self-balancing energy than God?

Neti, Neti

Many people, namely dualists, are appalled at the idea of God as immanent in the universe, God as the stuff of reality. They do not want to bring God down to earth; they like him decorously remote and removed.

Religion critic Harold Bloom has blasted the New Age for what he calls "obsessive immanence," and added that such "perpetual and universal immanence makes it difficult for a [New Ager] to distinguish between God and any experience whatsoever."

Bloom brings up a valid point, and idealists themselves are quick to point out the spiritual dangers of seeing God as purely immanent. Wilber is one who warns against overemphasis on immanence. He calls a completely immanent God a "flatland God," which creates a world that is "all surface, no depth...just equally flat and endlessly faded surfaces."

This flatland God, he added, drains all value from reality and blocks our perception of the true nature of Spirit.

Tielhard de Chardin likewise questioned whether we were in any danger of becoming lost in an immanent God. "Will [the belief] blur the outline of objects around us with an atmosphere of mirage?" he asked. "Will it take our attention from the individual and tangible to absorb us in a confused sense of the universal?"

But Tielhard concluded we need not worry about disappearing into an immanent God. He believed that in the act of union with the all, Spirit differentiates and accentuates the individual element. Unity, he declared, does not melt everything together into homogeneity, but allows us to see everything more clearly by revealing the context of each thing. The immanence of God and his love, Teilhard went on to say, "impregnates the universe like an oil that revives its colors."

It is important to know that God is always here, in the blood, the breath, the heartbeat of all life. Yet, it is also important to remember that God is not *only* here but exists beyond the realm of mere physicality.

Immanence, said Wilber, goes hand in hand with transcendence. Neither "is final, ultimate, or privileged, but rather, like the primordial yin and yang, they generate each other, depend on each other, cannot exist without the other, and find their own true being by dying into the other, only to awaken together."

God is the endless sweep of divinity that encompasses all we can know and all we cannot know, from the most dark to the most light, from the most immediate in here to the most inconceivable out there.

This is, of course, a contradiction, and one reason why the Hindus would describe God, or Brahman, as "Neti, Neti," not this, not that. God is both and neither, All and Nothing, Form and Emptiness, Being and Non-Being, Self and Not-Self.

Thus, in the New Age, it doesn't matter if your symbol of the divine matches up with mine. We each have the power to create God anew; we each bestow upon God the image that only we have the power to see. We understand that our different definitions of divinity are not a reason to fight and hate, but a reason to celebrate, for through our differences, God is enriched.

At the same time, the New Age reminds us that all differences are superficial. The reality of God is deeper than name, than symbol, than form. Regardless of symbol, *tat tvam asi*, thou art that. We are all one with God, and we are all united by this oneness. We are all in this together, we children of Jehovah and Allah and Brahman and the Tao and the god with the white beard. As long as we know that, we need never feel lost again.

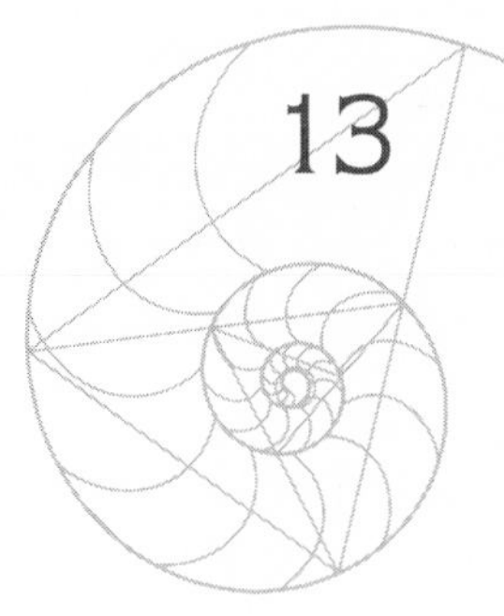

13 Reality: Land of Illusion

"The more clearly we see the reality of the world, the better equipped we are to deal with the world," wrote M. Scott Peck. "The less clearly we see the reality of the world—the more our minds are befuddled by falsehood, misperceptions and illusions—the less able we will be to determine correct courses of action and make decisions. Our view of reality is like a map with which to negotiate the terrain of life."

Indeed, it is with our worldview, our very own map of reality, that we chart our course in life and determine what is possible for us. This map sets the parameters of our experience, tells us what is important and not important, and whether we have succeeded or failed in our journey. Constructing a map of reality is literally the most important thing we will ever do.

For many, the most accurate map is the one drawn by science, which has categorized and measured and named the physical world on every level from infinitely vast space to the tiniest of subatomic particles. And although the New Age relies heavily on this map—as we all must if we want accuracy—it also recognizes that this map is grievously incomplete.

Despite its very fine details, the scientific map of reality offers us no symbolic legend, no compass to orient us, no pointers to anything beyond the flat surface of the map. Self-referential numbers and measures cannot impart meaning, cannot provide context. While they give us many fine classifications of "what," they tell us absolutely nothing about the all-important "why."

Of course, many scientists understand this and they themselves tell us that the more science advances, the more it stumbles up against the limits of measurement to explain reality. Which is why today we see all manner of physicists willing to speculate about the context of their numbers and measurements, and in the process, moving from objectivity to subjectivity, from materialism to idealism.

Holograms

As physics moves deeper and deeper into the nature of matter, reducing it to its smallest components, we find that a rock, a lake, a flower, a mouse—all are declared by science to be one similarly constituted thing, a collection of swirling particle-waves held together by the laws of quantum physics.

Physical reality is primarily emptiness, and throughout that emptiness are tiny electrical charges of energy dashing about at incredible speeds while taking up less than a billionth of the volume that matter seems to fill continuously.

In order to comprehend the tiny amount of matter in each atom, imagine that an atom is the size of a fourteen-story building. The nucleus of that atom would be about the size of a grain of salt. As for the electrons whizzing about, the salt grain of the nucleus has about two thousand times the mass of an electron.

Or, in the words of psychologist and philosopher Dr. Jean Houston, "Any single one of the atoms in the average human body has almost all its mass concentrated in a nucleus so small that if all the nuclei of all the atoms that make up the whole of humankind were packed together, their aggregate would be the size of a grain of rice."

The physical world is literally empty space that energy makes *appear* to be solid. Matter is literally nothing but a three-dimensional image of reality. To be more precise, matter is a hologram.

A cloud of possibility

The image of reality, which seems so real and solid to the human eye and hand, flickers toward surprising instability through the quantum microscope. When describing the constituents of atoms, physicists must refer to them not as actual things, but as probabilities and tendencies that display a distinct degree of unreality.

Subatomic particles show a marked tendency to fade in and out of concrete actuality depending on whether they are observed or not. The only way to truly describe these most basic constituents of the universe is as *possible* particles.

Science writer Nick Herbert elaborates:

> "A physicist observes the atom at a particular time, looks away for a moment, then observes it a second time...If the physicist tries to describe the atom in between observations as possessing definite attributes at all times, he finds he cannot predict correctly the results of his second observation. On the other hand, if the physicist describes the unobserved atom as...a 'wave of possibilities,' he will get the right result every time...What the math seems to say is that between observations, the world exists not as a solid actuality but only as shimmering waves of possibility."

According to this wave function, all unobserved atoms exist in possible places, not definite places. Of course, the wave function is merely a mathematical tool physics uses to describe reality, and not reality itself. Yet, for the physicist, the question remains: How do concrete things rise from the thingless world of quantum possibility?

The quantum question

There is apparently some disagreement on the answer to the quantum reality problem, and theories vary on why the quantum world behaves so capriciously. Interestingly, the theories put forth by different physicists often sound even more bizarre than that of a trance channeler's favorite entity.

For example, Hugh Everett's "many worlds" interpretation suggests that all quantum possibilities must be actualities that exist in parallel universes alongside ours. According to Herbert, the quantum reality problem has become, "strictly speaking, not a physics question at all, but a problem in metaphysics, concerned as it is not with phenomena but with speculating about what kind of being lies behind and supports the phenomena."

He adds that physics has reached a point where it can no longer answer such questions all on its own, and that without metaphysical "models of what is really going on in the world, quantum theory remains nothing but opaque mathematical formulism, a very sophisticated kind of ignorance."

In other words, it remains nothing but a map with no symbolic legend, no compass to orient us, and no pointers to anything beyond the flat surface of the map.

So here we have been given very exact knowledge of reality by physics, and still we are left to ask along with the physicists, what is really going on? What is the true reality behind its strangely behaving images?

The veil

Twenty-five centuries ago, when Plato was drawing his own map of reality, he did not have knowledge of quantum physics to aid him; yet, he intuitively felt that the world we perceive with our senses was not actual reality, merely a reflective image of reality.

Plato boldly declared that reality's true nature is contained in Ideas, and he considered the material world to be a shadow play cast by the eternal world of Ideas. He likened the ordinary person to a man sitting in a cave and looking at a wall on which he sees nothing but the shadows of the reality that unfolds unseen, behind his back. "The eyes," said Plato, "are full of deceit."

Even before Plato, the Hindus had grasped that the world is an illusion, which they called *maya*, the veil of appearances that hides reality. Maya, or the world of objects, is a playful creation, like an epic drama full of images spun from God's imagination.

The very nature of an image, whether mythologically imagined or scientifically defined, cries out the existence of a projection process and image source. For the Hindus, the image source was Brahman, or God.

For the idealist as well, the image source is God, or Spirit. We understand that the universe is quite literally made from nothingness, and science again provides evidence. When astronomers attempt to measure the energy in the entire universe, both positive and negative, they continually arrive at the total sum of *zero*. Zero! After all is said and done and weighed and measured, there's nothing really here.

Reality is indeed an image, an illusion of appearances. The *maya* thus spins out in dancing images from the void of nothingness, a dramatic illusion generated by the dreaming mind of God. Or, in twenty-first century terms, we might imagine the *maya* much as the Wachowski Brothers did in their movie, *The Matrix*, as a computer program that constructs the appearance of reality in the mind. And, just as in the movie, we all have a choice between taking the illusion at face value or waking up to reality.

The days and nights of God

When the Hindus first envisioned the creation of the *maya*, they imagined it emanating from the mind of God in an eternal rhythm of cycles. For a long stretch of time called a *kalpa* (4,320,000 years), the universe was manifested and made real by a sleeping God's dreams. For another *kalpa* God was awake and no longer dreamed the world into being, and nothing was manifested.

Now suppose, said Alan Watts, that you were God and you had the power to dream whatever you wanted. At first you might dream yourself a life of riches and plenty, dream yourself up food and toys galore. You might dream yourself as a hero in an adventure. You might dream yourself as a saint.

But after awhile, for variety, you might also dream yourself into a terrible situation, in a prison, in a war, just to see what happens. After a very long while, even this might become a little dull and you would be constantly looking for something new and different and dramatic. And you would certainly not want to know what happens ahead of time, for that would spoil the fun and ruin the whole purpose of the dream.

In this way, life unfolds within the mind of God like a dramatic dream. And what is God's reason for dreaming up our ever-changing reality? The same reason that we humans invent stories and put on plays and make movies; the same reason that we sit enthralled in dark theaters or before the screen of a video game or stay up late at night with a good book. So that we might experience everything that is possible for us to experience, feel all there is to feel, and learn all there is to learn.

We carry within us God's purpose, we carry within us the drive of the entire universe—to continually expand consciousness by creating, by learning, by ever becoming something new.

The world as *maya* is a playful, educational drama acted out by and for God, who is both the actors and the audience. And, as we slip in and out of the *maya*, we find that the world is real as a stage is real with its hard wooden floors and velvet curtains and props and lights and the smell of greasepaint. And we, the characters on the stage are real as long as the soul of the actor within us says our lines and wears our costumes. But when the actor leaves the stage, and the soul discards the body, we wake from our dream and the illusion becomes obvious.

Living a dream

For a New Ager, this long-enduring idealist map of reality-as-illusion is the map that most makes sense. It answers our heart's deepest question of why we are here and gives our lives the stability of clear purpose without weighing it down with heavy religious consequences, or without making us feel lost in a sea of random scientific processes.

This view of reality also gives us a profound sense of security. By allowing us to see through appearances, see through fleeting and ever-changing materiality to a constant spiritual reality, we discover that we have nothing whatsoever to fear. No matter what happens in the drama, we succeed in our purpose, we cannot fail. And no matter what happens in the drama, we, as part of God, are always safe.

Of course, this doesn't mean that the *physical* world is entirely safe or even that the world will survive. I feel quite certain that in the greater scheme of things, God is not attached to any particular outcome of the drama he/she has set in motion, and is content to watch us play it out according to our free will. And if we choose to destroy the planet and ourselves as long with it, well, that just might be a fitting end for the human experiment. The drama demands that if we want it to continue—if we want our children to have their turn to play their roles—then it is no use relying on God to save the day. If we want to survive as an embodied species, we are going to have to rise to meet the challenges of our times.

Still, we ultimately know that no matter what unfolds in the theater of life, we are always secure in the ground of being and have no reason to be afraid. And when fear goes out the window, fun comes in. When all is a game, a play, a show, we are free to enjoy the adventure. When all is a game, we can more easily laugh about our foibles and falls. We can also approach our lives as would any actor playing a role. The more challenging the role, the more satisfying it is to play it.

Tragedy and comedy, horror and suspense, romance and adventure—no matter what kind of role we find ourselves playing today, the New Age tells us we might as well laugh out loud and cry real tears, and keep ourselves on the edge of our seats. As everyone knows, life is not a dress rehearsal. We might as well give it everything we've got.

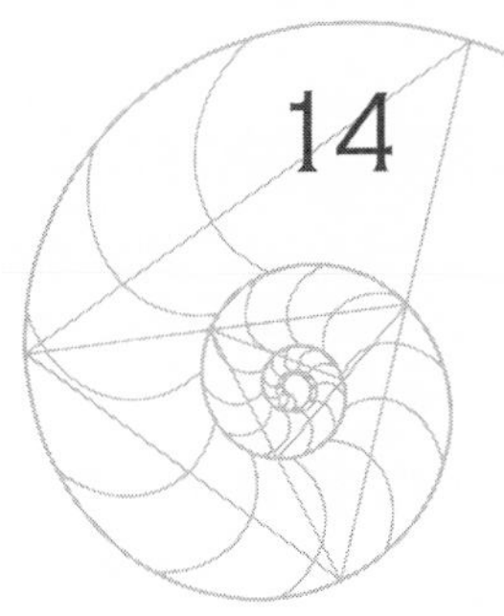

14 Creating Reality

In the divine drama that is reality, we've seen that the stage, the props, and even the characters are all part of One God, striving for self-consciousness. And we, as part of God, are creating the drama too. With our share of God-consciousness, we are actually writing the script along with God.

In other words, we create our own reality.

This is a fairly radical idea in these "poor me, it's not my fault" times. We live in the era of the victim, and many of us spend a lot of time on a therapist's couch, discovering how many of our problems can be blamed on Mom or Dad, or in a lawyer's office, demanding compensation because we took up smoking and became ill.

We are supported in our feelings of powerlessness by traditional ways of looking at the world. From the dualistic point of view, everything unfolds according to God's mysterious will, and who are we to question God's wisdom? We have no choice but to submit to it.

Meanwhile, from the materialistic point of view, everything is also determined, although not by God. Events unfold due to biological and environmental causes, with events falling like dominoes along the causal chain and sweeping us along with their momentum.

Those of us who are tired of feeling helpless before the whims of fate hear idealism's assertion that we create our own reality as glorious news. We feel immediately liberated, immediately empowered.

But there is a problem: The concept of mind as matter has always been subject to diverse interpretation. There is a Hindu interpretation, an ancient Greek interpretation, a Cartesian, a Theosophical. There is also a New Thought version (see Ernest Holmes), the channeled version (see Jane Roberts or Neale Donald Walsch), and the science-based version (see Fred Alan Wolf).

Which interpretation is right? In what way can we truly be said to create our own reality?

Manifestation mania

In the New Age, the most common interpretation of you-create-your-reality is hard to miss. It's known as conscious creation or manifestation and dozens of New Age gurus and teachers churn out books and travel the country to teach seminars on the subject. These teachers tell that we can manifest whatever we want in our lives by thinking correctly. Money, love, health, long life—God wants us to have everything we want for ourselves. It is, they say, our divine right.

Money, they say, is energy, like everything else. Just as the proper flow of divine energy within the body is believed to lead to good health, so the flow of divine energy through abundant thinking is believed to lead to prosperity.

On the other hand, a sluggish flow of energy—called scarcity thinking—will keep us locked in poverty. If we don't have a free flow of good things into our lives, it's only because we haven't learned to manage our thoughts correctly.

This basic reasoning was the foundation of the harmonial New

Thought religions that gained prominence in the early twentieth century. Ernest Holmes' Religious Science and Mary Baker Eddy's Christian Science were both built upon the assumption that by putting ourselves into spiritual harmony with the universe, not only will we enjoy happiness, we will also enjoy perfect health and financial success.

Both religions claimed to discover an impersonal divine "Law of Attraction" that works with mechanical accuracy. "We do not will things to be done," wrote Holmes. Through our thought "things are brought into being, not by will, but by the power of self-assertive Truth." As soon as we truly understand this, then "we shall reap a harvest of fulfilled desires."

The pagan religion of Wicca and other magickal belief systems are likewise based on the principle of harmony. Although they may add certain rituals to our carefully directed thoughts to help us better align ourselves to divine power, they also assert that the ability to create desired outcomes is ours by divine right.

The New Age movement shares the same idealistic underpinnings as New Thought and magick belief systems, and many New Agers—with the strenuous support of the ego—have taken the idea and run with it. In fact, they've been running with it so well for so long that in 2007 they ran it up the bestseller list yet again with Rhonda Byrne's book, *The Secret*.

But the mere popularity of the idea doesn't make it a sound idea.

Explaining the unexplainable

The inner workings of "you create your own reality" are sometimes vaguely explained in the popular literature on the subject. One channeled entity posited "mental enzymes," which waft from the skin and enter the atmosphere and thereby mold reality. Another stated that a thought repeated a great many times will eventually grow heavy enough with collective energy to attract the reality.

Others go into even greater detail. The more science-minded, for example, might take the well-known observer effect of quantum physics, in which subatomic particles do not exist in any specific location until they are observed by a perceiving consciousness, and build up from there. Add in the "many worlds" interpretation of physics, in which all possibilities exist as actualities in parallel universes, and some writers explain that a shift in thought or focus can cause a shift in one's reality. One merely changes tracks, so to speak, and heads into a parallel world.

Most, however, are content to allow the workings of thought-as-reality to be essentially unexplainable, or a divine mystery. Fortunately, the knowledge of how it works is not a necessary component of the manifestation equation. Only one's personal readiness and persistent belief are required. If more people don't take advantage of it, it is only because they don't know they can or they aren't spiritually ready to be limitless. Either that, or they're not doing it right.

One popular writer suggests that we err when we first desire something because within that desire is the belief that we don't have it yet, and of course, that is the belief which is made real. The trick, he says, is to circumvent the law and be grateful in advance. We have to *know* that we already have what we desire (even though we don't). If that doesn't work, it's only because we secretly harbor the belief it won't work. A failure to tap into our divine power is our own responsibility as much as anything else.

Still, despite pesky technical questions, the ego wants to believe. The ego hears the New Age message of manifestation and shouts, "Goody!" Like a kid in a candy store, the ego asks, you mean I can have anything? Yes, anything, says the smiling New Age guru from the cover of his book, all you have to do is believe.

And so we do believe, because it is so wonderful to think that we can be spiritual and acquisitive at the same time. We go faithfully to work at directing our thoughts, saying affirmations until they wear ruts into our minds. There is a feeling of great peace in knowing your wishes are about to be granted. It really isn't all that difficult to believe in magic, not when you want something badly enough.

Oh yes, the New Age guru adds, don't forget not to be attached to results. But it's too late. With all that thinking and believing and expecting, we have become very attached. Not to mention a little crazy after talking ourselves into the cognitive dissonance of *believing* in things that aren't there.

Of course, sometimes our desires *do* show up at the door, occasionally accompanied by odd coincidences or synchronicities, and we can become very excited to have the law verified in this way. But much more often, the desired reality doesn't show up, and we can spend months, even years, angry at ourselves, trying to catch the wrong thoughts that we are supposedly sabotaging ourselves with.

But what really disturbs is how we are left to interpret the law of attraction whenever true disaster strikes. Those who happen to fall ill or get cancer—or who are involved in a car accident where they or someone they love are seriously injured—are tossed into terrible anguish, wondering if they somehow *created* the event with their own thoughts.

The majority of manifestation gurus would insist that, yes, they did create such an event and probably even planned it out sometime before incarnating in this life as a way to learn a particular lesson. The other people involved in those events also either agreed beforehand to participate or agreed on a telepathic level as it was happening.

Thus, a murder victim is sometimes said to have agreed to be murdered, a child who is abused is said to have agreed to the abuse, three thousand Americans are said to have agreed to be crushed to death in the 9/11 attacks, and six million Jews are said to have agreed to walk into the ovens at Nazi concentration camps, all for the valuable learning opportunity.

This is not only nonsense, it is deeply offensive nonsense.

True learning is not a pre-arranged exercise but a spontaneous connection between cause and effect. If a murder happens because of an unknown decision made before our lifetimes, then cause and effect do not unfold organically, in this moment, as we know they must. And, if the murder was agreed to beforehand, then clearly that agreement was the *cause* of the murder, and the only thing to be learned is that one shouldn't make such ridiculous agreements in the first place.

The idea that we literally create our own reality, says Ken Wilber, is an "ungraceful interpretation" of basic idealistic premises. He then goes on to point out the obvious: "Only psychotics believe they can create their own reality."

Indeed, no matter how many mental somersaults we are advised to perform, all empirical and rational experience shows us that believing doesn't make it so. We are continually disappointed by expectations unmet and surprised by events unimagined. Meanwhile, the destitute woman in the mental hospital who fervently and sincerely believes she is a millionaire will not suddenly find her bank account overflowing. The convicted murderer who sits in prison and thanks God in advance for his release is not likely to see the gates open for him no matter how great his faith.

Perhaps it's unfair to expect the creative law to work for criminals and the mentally ill, but what about children? Children, more than anyone, have complete faith in magic and only vague knowledge of limits, so it should follow that children would be the most accomplished creators of reality. But, in fact, children prove to be the most helpless over their fate.

Spiritual materialism rears it heads

The Tibetan teacher Chogyam Trungpa warns that any interpretation of spiritual principles which claims to deliver the ego's desires is an example of "spiritual materialism." We Americans, raised with an infamous sense of entitlement, are especially prone to it.

In this common malady, the ego insinuates itself as our spiritual advisor and tries to bend spiritual principles to its will. Spiritual materialism, Trungpa adds, whispers to us with such sincerity, such rational justification, that we rarely become suspicious of what the ego is up to.

The ego is quick to agree that we are one with Spirit, and quick to assume we should have Spirit's creative powers. But as Wilber points out, if the reality I want to create is "nothing but getting a new car, a new job, more money, fame, health instead of disease, happiness instead of sadness, joy instead of pain, light instead of dark, [then] I am no longer being one with everything... I am only being one with a small slice of the universe that is governed by my small desires and wants."

The New Age movement needs to shake itself free from spiritual materialism and manifestation mania. This way of thinking not only leads us astray personally, it chokes off any possibility of a true new age of harmony for all of us.

"Limitless consumption without consequence [has] a devastating affect upon our moral, social, and ecological landscapes," writes David Spangler. "It is part of the modern attitude that the New Age is trying to change; it should not be made an attribute of the New Age itself. When it is, we are boldly going back to where we've been before. No transformation, no emergence, no imagination, no New Age."

Genuine idealism discourages us from seeking riches; instead, it asks us to let go of the old paradigm, the old value systems and its external validations such as money and status. It tells us that power over one's life is not the ability to conjure up gold, for if the gold is lost, then so is the power.

True power over one's life is the ability to think freely, act freely, and love freely, no matter what happens. And responsibility for one's life comes not in the creation of particular circumstances, but in the ability to choose how we react to circumstances. We change our beliefs not to change life but to help us change our *response* to life.

Today, whenever I see another create-your-own-reality book that makes my ego itch to buy it and try it, I stop and ask myself: Would the Buddha or any other enlightened person sit down to say affirmations for greater prosperity? I think not. An enlightened soul is completely self-sufficient and has no need for anything other than the here and now experience.

So then what about the idealistic notion that mind creates reality? If one cannot exert conscious control over the process with one's thoughts, is this principle still valid? And if we do not have control, then how can we still be considered responsible for what happens to us?

Esse est percipi

In Western idealism, "mind as matter" means that the mind, through the act of perception, dictates how reality appears to us. What reality might be outside our perception of it we cannot possibly know. As the eighteenth-century philosopher George Berkeley famously phrased it, *esse est percipi*, to be is to be perceived. Thus, mind creates reality. Or to be more precise, perception creates the look, the sound, and the feel of reality.

At first glance, it would seem that we have no choice in how we perceive the world. The sky is blue no matter how many different eyes look upon it, and that is a fact. Yet, as we move into the more complex realm of human experience, we find that facts begin to slide all over the place.

Although we may see the same things, we each experience them in our own unique way. Our egos mold our experience of the world, selecting which sense information to bring to the forefront of the conscious mind and which to ignore. This means we perceive things not as they really are, but as *we* are.

The outer world is always a reflection of the inner reality. We take all we encounter and pour it into our preconceptions like a paint-by-the-numbers set, and so we largely see what we expect to see.

Reality is therefore a personal phenomenon, which the mind contributes as much by its molding forms as does the outside world. And it is this self-shaped reality in which we operate and on which we base our decisions and choose our actions.

For example, if I believe that human beings are essentially selfish, then when I look at the world, I will see plentiful evidence of selfish people. I might perceive the driver who changed lanes in front of me as rudely cutting me off. I might perceive the woman applying for welfare aid to feed her children as looking for a free handout.

The ego forms a preconceived "frame" through which the mind views all events. Anything that happens contrary to my preconception will be reinterpreted or ignored. The ego, however, is not a solid entity. With a little work, it can be changed, or at least made a little less opaque, a little more flexible.

One way to reshape the ego is to change our habitual thoughts and beliefs. In this respect, at least, the manifestation gurus do us a service when they ask us to look at how our assumptions are reflected back to us and how our thoughts impact what happens around us. Or, as Peter Block puts it, we need to look at the "story" we tell ourselves, "our version of the past [which] becomes the limitation to living into new possibility."

When we become more aware of our habitual way of thinking and believing, or what the Buddhists call our "conditioning," we then give ourselves the opportunity to stay open to the moment instead of shape it to our expectations. When we free ourselves from our preconceptions, we automatically reframe reality. We change how it looks to us and what it becomes to us. More importantly, by changing our beliefs, we change our actions. And it is through our actions that we take reality in hand, so to speak, and mold it anew.

By changing our thoughts, we quite literally change our world. And although it may happen in a more practical way than the manifestation gurus suggest, it does happen, at least according to the interpretation of idealism put forth by Western philosophers.

From the Eastern point of view, however, this interpretation, while accurate, is incomplete.

Creating reality

In Eastern idealism, mind as matter is much more than the molding of appearances. In the East, mind as matter means that matter itself is a mental image, dreamed up in the mind of God. And each of us, as one with God, is dreaming the dream along with God. One might even say the dream would be impossible without us, for we bring it into existence through our awareness.

If we feel we are merely passive observers of this process, responsible only for what we do and not for what happens to us, we are mistaken. As Alan Watts explains, humans are not stand-alone organisms. Each of us is inextricably linked to our environment, one with the whole.

We are each, said Watts, an organism-environment, a "do-happening." All is One and if we pretend we are not responsible for the "happening" half of the equation, then we play a game with ourselves known by the Hindu name of *avidya*, or ignorance.

"Basically," Watts continues, "the place in life where you are is where you have put yourself. Everyone is in their true place. In whatever language you say it, everybody is a manifestation of the divine, playing this game and that game. Your not knowing it, if you do not know it, is part of the game…It is all happening because you are doing it." We are each doing it. We are each dreaming the dream, we are each creating the universe through our awareness.

Of course, few of us are aware of our creative involvement in the universe, for it exists far below the noisy ripples of thought that froth up on the surface of our daily consciousness. And that is how it is meant to be. To try and drag such creation into the conscious world would be like trying to dream while awake. It is a contradiction in terms.

As in dreaming, we create reality not by controlling what happens but by observing what happens, allowing what happens, experiencing what happens, feeling what happens. As soon as we try to direct the dream or exert control, we wake up and the dream ends.

Our dreams unfold beyond our choosing, and yet a lack of control does not imply a lack of responsibility. When we dream we are, without a doubt, still the creators of the dream. We cannot control it, but we are still the ones doing the dreaming, and therefore still responsible for its existence.

In the same manner, each of us creates the universe through our mind, through our share of consciousness. And each self-created reality is reflected in the whole. Indeed, this is how the whole is seamlessly created, my reality reflecting yours, reflecting his, reflecting hers, and on and on, each of us dreaming the world into existence. It is all happening because we are all doing it.

The New Age thus challenges us to take responsibility for it all. It asks us to examine our own encounter with reality, to observe how the beliefs we hold in our minds come to life before our eyes. It dares us to step into our role as co-creators of the universe and create a reality that is a welcoming and supportive environment for all.

15 The Riddle of the Self

There are moments when my eyes meet a mirror in passing and I don't immediately recognize myself. With a delayed jolt I realize that the stranger in the mirror is me. It doesn't seem possible that the woman staring back so blankly could be the same emotional swirl of a person I feel myself to be. At such times, I have the disquieting feeling that I am two people—the noisy me, running about with too much to do, and the more silent me, who gazes startled from the mirror.

There is an uneasy, sometimes even hostile, relationship between these two halves of myself. The woman in the mirror falls grievously short of what I want her to be. She's not thin enough, not kind enough, not secure enough, not disciplined enough. I feel certain she is the one holding me back, preventing me from being happy, so I criticize her and nag her to improve.

There is some small comfort in knowing that most of us feel something similar, this split in the self, with one side at war with the other. Many of us have spent a great deal of our lives, and great deal of our money, in the effort to get the contrary person in the mirror under control.

Yet, at some point, we grow bruised and weary of the battle. At some point, even more than we long for improvement, we long for peace. We long to heal the rift between our two selves and become one whole person. More than anything, we long to discover who we really are.

Searching for myself

The desire to find oneself is apparently a modern phenomenon. Before the rise of science, most people accepted what local religions and myths declared them to be.

In the Christian West, that meant each man, woman, and child was born a sinner, and any interest in the self other than the matter of one's salvation was unseemly vanity. Any feelings of inner conflict were laid at the devil's door, and one could only hope that God on his throne would hear one's prayers and be moved to grant one peace.

Then along came unsentimental science and, suddenly, who we are became something different entirely. The brain was declared the seat of the self, and all our troubles became issues of bodily mechanics. Depressions, dissatisfactions and other "ill humors" could be warded off with garlic or vaccuumed out of the blood with leeches. (We still do something similar today, trying to treat our ill humors with antidepressants.)

As science sucked away at our souls on one side and religion held unhelpfully to its archaic pronouncements on the other, we human beings were left to flounder somewhere in the middle.

By the turn of the twentieth century, being a human self had become something of a problem. In an effort to help solve the problem, science developed a new branch called psychology. Yet, despite its many successes in treating the various glitches produced by the meeting of mind and life, it never satisfactorily addressed the lingering question mark of who we are.

Indeed, increasing numbers of people, even after growing up on a church pew or spending years on a psychiatrist's couch, are still searching for themselves. But despite the connotation of narcissism attached to the search, the effort to find oneself has always been an important philosophical endeavor.

Know thyself

The words "know thyself" were first inscribed by the ancient Greeks at their Temple of Apollo at Delphi, and ever since, this dictum has been considered the foundation for all wisdom. After all, the self is the door through which all experience of reality flows, which necessarily means that understanding who we are is the key to understanding all else.

The New Age actively encourages us in this vital task and offers up a variety of self-discovery tools to assist us. I can head off to the bookstore and find any number of metaphysics-based self-help books by any number of gurus and shamans that will help me identify what I'm looking for.

Meanwhile, in my local *Whole Life Times* directory, I can find help in integrating myself from hypnotherapists, transpersonal psychologists, spiritual counselors, bodyworkers, intuitive advisors, and meditation masters, among others.

Many of these teachers and healers begin by turning us back toward the mirror. They ask us to examine the voice that scolds us so relentlessly. Where does that voice come from? Why do we feel it somehow separate from us? Just who, the New Age asks, do we think we are?

I think, therefore I am

When I try to put my finger on who I am exactly, I find myself sorting through a list of words I use to describe myself. I am a woman, I am a writer, I am a mother, an American, a Democrat, a blonde, a book lover.

But as I read my list I realize that most of these things are easily changeable. I can change my career, my political party, my place of residence, the color of my hair, or most any other thing about me, and I would still be myself.

Science, of course, could map out my DNA and give me a printout of my body's genetic code, which is not changeable. But that would be mere number identification, like my social security number. While unique, this information tells me nothing about *who* I really am.

To find out the *who*, I must go deeper than adjectives and other classifications and ask, who is this person that writes? Who is it that mothers my children? Who is it that asks these questions and thinks these thoughts?

Ah yes, thoughts. My thoughts seem intimately connected with who I am. And yet, my thoughts come and go so quickly. Some common themes are repeated, but my thoughts can change entirely, head off in new directions, and I would still be myself. Obviously, I cannot really rest my sense of self on the content of my thought.

Yet, if I look deeper, beneath the ever-shifting river of my thoughts, I find a steady sense of consciousness of those thoughts. If nothing else, I am a being that is conscious of its thought.

Then again, that's exactly what everyone else is, too. Each and every one of us is a being who is conscious of its thought, and if I cannot use a list of adjectives to describe myself, then in what way am I unique, in what way am I me, and not you?

Despite my earnest efforts, I can think of nothing that makes me essentially different from any one else, at least not in this particular moment. But wait, if I collect all my moments together, I can identify a pattern that is unique.

"According to convention," writes Alan Watts, "I am not simply what I am doing now. I am also what I have done, and my conventionally edited version of my past is made to seem almost more the real 'me' than what I am at this moment. For what I am seems so fleeting and intangible, but what I was is fixed and final."

Memory provides us with an image of ourselves based on our remembered strengths and weaknesses, remembered likes and dislikes, remembered skills and talents. Memory gives our successive moments of consciousness the image of unity, and it is this image that forms the ego of a human being.

Self, meet ego

It would seem we have arrived at the source of self in the ego, a memory-based image that represents who we are. But on close examination, we discover that this image isn't real either. A memory of the past is nothing but a thought that we have *now*. Whenever we remember something that happened in the past, we are remembering it in the present.

Ultimately, even memory leads us back to this particular moment. The ego we think to be firmly based in the past is actually an illusion of the present.

Alan Watts again describes it best when he says, "The image you have of yourself is a social institution in the same way it is a social institution to divide the day into twenty-four hours, or to draw lines of latitude and longitude which are purely imaginary over the surface of the earth. It's very useful, but there are no actual lines. They are imaginary. Ego is an imaginary concept that is not the organism."

This is not to say that the ego is an accidental by-product or somehow unnecessary. The ego serves a vital function by making the physical world accessible to us. I sometimes think the ego must create a sticky force much like the force of gravity which keeps us fastened to the earth. Without gravity, we would go tumbling out into space and find ourselves dissolving into the void.

In the same way, the sticky ego makes it possible for us to exist outside the absolute from which our existence flows. Indeed, neuroanatomist Jill Bolte Taylor describes the way the ego helps us make sense of a relative world in her stunning book, *My Stroke of Insight*. After a stroke shut down the "ego center" of the left side of her brain, Dr. Taylor says she became incapable of differentiating herself from the flow of life around her. Without the brain chatter that normally churned from her left brain to keep her anchored in her version of herself, she felt herself become fluid and peacefully at one with the universe. Yet, however much she enjoyed that peace, she literally could not orient herself in physical space, nor relate to other people. She movingly describes a tough decision to "heal" the left side of her brain and rebuild her ego so she would be able to function normally in the world again.

Taylor's experience, grounded in a modern scientist's knowledge of the brain and its functions, marvelously confirmed for me the ancient truths of idealism. Without the sense of separation provided by the ego, the world and all its divisions would have no meaning for us, and we would be unable to learn from it. The ego is a necessary escort into the world of form, and we all need a strong and healthy ego in order to serve our purpose here.

But that doesn't make it any less an illusion.

Seeing through the illusion

The ego is usually blamed for all our troubles. Eastern religions have long taught that a man's ego is the part of him that keeps him unnecessarily separate from God. The part of us that hates and judges is pure ego. The part of us that clings and fears is ego. The part of us that is threatened by the opinions of others is ego.

But our problems do not arise from having an ego; rather, they arise from our *identification* with the ego. Instead of recognizing it as our persona, or what Jung calls a mask or false face, we take it as our true face. We jump into the shoes of this false, solid-seeming self and, in the process, separate ourselves from who we are in this moment. We literally split ourselves in two.

To be internally divided is a pretty painful condition, and so we begin to wrestle with ourselves, try to fix ourselves. But it is a hopeless task. As Watts phrased the problem:

> How on earth are you going to get at yourself, to do something about yourself...? In other words, if you feel that you need to make some sort of psychological or spiritual improvement, obviously you are the character who is going to have to bring this about. But if you are the one who needs to be improved, how are you going to accomplish the improvement? You are in the predicament of trying to lift yourself up off the floor by pulling at your own bootstraps, and you are likely to land with a bang on your fanny and end up lower down than you were in the first place.

The only way out of our predicament is to stop identifying with the ego, learn to understand its basic unreality. Yes, the ego will continue to tag along with us, noisy as ever, ranting at us in the mirror. But if we refuse to identify with it, refuse to take it seriously, then the ego's voice can become exactly what it is: the background noise of being human.

When we begin to understand that the self is not found in the ego, but in the soul, we step through the mirror into a magical looking glass world where everything is exactly the same but completely different. The ego-identity that once seemed such a solid self becomes a wavering illusion, and the past on which we based that identity becomes as insubstantial as a dream. Meanwhile, the present moment that was once so fleeting opens into an eternity and brings us into the presence of our true self—the soul.

Locating the soul

Below the ego's noisy river of thought, there is always consciousness. This consciousness, which we also know by the name of soul, is the elemental energy at the core of each individual. The soul does not belong to us, we belong to it. It is not a part of us, we are a part of it. Which is why it is so notoriously difficult to locate.

As religion scholar James Carse writes, "When I look for the unnameable within myself, I don't know what to look for. But then, I couldn't see it anyway, it is not to be seen, for it is indistinguishable from the act of seeing." Or as St. Francis of Assisi said, "Who you are looking for is who is looking."

The soul is like the eye that cannot see itself, or the hand that cannot grasp itself. It is not a describable object, not a thing that acts. The soul is not a thing at all, it is a moment, a simple moment of conscious being.

This may seem too small a substance on which to base an entire self, especially when compared to the dense layers of ego. How can this one moment of consciousness be all there is?

The soul's frequency

Joseph Campbell likened soul energy to electric energy, and the body to the bulb that turns the energy into visible light. The bulb may burn out, we may change it many times, but the energy current still exists and is always connected to its source.

Comparing the energy of soul to the energy of electricity can be helpful, but again we find that electric current is pretty much all the same, no matter how many different kinds of bulbs it lights. And beings that are conscious in this moment are essentially the same as all other beings, no matter how different the egos that come with them.

This is the basis for the Buddhist concept of *anatta*, or no-soul, which says the soul is not individual or separate from the one life-force and so does not endure after death.

Ultimately, say the Buddhists, there is no see-er, there is only seeing. There is no knower, there is only knowing. There is no particular being at all, only being itself, consciousness of being that pools within an individual for the duration of his or her lifetime. The separation between subject and object, or between one soul and another, is an illusion.

We Westerners cannot conceive of a self that is indistinct from all others. Our very definition of self is based on the self as an individual. The idea of *anatta* or no-soul strikes us as either appalling or ridiculous, and is quickly discarded. Indeed, I believe one of the main attractions of Christianity is its devotion to the individual ego. Christianity insists that each person keeps the same identity forever and criticizes any philosophy that appears to threaten individuality.

Yet, just because the soul is not individual and separate doesn't mean it is not unique. Yes, the soul is energy, but as in the electromagnetic field, energy is expressed in waves and can be measured by the frequency of those waves. An infinite number of frequencies can carry the exact same energy; there is no separation in energy, and yet each frequency is unique.

That is why, in the New Age, one often hears the term "vibrational frequency" to describe a particular soul. Although we are each made up of the same universal energy, each soul is understood to generate its own unique and constant frequency, giving our particular consciousness continuity.

According to Dr. Bruce Lipton, a biologist who spent decades studying the workings of cells, the membrane of every human cell is packed with receptors to pick up numerous chemical and energy signals that move through the body and communicate with the cell. And one kind of receptor he calls the identity receptor. Each person has unique identity receptors, says Lipton, and his research has convinced him that these receptors literally act as antennas that "*read* a signal of 'self' which does not exist within the cell but comes to it from the external environment."

Consider the human body a television set, Lipton continues in his book, *The Biology of Belief*. "In this analogy, the physical television is the equivalent of the cell. The TV's antenna, which downloads the broadcast, represents our full set of identifying receptors, and the broadcast represents an environmental signal." To believe that our cells are the source of the self "would be the equivalent of believing that the TV's antenna is the source of the broadcast." The cell and its receptors are not the source of the self, "but the vehicle by which the 'self' is downloaded from the environment," downloaded from Spirit. Lipton goes on to describe his belief that not only are our bodies designed to tune in to a particular spiritual frequency, they are also designed to experience the physical world and send that information back to the environment, or Spirit.

In other words, we are each of us different frequencies of the energy of one God, unfolding Himself/Herself into physical being, and each of us contribute our own small part to God's greater self-knowing. Yet, as the Buddhists understand, there is no individual soul. We are different expressions, or vibrations, of one divine soul. We are all God in disguise.

Does this mean that after death and the loss of ego that we are absorbed back into God, destined for oblivion? It seems to me that if we were never really separate from God in the first place, then we cannot somehow disappear back into God. In the words of Joseph Campbell, "If the self participates in the power of being-itself, then it receives itself back."

The soul is not absorbed away—we simply remember what we are and have always been, an eternal aspect of God.

New self, new world

The New Age considers this new understanding of ourselves to be vital to our future, for when our conception of ourselves changes, then everything changes. If we see ourselves, and each other, not as ego-based sinners who must be controlled but as divine souls worthy of trust and respect, then we will act accordingly. Our relationships, our values, our politics, our philosophy of education, our system of law and justice—all these will reflect a profound and positive change.

Personally, the changes would be immediate. A self understood as soul is no longer doomed to be divided within, no longer trapped within the ego and controlled by its whims. We suddenly have a choice between identifying with the ego's drama or identifying with the much simpler present moment. The problem, and pain, of being human eases greatly.

But certainly the most dramatic and far-reaching changes allowed by this understanding of self would be in the social arena. If we could learn to discern the divine frequency vibrating in the other, we would no longer feel so easily threatened by others. Those who used to inspire our fear might instead inspire our compassion. And rather than feel a need to punish others, we would feel the need to help them, care for them, educate them. Rather than spending all our resources protecting ourselves, we might feel compelled to invest some of our resources in others and empower them to become what they deeply need to become.

The New Age understanding of the self brings us a new understanding of the self in others, a new understanding of our essential oneness. And that, more than anything, is our dire need. For that, more than anything, is the true foundation for a new age of peace and harmony between men.

16 Karma and Destiny

Life shows a disconcerting tendency to change directions based on nothing more than chance timing or a stray whim. If I hadn't gone for pizza on a particular Thursday night, I wouldn't have met my daughter's father. If I hadn't scanned the classifieds on a particular Tuesday, I wouldn't have applied for the job where I met my best friend.

When we measure the impact of such fortuitous events, it is difficult to believe they happened by mere chance. Surely these life-changing moments are arranged by fate, or were meant to be. Indeed, most New Agers insist there is no such thing as a coincidence, no such thing as an accident. But if so, does that mean everything from lost keys to pizza cravings are meant to be?

On one hand, life seems to tumble straight out of this moment, without rhyme or reason; on the other hand, it seems that greater forces are always at work in everything we do.

Perhaps we see it both ways because we want it both ways. We want the freedom that puts our lives in our own hands, but we also want to know that the universe has a special purpose in mind for us. We want the power to change our lives according to our choices, but we also want the pattern that tells us where we've been and where we're supposed to go. We want both freedom and destiny, yet how can it be possible to have both?

"See how fate slides into freedom and freedom into fate," wrote Emerson. "This knot of nature is so well tied that no one was ever cunning enough to find the two ends." In the New Age, we find we cannot leave the knot alone. We puzzle over it, turn it, poke it, prod it. We want to know exactly which end is which so we can find our balance on its sliding surface. For help, we turn to the East and the elegant law of balance called karma.

The law of balance

In the last four hundred years, science has arrived at a remarkable understanding of how the universe works. A procession of brilliant minds has studied life in its smallest details, and they have unanimously concluded that the universe is held together by a number of irrefutable laws.

One such law in the realm of matter is the law of motion, discovered by Newton, which says that for every action there is an equal and opposite reaction. A similar law, which applies to the realm of energy, is the first law of thermodynamics, or the conservation of energy. This law says that all the energy in the universe remains at a constant level, and a loss in one area is balanced by a gain in another.

We are confident of these laws because some extremely intelligent people have assigned them mathematically exact formulas and verified them with empirical experimentation.

But what about those levels of existence such as consciousness in which empirical formulation is not possible? If, as physics claims, our balancing laws are universal and applicable to all parts of the universe, wouldn't it follow that balancing laws must operate on the level of consciousness as well?

Hence, the law of karma, discovered by the Hindus, which

says that even in the realm of the unseen and unmeasured, cause is inevitably followed by effect.

Karma is a universal structure, like the structure of time, built into consciousness itself. The idealist philosopher Gottfried Leibniz described causality as an innate idea within the mind, while Immanuel Kant called it *a priori*, or prior to, and necessary to, all conscious experience.

Without the innate mental structure of karma to connect cause and effect, we wouldn't be able to organize the flux of sense impressions that flood the mind. Victims of stroke or brain injury have been able to confirm this. In *My Stroke of Insight*, Dr. Jill Bolte Taylor describes being literally unable to make the connection between causes and effects after a massive brain hemorrhage, and how she floundered in a meaningless world where all events popped up at random and made no sense to her.

Without karma, we literally wouldn't be able to understand our experience. In fact, without karma, there would be no way for life to evolve toward consciousness at all. Without the ability to connect cause and effect, there would be no basis by which an organism could choose differently in its behaviors, no impetus for adaptation to a higher level. This is why the Buddha asked of his cousin, "If, Ananda, there were no karmic ripening in the sphere of the senses, would there appear any sense sphere existence?" And his cousin naturally replied, "Surely not, O lord."

In Buddhism, karma is therefore not only part of the *maya*—the illusion of material reality—it actually holds the *maya* together in the same way the physical laws hold it together. Karma, say the Buddhists, is the womb from which we spring, the true creator of the world and of ourselves as experiencers of the world.

Blaming karma

Understanding karma as a feature built within consciousness is probably not the definition familiar to most. In the popular imagination, karma is a grubby little law, on par with a hard-hearted accountant who pitilessly puts red marks on our books of what we owe life. Such a law is seen not as a blessing, but a curse.

This point of view originated in the Hindu imagination, which sees karma as the intractable force that keeps the miserable masses lashed to the wheel of life. Only when karma is satisfied can we be released from the cycle.

We Westerners like this interpretation, probably because it bears such a close resemblance to our concept of "eye-for-an-eye." Indeed, most of us who adopt the idea of karma expect it to work like a basic one-to-one equation computed by that cosmic accountant, wherein every deed is rewarded or punished with an equivalent deed.

Many find this interpretation very comforting. I know one unflappable woman who attributes everything that happens in her life to her karma. No matter what manner of disaster befalls her, she doesn't take it personally. She's convinced that karma brings her only what she deserves and will exact ruthless revenge on any who harm her.

Sometimes it really does seem to work out that way. As a teenager torn between morality and being cool, I once stole fifty dollars from a stranger; just a few months later another stranger stole eighty dollars from me. It was a vivid lesson, and I have never again felt tempted to steal. Nor have I been a victim of theft again.

Yet, most often, karma does not to work in such a straightforward way, and we cannot help but notice that bad, selfish, and horrible people often prosper undeservedly, while good and wonderful people often suffer undeservedly.

This clear lack of balance in the law of balance is often justified by adding in the concept of reincarnation. We tell ourselves we must have done something in a *former* life, or at a *former* time, that is now having this particular consequence.

But according to Watts, "You do not need to believe in reincarnation to understand karma." Karma literally translated means action or doing. When a Buddhist says, "That is your karma," he is saying, "That is your doing." Karma is simply the knowledge that you are "both what you do and what happens to you," Watts concludes. It is not an equation that stretches across time but the balancing of your actions here and now.

The fact that we cannot predict what form this balancing act will take, or how it will manifest in our lives, is besides the point from a Buddhist perspective. So while it is wise to have a care for the workings of karma in our lives, it is most unwise to expect it to work in any particular fashion. That is why the Buddha declared karma to be an "unthinkable," and warned against treating it as a subject of speculation.

We would do better, said the Buddha, to look at life as a state of mutual arising. Or as Campbell described it:

> A great number of things round about, on every side, are causing what is happening now. Everything, all the time, is causing everything else... nobody and no thing is to blame for anything that ever occurs, because all is mutually arising. All is one thing.

The Present Moment

According to my clock, this one little moment barely exists. Blink and it's gone. The next moment is gone just as quickly, and the next. With so many moments disappearing so fast, it is no wonder that we feel we have to hurry, that we can never catch up.

But my clock has it backwards. Time as my clock measures it simply doesn't exist because this one little moment doesn't disappear at all; it is always here, and it quite literally lasts forever.

Time is an illusion we have created for our convenience. It is a structure that we all use by general agreement, much in the same way that we have agreed that certain words represent certain objects. Words aren't real either; the word hot has no heat in it. Yet, these symbols of reality allow us to communicate with each other—and show up in the same place at the same time.

Yes, we can remember moments that came before this one, but we are not remembering previous times so much as we are remembering previous events—previous motions of matter. These events seem separated in time because we experience them in succession. But as each event happens, it is now. When any past event happened, it was now. When future events happen, it will be now. All events happen now because now is all that exists.

Our clocks perpetuate the illusion of time by adding another number with each sweep of the minute hand. But we can't actually add to time because this moment has no beginning and no end. The ticking of a clock is nothing but matter in motion, as is the rotation and orbit of the planet by which we measure days and years. Clocks do not measure time after all; they merely measure movement.

It seems a radical assertion to say the past does not exist. Some might even call it a ridiculous assertion. After all, we build our identity upon the past. We look at the person we are today as a result of what happened yesterday. But if we understand that linear time is an illusion, we see that the people we are today is not a result of what we've done in the past, but of what we do today.

Alan Watts' analogy is that of a ship crossing the ocean. The ship moves in the present while the wake fans out behind it, marking its past. We wouldn't say that the wake is propelling the ship; it only marks where the ship has been. Likewise, we cannot say that the past propels us into the present. It is the present that creates the past. A ship may change directions at any time, and so may we.

And the moment we change directions, change our actions, we change our karma. We don't change it so that we can get a reward at some later time, or in a later life. We change it here and now. The cause is now, the effect is now, it is all mutually arising right now. And now. And now.

Karma is not justice

Clearly, karma is not a transparent system of debits and credits. The karmic accountant is simply not going to play the human game of ensuring justice or redressing wrongs. Whatever karma brings to us is in the interests of balance and harmony, not of justice.

Although we may think of justice and balance as the same thing, justice is the social invention of humans, not of God. From the perspective of the infinite, there is no innocent or guilty, no fair or unfair. There is only the endless rhythm of positive and negative energy flowing between chaos and order, separation and union, darkness and light—all of it seeking balance through karma.

Karma does not decree that a person deserves punishment for his crimes, nor does it spare the innocent from pain. That is why we cannot conclude that the circumstances we are born into, whether we perceive them as good or bad, are the result of karma we carry from a previous life.

Of course, some interpreters of Eastern religion do consider the soul to be the repository of karma, which allegedly follows us from life to life. But karma is the law of balance that applies to the *maya*, or material reality. The soul, meanwhile, exists outside of time and space. The soul is therefore not subject to causality. The action or doing of karma unfolds in the present, unfolds in a state of mutual arising. Karma cannot compel the soul; rather, it is the soul that compels karma into its service.

Yet, if we cannot blame karma for all that happens, if all is but a state of mutual arising, does this mean there is no pattern after all? Do we slide off willy nilly along the slope of freedom with no fate to ground us? Are all our efforts to discover our destiny wasted effort?

The knot of destiny

The concept of karma was first preached to Americans by the colorful founder of the Theosophical Society, Helena Petrovna Blavatsky. In her book, *The Secret Doctrine*, Madame Blavatsky writes, "those who believe in karma have to believe in destiny, which, from birth to death, every man is weaving, thread by thread, around himself, as a spider does his web." But Blavatsky is also quick to add that karma does not design our destiny, we design it ourselves with our actions.

The New Age often amplifies this point of view and declares each person to be the sole creator of his or her future destiny. Many writers even go so far as to depict our souls waiting backstage for our entrance into the world, freely choosing the circumstances of our birth as well as the details of the life we will lead.

This idea goes all the way back to Plato's *The Republic*, in which Plato elaborated in fanciful detail the between-life scene of souls choosing their next lives. "The responsibility lies with the one who makes the choice," he wrote. "The gods have none."

Like Plato, many New Age writers have elaborated on the between-life process in colorful detail and have described rooms made from walls of light, and benevolent spirit guides who show us our futures on magic screens. But since most of us do not remember this pre-incarnation experience, we are left to try to ferret out our destiny by other means. And of course, the New Age is ready to help us with an entire industry devoted to divining our destiny for us. Psychics, tarot card readers, numerologists, astrologists stand ready to lend us their all-seeing talents.

But if we understand that all existence is a state of mutual arising, then we understand that trying to see into the future is basically meaningless conjecture. Destiny is not laid out ahead of time but unfolds spontaneously according to our ever-changing karma. We do not move along as on a straight thread that stretches out into the future. Rather, destiny unfolds from this very moment, continually looping back around to where we are in this moment, much like a spinning circle. Fate, said Emerson, is "a series of concentric circles," eternally generating.

In the end, destiny is not really about one's future at all, it is about one's purpose. Destiny carries what the Greeks called our *telos*, our reason for being. And, as we know from the story of our creation, our reason for being is to expand God's self-awareness through our varied experience. Destiny is therefore not a datebook filled with meetings and things we are fated to do. It is simply our innate knowledge that we have important work to do.

But this work is not predetermined. Now is all there is, and who we are today is not the result of yesterday's decisions but of the decisions we make today. We create ourselves, and our destiny, each day, brand new. The outcome is never fixed; all is at risk each moment, in each choice.

Destiny does not lie in past or future but in purpose, in the need of the gods to find themselves through us.

Like most New Agers, I often ponder my own destiny, and I try very hard to discern its shape. I suspect that we may indeed wait backstage before our birth and perhaps even choose our parents and a few grand ideas to explore. But after that, I think we hold our breath and jump into time and the sliding unknown with all its determined certainties and perilous uncertainties. And I think we struggle mightily to learn that we don't have to struggle at all.

Meanwhile, I imagine the gods up above, watching and cheering us on. Sometimes I can almost hear them laughing at our mistakes and raining down the tears of their sympathy.

17 The Problem of Evil

As soon as our children are old enough to talk, we begin the ritual chant: Don't talk to strangers. Like every other parent on the planet, we must figure out how to make three-year-olds understand there are "bad guys" who want to hurt children. By the time our children turn four or five, they know about the existence of evil. By the time they become adults, they know that evil exists everywhere.

There is no way to avoid this knowledge, especially not in our post 9/11 world. We all have heightened awareness now. We continually read about evil in history books and today's newspaper. We find it in the rich nations and poor countries, big cities and small towns, a plague on every society in every corner of the earth. And at least once in our lives, we are likely to be touched by evil's destructive power as victims of abuse or crime or war.

Evil challenges us not only in creating a secure world in which to raise children, but also in creating meaningful lives for ourselves. It requires us to daily wrestle with questions of how we can possibly accept—let alone live peacefully within—an existence that roils with such horrors.

Thus far, the Western approach to these agonizing questions has been to insert as much distance as possible between evil and ourselves. With our religions we have created unholy devils on which to cast the blame for dark deeds, and a host of prayers and rituals to keep it at bay. With our sciences we have discovered mental disorders and illness and invented drugs and treatments and hospitals to keep them at bay. And with our governments we have built prison after prison in which to lock up those of us who seem susceptible to evil and keep them out of sight.

We have done everything humanly possible to push evil away, get rid of it, banish it. And yet, it remains with us still.

The problem of evil is a particular challenge for the New Age. Since we have loudly declared that "All is One," we cannot possibly disown evil. We have no choice but to recognize evil as part of Spirit, part of God, as a darkness that lurks on the underside of light.

This position can be difficult to sustain. Indeed, it is the "evil is an illusion" assertion that draws the most heated attacks from critics of the New Age and others who prefer to battle evil as a separate foe. Lawyer and professional realist Wendy Kaminer, for example, describes the New Age's "refusal to acknowledge evil" as "offensive gibberish."

I think Kaminer is correct in that it is clearly offensive to make light of evil. And if the New Age is going to assert that Spirit is the only reality, then it must meaningfully account for the darkness we daily encounter in the world.

More importantly, it must empower us to effectively address evil so that it may no longer flourish.

The eye of the beholder

Most often, when idealists turn to the question of evil, they talk about polarities, how we must have dark in order to recognize light. Contrast is built into "the very nature of awareness," Watts writes, and all things must "be experienced as good/bad or plus/minus in order to be experienced at all." As finite creatures, we exist in a relative world where everything is inevitably better or worse, according to our particular point of view.

Yet, as Watts also goes on to say, describing the nature of human perception is not the same thing as describing the nature of reality. Our perception of two distinct forces—good and evil—does not mean that these forces are distinct in reality. From a perspective of infinite reality, polarities are meaningless.

It might be true that human perception needs to create bad in order to delineate good, but this division is completely arbitrary. Each person places it where he or she likes, according to cultural convention or family history or personal taste or any combination thereof. That is why in some countries it is perfectly acceptable for a woman to be rewarded for sex with money, while in other countries a woman may be punished for sex with a horrific death.

Mystics who have transcended ordinary human perception unanimously agree that reality is not divided into two forces. Reality is One, and within this One lies both negative and positive energy, both darkness and light.

Still, we cannot help but ask, *why* must there be darkness? Why can't all be light? Why does spirit unfold in such a way that the negative so often sweeps across the face of the world, knocking us all down, again and again?

It was Georg Hegel, the brilliant German idealist, who described the process of Spirit unfolding as a process of dialectic. Separation and union is the essence of creation, said Hegel. Spirit must be able to divide in order to be able to join together and give birth to the new.

According to Hegelian idealism, as the One descends into the many forms of matter, it splits into multiple fragments. Some of these fragments are positive and negative, which allows them to push and pull against each other, separating and joining in new patterns, creating more forms, more reality, more experience.

If energy were to somehow reach stable equilibrium, there would be no more push and pull, no more flow of energy, no more life, period. For matter to come alive, there must be a continuous flow of energy racing from the positive to the negative and back again.

This rhythm is the essence of being; all life beats to this alternating pulse. The negative, Hegel concluded, is an intricate part of—and even necessary to—Spirit becoming.

The evil that men do

Let's say we theoretically accept the dialectic nature of life and acknowledge that All is One. Let's say we can agree that there is no separate force, no dark lord intent on our destruction. The stubborn fact remains, the effects of evil are still with us. Slavery, war, murder, oppression—all of these still exist, devil or no. We still have to deal with the malignancy that steals across the human heart and compels someone to knowingly hurt others. And we still need to figure out what to do about it.

The New Age tells us that the vital first step in winning the fight against evil is to abandon the idea of a separate force intent on destroying us. This assumption is in itself the *source* of so much of the evil we encounter. This assumption allows us to demonize our fellow man and treat them as objects of fear and hatred.

Worse, this assumption not only allows us to hurt others, it actively encourages us to battle against evil by killing those we have perceived to have wronged us. Thus, we ourselves become killers; we end up becoming the very evil we are trying to destroy.

History bears this out, over and over again, from the Nazis and their concentration camps, to the suicide bombers and terrorists of today. In trying to destroy the evil *out there*, we only end up perpetuating the cycle of destruction that causes us so much pain.

But the moment we stop disowning evil, the moment we recognize that evil is not "out there" but "in here" with us, all of us, then we find ourselves in possession of the power to change things.

In that moment, we are able to clearly see that at the root of every abominable act perpetrated by a human being is a human ego lashing out, an ego blinded to others by its own pain and anger. In that moment, we are able to see that negativity only breeds more negativity, and if the world brings suffering to a child in the beginning, that child will grow up to bring the world suffering in the end.

Evil is real, said Gandhi, only insofar as we give it credence. In his preface to Gandhi's writings, Ecknath Easwaran tells us that Gandhi tried to teach that "the essence of holding on to Truth is to withdraw support of what is wrong." And, "if enough people do this—if even one person does it from a great enough depth—evil has to collapse from lack of support."

When we stop disowning evil, stop demonizing and hating and fearing, we are given the opportunity to escape the negative spiral. We are given a choice in how to respond. We may choose to meet negative energy with positive energy, choose to meet pain and fear with love and compassion.

This does not mean that we allow others to harm us, or permit people to avoid consequences when they inflict pain on others. But the rule of law does not require the context of evil to function. In fact, the rule of law and exercise of power works much more effectively if it is not muddled by hysterical notions of evil.

We must always insist that negative actions be given the appropriate consequences. But know this: When we no longer require revenge for our pain, we remove evil from the world. As soon as we are able to accept and forgive others, and help them to heal, then, in that moment, evil is no more.

The problem of pain

I absolutely believe it is in our power to banish evil from our lives. I believe we can collectively decide at any time to see differently, choose differently, live differently. But it must be acknowledged that even if we were to create such a miracle together, that would not save us from pain.

I think the problem of evil ultimately boils down to the problem of suffering, the problem of pain. More than anything, we do not want to feel pain. More than anything, we want to live in a world where no one, especially those we love, will suffer pain.

Of all the difficulties life throws our way, pain is the most difficult to reconcile with the notion of a loving God. Why, oh why, does God allow us to suffer? I have sat with my suffering child in the hospital, weeping and despairing over this question. Why are the innocent so often allowed to be hurt?

I have found comfort in the idea that perhaps God allows us to feel pain for the same reason that I allowed my toddlers to leave their cribs even though I knew they would fall and hurt themselves many times during the day.

Yet, if I could, wouldn't I design a world in which a child would not suffer pain each time she banged her head? Maybe not. If she was unable to feel pain, she'd have no reason to learn to duck her head when she crawled under a table. Without pain, she'd have little motivation to learn this important lesson. Without pain, she might come to even greater harm.

"Unless the organism can feel pain," Watts wrote, "it cannot withdraw from danger, so that the unwillingness to be able to be hurt is in fact suicidal, whereas the simple retreat from pain is not."

Sadly, in our unwillingness to feel pain and our efforts to anesthetize ourselves against it, we end up bringing much greater suffering to ourselves and those we love. Alcoholism, drug addiction, food addictions—these are just a few examples of pain avoidance turned sources of even greater suffering.

We Westerners have forgotten, or perhaps have never truly realized, the value of pain. In modern America especially, we assume that a pain-free life is a promise of democracy and have therefore become a society of litigation and punishment. We believe that if someone causes us any pain or difficulty, even unintentionally, he or she must pay.

This is progress of a sort, for we have finally realized that it is wrong to hurt each other. But we have taken this realization to the illogical conclusion that it is wrong to be hurt or feel pain at all. The result is that all our suffering has become senseless, pain without redeeming purpose, pain that hurts without the ability to instruct.

The first noble truth

Pain is braided into the very experience of being alive, a natural feature of biological life. In the grand drama of God's self-exploration, we will all be hurt, we will all be broken, we will all die.

"The earth must be broken to bring forth life," Campbell wrote. "If the seed does not die, there is no plant. Bread results from the death of wheat. Life lives on lives."

This may seem an absurd way to look at pain that is the result of senseless evils like assault and murder. These horrors certainly do not bring forth life. But it is not the events themselves that are meaningful, it is what the events cause to happen within us.

"Evil facts," said William James, are "possibly the only opener of our eyes to the deepest levels of truth." We learn courage by coming face-to-face with fear; we learn to love by overcoming hate. Through the negative we are brought to the positive. Evil, as much as awe, brings the heart to God.

Many people approach their philosophy or religion as a way to help them escape their pain. A good belief system, however, will not insulate us from pain, but help us better yield to it.

Thus, the Buddha's First Noble Truth: life is suffering. To truly accept that pain is part of being alive is the beginning of all wisdom. And only from this beginning will we learn to transform the negative to the positive, turn straw into gold.

The love of fate

In the New Age, we have learned that to reject the pain and ferocity of life is to reject life itself. To say no to one little detail is to unravel the whole. We need to say yes to all of it so that we may learn what it has to teach us. We say yes not only to pain, but yes to the challenge that evil throws in our faces: the challenge to accept, to forgive, to love, and to heal the tortured souls that bring evil into the world.

This acceptance is captured by Neitzche in the words *amor fati*, or love of fate. No matter what happens, we accept that we are being given something we need to learn. No matter what happens, we accept it as an opportunity we are privileged to have received. We say yes to it all, for as Campbell again explains, "The demon that you can swallow gives you its power, and the greater life's pain, the greater life's reply."

The New Age tells us that if we say yes to it all, and "participate with joy in the sorrows of the world," then we have found the whole, the One, the universal life. In saying yes, we gain a larger context and we see that we are not alone with our pain.

We move from the individual to the universal. We move from my pain to *the* pain, from my drama to *the* drama, the whole of six billion individual dramas happening all at once. And from this universal perspective, we gain a bittersweet understanding that pardons all, accepts all.

As Campbell writes of the mythological hero who endures many trials, "The hero transcends life with its peculiar blind spot and for a moment rises to a glimpse of the source," and with the "horror visible still," he sees an all-suffusing, all-sustaining love. And he knows that no matter what he endures, his essence is eternal, indestructible, and always safe.

Still, no matter how strong these arguments, they are bound to sound hollow when the shadow of evil looms over one's life. No amount of expounding on God's purpose can console the woman who must bury a murdered husband. No shift in perspective will ease the pain of a child suffering from abuse. No set of beliefs can save us from pain, and certainly no philosophy can take the place of human action in the effort to prevent evil from flourishing.

The problem of how to live in a world with evil is surely the most difficult problem we will ever encounter, and try as we might, we may never come up with satisfactory answers. But surely that is as it should be. It would be wrong to become comfortable with evil, wrong to ask that we not be disturbed when it strikes.

The problem of evil can and must continue to challenge us, each and every day. As Jung also pointed out, "The serious problems of life, however, are never fully solved. If it should appear that they are, this is the sign that something has been lost. The meaning and design of a problem seem not to lie in its solution, but in our working at it incessantly."

Teena's Favorite New Age-Friendly Web Sites

Integral Life **integrallife.com**

A rich resource of fascinating articles, audio dialogues, and discussions that are mostly specific to integral spirituality and philosophy. Probably more depth here on spiritual idealism than any other site on the Web. Some of it is available free, but to really sample the good stuff, you will have to pay a monthly subscription fee.

Reality Sandwich **realitysandwich.com**

With the catchy slogan of "Evolving Consciousness, bite by bite," this site calls itself a "web magazine for this time of intense transformation." Subjects run the gamut from sustainability to shamanism, alternate realities to alternative energy, remixing media to reimagining community, holistic healing techniques to the promise and perils of new technologies. Very tasty.

Shift in Action **shiftinaction.com**

Packed with profound ideas, stories, articles, reports, audio and video downloads, interviews, ideas, and inspiration on many subjects dear to an idealist's heart, this Web site is a profound education. Plus, an interactive community encourages connections. A project of the Institute of Noetic Sciences, Shift in Action was designed "to create expanded access to ideas, teachers, pioneers, and allies who are advancing the new perspectives our planet needs." While there is plenty of free information, a small monthly subscription is absolutely worth it for the extras. Support this site!

Brezny's Free Will Astrology **freewillastrology.com**

Rob Brezny does not just provide weekly horoscopes, which manage to be deep and thoughtful meditations on one's relationship to reality in one hundred words or less, his site is full of positive essays, suggestions for reading, and links to other resources. Mondo friendly and uplifiting site.

NewAgePride.org **newagepride.org**

This is my site, built in a burst of idealistic optimism to help build community and help restore some luster to the New Age moniker. (It ultimately evolved into this book.)

Lorian Association **lorian.org**

Back in the early 1990s, I asked my bookseller for the best book that would explain the New Age, and she handed me *Reimagination of the World*. And so I got to know, and was richly rewarded by, the work and thought of David Spangler, often called an "architect of the New Age," or sometimes "Father of the New Age." (He prefers to call himself a fond "uncle.") Spangler founded the Lorian Association, a spiritual research center, and its Web site offers a plentitude of educational resources and support, not to mention valuable insights from the very wise Spangler himself.

Beliefnet **beliefnet.com**

A comprehensive resource for body, mind, and spirit approached from many different spiritual traditions. Fun to click around, most of the features are light and entertaining, so you may have to click around quite awhile to find real food for thought.

Conscious Media Network **consciousmedianetwork.com**

This is an eclectic site of video, audio interviews, and music that is a true reflection of the New Age movement – equal parts serious philosophy and social theory mixed in with holistic health advice and occult speculation. Literally something for everyone.

Wisdom Page **wisdompage.com**

A goldmine of wisdom resources, including various on-line texts concerning idealistic wisdom, references to books about wisdom, information about organizations that promote wisdom, wise activities, and listserv groups concerned with aspects of wisdom.

Café Press New Age Stuff **shop.cafepress.com/new-age**

The best place to shop for cool T-shirts, bumper stickers and more with a New Age theme.

PART V

New Age Politics

Ideas are great arrows,
but there has to be a bow.
And politics is the bow of idealism.

— BILL MOYERS —

18 Politics and Spirituality

The word politics comes from the Greek word *polis*, meaning the state or community as a whole. In *The Republic*, Plato confidently detailed his version of the ideal state and how it could be achieved. So from the beginning, politics has implied the ways in which to create the ideal society. And the creation of an ideal society is, of course, the hopeful aim of the New Age.

It should come as no surprise then, that the idealism of the New Age asserts the importance of becoming politically active. "To heal the world you must be in it," writes George Lakoff, founder of a progressive think tank. "Spiritual commitment requires political action, or it amounts to nothing."

Politics is philosophy brought to life in the community. It is the process by which groups of people make decisions, by which we put our ideals to work in the public sphere, and by which we rank priorities for the common good. Every part of our lives is influenced by political decisions—from the jobs available to us, to the food we eat, to the cars we drive, to our personal safety, even to the very air we breathe. Any true peace and harmony brought to society will be developed and refined through political means.

Yet as we look back at the past forty years of our political history, we see that Americans are drifting ever further from peace and harmony, not closer. The Right has become stridently religious, the Left has become stridently non-religious, and the center is caught in the tug-of-war between both, and feels served by neither.

What is going on?

The political mirror

American democracy has been a light unto the world for centuries. And when we look at many Third World countries, oppressed by dictators or torn apart by wars or devastated by disease and poverty, we Americans have good reason to count ourselves lucky. However, when we look at many of the more advanced nations of Europe, who manage to achieve a greater quality of life for their people with fewer resources, we Americans have good reason to hang our heads in shame.

Here in the richest nation in the world, millions upon millions suffer from discrimination and poverty, poor education and lack of health care. Meanwhile, we divert our resources to military attacks on other countries, and we are contributing more to global warming than most other nations combined. We identify these problems year after year, decade after decade, but make almost no progress in solving them because of a political system that is so deeply divided it cannot respond to the needs of the people it is supposed to serve.

If we look at this problem in light of our map of spiritual growth, it becomes clear that the failure of our political system is a direct reflection of where we sit on the spiral of development. We are a people whose spiritual center of gravity hovers between Stage Two fundamentalism and Stage Three materialism.

Contrast this with European societies, which have had more time to mature and grow. Countries such as Sweden and France and England now operate solidly from Stage Three, with a great deal of influence from Stage Four idealism, which allows their governments to extend what seems to us extraordinary protections and benefits to their citizens.

Here in the U.S., our lower spiritual center of gravity creates a politics that doesn't serve our best interests, primarily because we have no idea what our best interests really are. A good quarter of the electorate live by Stage Two priorities established by the ego and its considerable list of desires and fears and insecurities. This population chooses to pour their money and effort into punishing and controlling largely harmless activities like consensual sex and pot-smoking, while ignoring and even abetting truly harmful practices like baseless military aggression. Add to this another third of the electorate that operates from Stage Three priorities established by materialism and slavish devotion to capitalism and the market—causing them to turn a blind eye to things like the corporate ravaging of the environment and exploitation of the labor force—and we can see why our government is unable to address the actual needs of the people.

Michael Nagler, co-founder of the Peace and Conflict Studies program at UC Berkeley, compares our current situation to that of a snake unable to shed its skin. After awhile, a snake that cannot grow from the overtight skin will not only suffer pain, but will get sick and perhaps even die. "A spiritual crisis," Nagler continues, "occurs when a culture finds itself trapped in an outmoded, suffocating network of values and conceptions in a worldview, a 'creed outworn,' that has become too small to allow the people to get on with their cultural evolution."

Our spiritual center of gravity, stuck between Stage Two and Stage Three, has our society caught in a chokehold that literally threatens to end life as we know it.

Of course, long before any of us ever heard of spiritual stages, progressives were operating from the assumption that the Right was behind the times. The word "progressive" shows that we have always understood that liberal policies come from a more advanced way of thinking.

The irony is that progressives, who supposedly operate from a higher understanding, have been terribly ineffective these past forty years—ineffective not only in leading, but in appealing to the electorate. Even in the 2008 election, coming on the heels of the most disastrous presidency in history and the ideological meltdown of the Republican Party, progressive issues were a difficult sell, and the popular vote was perilously close.

Now it may be that President Barack Obama will be able to deliver on his campaign promises of pulling together the nation and inspiring us to effectively deal with the monumental challenges we face. We should certainly give him the benefit of the doubt, along with our wholehearted support, as he progresses through his first term. Yet the odds of success for all of us can only increase if we better understand why the political impotency of the idealistic Left has so often turned out to be our biggest problem of all.

Old Left, New Left

After the 2004 re-election of George W. Bush devastated the progressive cause, a spate of books came out examining the reasons for our ignominious defeat. One of the best was *Start Making Sense*, a collection of essays that looked at the state of the Democratic Party from all sides.

In his essay, former Sierra Club president Adam Werbach suggested that, in many ways, the Left has been a victim of its own success. Progressives did very well back in the early 20th century, when larger numbers of people were struggling to survive. The "liberal project" created the minimum wage, the forty-hour workweek, Social Security, and civil rights, as well as greater gender equality. Because of these triumphs, basic survival is no longer a concern for most of us. We now have the luxury of voting for our meaning needs instead.

"Most Americans today are not survival oriented; they're fulfillment oriented," Werbach wrote. "People are looking for something to believe in. They're looking for meaning in life. They're looking to be part of a broader project."

In other words, they are looking for a sense of connection to each other, a sense of belonging to a greater community, a sense of common purpose. They are looking for confirmation that their lives, and what they do or don't do, matters in the greater scheme of things.

And who has been addressing meaning needs? Which political side has loudly claimed to represent meaningful values? Well, it certainly hasn't been the Left. The only spiritual representative on the political scene—the only one clearly articulating the pain inherent in the materialistic American way of life—has been the Right. And by default, they have continually walked away with the vote of the spiritually hungry.

The Left, fighting a class struggle for economic justice, effectively served us when the leading edge of the population was still moving from Stage Two religion into Stage Three rationalism. But in the last forty years, the leading edge of growth has reached Stage Four spiritual idealism. We spiritual idealists are especially oriented toward big-picture meaning needs. The Left, however, still operates from the Stage Three version of progressivism, what George Lakoff calls "Old Enlightenment" thinking, which deems *all* spiritual values as regressively religious.

The Democratic Party of today is still very much the party of an outdated old Left, hobbling along on a cobbled-together platform of individual policy issues such as environmentalism, antiwar, pro-choice, gay rights, etc. And we are now, adds Werbach, organized into "stovepipes rather than toward a single end." Lakoff calls these stovepipes "issue silos."

Each group pursues its own specific legislative goals, addressing them from the Old Enlightenment model that, Lakoff observes, deals primarily in economic concerns, and develops policy around the numbers and statistics that apply to different demographic groups. Rarely do progressive groups work together toward a common goal, building social capital and the political power to create a world that works for everyone. Sadly, the Right has been partly justified in their criticisms of the Left as ineffectual stewards of the public good.

The fact is, progressives have been like specialists running around treating the symptoms of our diseased society—global warming, war, discrimination, corruption in government, economic collapse—without ever mentioning the disease itself. The disease is, of course, failing paradigms that perpetuate spiritual bankruptcy in the public sphere and keep us isolated from each other. But because Stage Three rationalism refuses to admit spirituality into politics, we actually end up helping the disease grow, and the symptoms intensify.

In search of meaning

This unfortunate state of affairs within the Democratic Party is particularly ironic, says Michael Lerner, founder of the Network of Spiritual Progressives, because for the majority of us, our political positions are explicitly drawn from strong spiritual beliefs about what is good and right and moral, beliefs such as: we are all connected, interdependent, and responsible for each other. We are often passionate about politics for spiritual reasons, then we force ourselves into the absurd position of operating as if politics should be stripped of all residue of spirituality.

If we are going to effectively treat the disease of failing paradigms, we are going to have to move past the Old Left idea that a healthy separation of church and state requires us to separate politics and spirituality into independent spheres. Idealism tells us that "All is One," all things are interrelated and interdependent. Politics and spirituality (or its lack) mutually create each other. To insert a sharp knife between them is to harm both, and this harm is perpetuated in a never-ending negative spiral.

If we spiritual idealists want to see our ideals represented in the public sphere, then we are going to have to stand up for them in the public sphere. We are going to have to talk about spiritual values like compassion and empathy as valid reasons for universal health care. We are going to have to talk about values like peace and non-violence as valid reasons to end the war in Iraq. We are going to have to talk about values like unity and interdependence as reasons to reform our justice system. We are going to have to do as Lerner suggests in *The Left Hand of God* and "come out of the closet and identify publicly as spiritual beings and claim [our] right to be heard and respected as spiritual people."

This is not a new observation. Walt Whitman, the great nineteenth century mystic poet, felt that democracy was a concept "the real gist of which sleeps, quite unawakened." He believed the solution was the "spiritualization" of the political sphere. "The core of democracy, finally, is the religious element." He talked about a universalized spirituality "which is adhesiveness or love, that fuses, ties and aggregates, making the races comrades, and fraternizing all."

Today, more than ever, we are in need of a spiritual story that will help us to recognize our oneness, to throw off fear and apathy, and to fight the influences of money and special interests that have been able to get such a death grip on our politics.

It is time, adds Lakoff, for a "New Enlightenment," a new age which "comes with a new consciousness." This new consciousness, he continues, starts with the understanding "of our connection to the natural world and to each other" and ends with "the realization that empathy and responsibility are at the heart of the moral vision on which our democracy is based."

Surely it was no coincidence that in 2008, when Democrats nominated a candidate who was upfront about being a spiritual person, and who openly spoke of the relevance of spirituality to public policy, they won the White House. Like John Kennedy and Bill Clinton before him, Barack Obama clearly operates from the leading edge of Stage Four spiritual growth. In fact, to hear him talk, there is reason to hope he might actually be looking at the world from Stage Five.

Time will tell, but it seems entirely possible that America has elected its first integral president with the ability to speak to the needs of all of us, no matter where we sit on the spiral of development. I fervently hope so, for only when our politics addresses the needs of those on every stage on the spiral will we truly be able to work together and solve the problems that threaten tomorrow.

19 Politics and the Spiral

From the integral perspective, American politics is not divided in half as it would appear by the close outcomes of so many of our elections. We do not divide ourselves into clearcut groups of Republican and Democrat, or conservative and liberal; rather, we arrange ourselves politically up the spiral of development into four large contingents that correspond to different stages.

On the far right, we have Stage Two traditional Republicans, fundamentalists and hardcore religious conservatives who are comforted by ethnocentric homogeneity and authoritarian leaders. They are highly motivated by social issues like gay rights and abortion, and feel obligated to punish and censure those who do not fit within their own religion-mandated categories of right and wrong.

Also on the right are the Modern Republicans, made up of Stage Three fiscal conservatives who are less concerned with social issues and more concerned with free markets and fighting off government regulation. They are famously willing to align with traditionals, and have been known to espouse traditional priorities they themselves may not hold in order to win on election day.

As we've seen, there are also plenty of modern Democrats who operate from Stage Three on the spiral. This secular group appreciates healthy markets but, generally speaking, also wants to manage those markets for the benefit of the many rather than the privilege of a few. Stage Three Democrats are concerned with equality in social issues, but not overly so. In fact, not since the civil rights era has this group pitched any real battles on social issues. This is one reason why gay people still do not have the right to marry, abortion doctors still have to wear bullet proof vests, and non-violent drug offenders still languish in prisons. This is the old Left, struggling for relevance in today's political climate.

The new Left, made up of postmodern Democrats and greens, is based in a Stage Four understanding of reality. We see most of the "spiritual but not religious" contingent here, as well as liberal Christians and Jews and so forth. The postmoderns are peace-loving, environmentally-concerned and ecologically aware. They passionately care about social equality and justice, and not just in economic terms but in personal terms as well. They will not just vote for gay rights but will speak out for them and march for them.

This contingent usually votes with the old Left, but is often frustrated and dissatisfied with the candidates presented to them. Sociologist Paul Ray calls this group "Political North," neither left nor right, but forward or above. He is absolutely right that this is a higher stage of political thought informed by strong spiritual values. He is also right that this group is so recently arrived on the political scene that it suffers from a "cultural identity crisis" and is in need of a unifying identity so that it may get a sense of itself as a group. (Might I suggest unifying under the term New Age?)

These are the four main strains of thought at work in American politics today, but this is such a new way of looking at the electorate it is not yet well-understood. Maybe that's because it is only from a Stage Five integral perspective that this political grouping according to stages becomes clear. And it is only from an integral perspective that we begin to grasp the importance of safeguarding the structures of each stage.

The culture wars

For those of us who haven't reached Stage Five (most of us), we often feel an irresistible temptation to declare our own stage as the only *right* one. In the earlier stages we might go even farther and try to stamp out all the others. We've seen fundamentalist religion do this for centuries, but it has lately become fashionable for skeptics to aggressively attack religion in return.

In his 2004 bestseller, *The End of Faith*, Sam Harris advocated the end of all religions, but particularly Christianity. Other atheist-leaning authors, and filmmakers like Bill Maher, have joined him in arguing that Christianity and other religions are too dangerous to let stand. They believe that because so many dualists use their religion as an excuse for violence and repression and exploitation of the environment, if we get rid of the religion, we'll get rid of the problem.

Yet, fundamentalism is an inevitable expression of Stage Two thinking, and there's no way to get rid of Stage Two. Fundamentalist thinking is not created by Christianity, or Islam, or any other faith—and taking away the dogmatic structure of religion will not make the fear-fueled, Stage Two drive to defend and conquer go away. People in Stage Two, with their high need for authority and order and "being right," would simply attach themselves to some other militant doctrine—a doctrine that might not be balanced by Christianity's emphasis on love and forgiveness (i.e. communism, Nazism, etc.).

Harris naturally wishes that everyone would hurry up and grow into the Stage Three rationalism from which he preaches his no-religion gospel. Actually, Harris appears to be more of a Stage Four idealist who points hopefully to higher forms of non-religious spirituality that unite us rather than divide us. The problem is, we cannot make people grow any faster than they can grow. And since being able to move through Stage Two is the only way to get to Stage Three, if we want more Stage Three and Four thinking, then we shouldn't try to destroy Stage Two structures, or give Stage Two believers a reason to cling more tightly to those structures. Furthermore, if we cut off access to Stage Two beliefs, then we give people thrashing around in Stage One chaos and egocentrism nowhere to go.

This is one reason why Wilber says the attacks launched between stages is one of our biggest "threats" to the future.

Yet, I do believe religion critics like Harris and Maher are right in one thing. Those with a more liberal understanding of the Christian religion—those in peace-loving Stage Four—too often provide cover for conflict-loving fundamentalism to run amuck. From a 2008 Pew report on the U.S. religious landscape, we know that while 78 percent of Americans identify themselves as Christians, only about 26 percent are actually fundamentalist or "evangelical" Christians. Stage Four Christianity is a very different religion than Stage Two Christianity, and yet because so few take the trouble to point out the difference, the divisive Stage Two version is lent disproportionate strength and influence. Meanwhile, the path to growth out of Stage Two is mixed and muddied and hard to find.

We would go far in addressing this problem if we had a culture-wide common knowledge of spiritual stages. With such a knowledge, we might also be able to calm the destructive culture wars that now roil the political landscape, with each stage attacking not only each other, but attacking those within each stage who dare to evolve to the next level. Right now, Stage Two religious types banish and demonize their perceived deserters who grow into materialism. Stage Three materialists, in turn, mock and marginalize those who grow into idealism. Meanwhile, Stage Four idealists deride those who grow into Stage Five integralism as hierarchal and elitist. If we better understood that all these stages follow a natural and inevitable progression, surely we would have fewer reasons to fling so many stones at each other.

A common knowledge of spiritual stages may also be the best way to start raising our nation's spiritual center of gravity so that we are better able to politically address our mutual problems. With maps of spiritual stages in hand, we Stage Four idealists are more likely to get ourselves unstuck and moving up the spiral to the more profound and active idealism of Stage Five. And from there, we will be more likely to help Stage One grow into to Stage Two, and Stage Two into Three and so forth

We will do this as progressives always have, by addressing the economic and social issues like poverty and the lack of education that keep so many trapped in the earlier stages. But we'll also do this by protecting the conceptual frameworks for each stage so that the entire spiral is healthy, and people have the ideological space to grow. All stages, says Wilber, "must become stable, respected stations in life."

We are all at different stages of spiritual development, and that is a fact. It is time to create a more inclusive politics that gives each of us, no matter our stage of growth, a dignified place at the table. It is time for a truly integral politics.

Integral politics

In the two-party system that divides American politics today, we see an often bitter difference of opinion on the cause of our social ills. The conservative opinion—anchored in Stage Two and a moral order based on rules and discipline and obedience to authority—sees the individual as entirely responsible for his or her own suffering. All the problems of society are understood as the failures of individuals, which is why conservative solutions focus on scolding or controlling individuals rather than funding social programs.

Meanwhile, the Democratic and Green Party point of view—anchored in the empathy-based moral order of Stages Three and Four—says the failures of society are entirely responsible for the suffering of individuals. That is why most liberal solutions focus on developing social programs rather than encouraging individual responsibility.

Each side argues so adamantly for its own point of view, and gets so caught up in power struggles over which approach to take, that our politics is now all but incapacitated. It's unfortunate, because seen from a Stage Five integral view, both sides are right. Or rather, each side is fragmented and partial. Neither individual or collective is primary, says Wilber, they are merely "different dimensions of the same occasion."

In other words, we are failing *both* as individuals and as a society, and our solutions must therefore integrate both approaches. We must insist on individual responsibility at the same time we accept collective responsibility.

Indeed, that was one of the unique features of Barack Obama's winning presidential campaign. Even as he talked about increased funding for public schools, he talked about a parent's obligation to turn off the TV and get involved in his or her child's education. Even as he talked about increasing economic opportunity for families, he reminded divorced fathers of their responsibility to continue to provide for their children. Even as he talked about funding alternative energy, he reminded us that we are all going to have to change our ways and learn to conserve.

An integrated politics, if embraced, is our best hope of breaking political deadlock by giving both sides what they want—by giving the individual and the community equal weight. Even as we enhance opportunities in the community, we insist on increased responsibilities for the individual. We pay for child care for parents who are working and paying taxes into the system; we pay for college in exchange for public service commitments; we pay for welfare in exchange for college or job training enrollment. Rather than handing out entitlements without asking anything in return, we insist on a return for our investment.

Unlike our current polarizing approach that leaves so many people stuck in their life circumstances, and likewise stuck in their level of spiritual growth, a more integrated approach would improve life circumstances and create movement up the spiral of development. This would create a positive feedback loop: As more people advanced through spiritual stages, the more enlightened our public policies would become, and the more people would be able to advance through spiritual stages. Individual and society would increasingly benefit each other.

Making peace with parties

An integral politics would allow us to respect and honor the truths contained within each stage of human evolution. Beyond that, it would allow us to see just how much common ground there is between us. When we stop competing over which stage of the spiral is best, and allow each to flourish in its own way, we discover many surprising areas of agreement on which to build consensus and meet common challenges.

The question is, how do we move beyond integral theory and bring it to bear in the actual world, starting from where we are today? How do we get the Left and the Right to integrate, especially in regards to political parties and the voting booth? Are we supposed to politically sit in the literal center? Vote for whoever seems the most moderate candidate, regardless of whether he or she is Democrat or Republican? Or maybe join a third party?

I don't know a good answer to that; I can only say how I deal with it in my life. Even though I am idealistically most compatible with the Green Party, I do not vote Green because it is so far to the left of the spiritual center of gravity that it doesn't seem to me a balanced, integral choice. I am all for visionary perspectives, and believe we need the empowering perspective represented by the

Green Party, but I also believe in the necessity of working within the scope of the reality at hand. And the reality is a majority of Americans still hang out in Stage Two and Stage Three. An integral approach must respect their worries and concerns, and address their priorities as well.

In my opinion, those who righteously insist on pushing hard Left only tear themselves away from the mainstream and leave it to sink to the right, as happened with Ralph Nader and the 2000 election. So rather than trying to lure Democrats away to be Green, I think the Greens could be far more effective if they joined the Democratic Party and helped widen and enlarge its vision.

To say such a thing is heresy to the Left, which deplores the two-party monopoly on politics. But it seems to me that life chooses a yin/yang, dialectic balancing act on its own, and we make ourselves crazy trying to make it happen otherwise. And perhaps if we stay and work within the system, we might then be better able to institute reforms like instant run-off voting which would make a multiple party system actually viable.

In 2008, thanks in part to the cataclysmic presidency of George W. Bush, the ranks of the Democratic Party swelled by millions. I'd also like to think that increase is due in part to more people growing up the spiral from Stage Two to Stage Three, and from Three to Four—and that the societal pendulum really is about to swing back toward the progressive values of empathy and sane public policies. But even though Democrats have recently won back the White House and Congress, they will have a hard time freeing the government from its paralysis without integrating both liberal and conservative approaches.

We cannot, of course, do their work for them, or change the system for them. We can only change ourselves. We can examine our own assumptions and step back from our own extremes. We can make sure our contributions to the political process are not divisive and blaming, but inclusive and respectful. This is not at all easy, as we learn every election year, when campaigns clash and drag us all into ideological conflict with each other.

Yet a change of vision never comes by making one's opponent *wrong*. We learned this long ago from great idealists like Thoreau and Gandhi and King, who understood that getting mad and attacking is counterproductive. There are already plenty of people furiously waving their arms, yelling about our troubles and making lists of those people and institutions they deem responsible for them. Negative thoughts and words only breed more negativity.

"You cannot dismantle the master's house with the master's tools," says the old proverb. In the end, confrontation only reinforces our feelings of alienation from each other.

Holding on to truth

Gandhi coined his society-changing method of nonviolent persuasion as *satyagraha*, or "holding on to truth." He also called it love-force, or soul-force. Gandhi proved that the way to heal an unjust situation is not to eliminate or defeat your antagonist—impossible anyway—but to transform the vision of the antagonist through consistent, nonviolent refusal to accept what is not true.

"There must be no impatience, no barbarity, no insolence, no undue pressure," wrote Gandhi. "If we want to cultivate a true spirit of democracy, we cannot afford to be intolerant. Intolerance betrays want of faith in one's cause...One's opponent must be weaned from error by patience and sympathy."

I thought of Gandhi's words a number of times during the 2008 election when the press continually marveled at Barack Obama's "cool under pressure." No matter what the opposition threw at him, either in the primaries or the general election, Obama famously refused to rise to the bait, and continued to calmly hold to his truth. In fact, many pundits ascribed his success in the debates, and his resulting surge in the polls, to his unflappable cool.

Like Gandhi, Martin Luther King, Jr., also exhorted us to rely on the power of empathy and love in the creation of what he called a Beloved Community. "This type of love," King wrote, "can transform opponents into friends. This type of understanding goodwill will transform the deep gloom of the old age into the exuberant gladness of the new age. It is this love which will bring about miracles in the hearts of men."

"By their fruits you shall know them," says the Bible verse. In the New Age, we might also add, by their attitude you shall know them. When we go out into the world to try to change the status quo, we must hold onto our truth without condemnation, anger, or blame. Each problem, each conflict, no matter how big or how small, presents us with the chance to either move forward in our evolution or move backwards.

The New Age urges you to "hold on to the truth" as you translate your dreams into practical action. Respectfully step up and help shape political solutions to the pressing needs of your community, your state, your nation.

Teena's Top Ten New Age Movies

Once upon a time, we humans spent our evenings sitting around the fire, listening to elders tell the stories that gave us clues about who we are, and why we are here. Today, the movie screen provides the fire, and Hollywood provides the stories that are still as important to us as they ever were.

Here is my list of the top ten movies that reflect an inherently New Age point of view. Generically spiritual or life-affirming films do not belong on this list, nor do many films about ghosts and the afterlife (although plenty of New Agers *do* speculate like mad about what happens to us after death).

Movies such as *Ghost* and *What Dreams May Come* present a dualistic view of reality in which spirit is separate from matter, and the bad is fundamentally separate from the good. A film expresses a unique New Age perspective only when it presents its version of reality in idealistic terms. For example, in the *Star Wars Trilogy*, reality is the expression of Spirit, or The Force which "binds the universe together." There is, of course, a dark side to The Force, but it is clearly made up of one all-encompassing energy. This understanding of The Force is idealism in a nutshell.

A few of these movies are relatively unknown gems, but most were very successful commercially, and a few, like *Star Wars* or *The Matrix*, became cultural phenomenons. I naturally take this to mean that an idealistic picture of the universe resonates hugely for audiences. I hope more filmmakers develop many more movies that feed our hunger for meaning.

1. The Matrix

Watching *The Matrix* can hit you like an enlightenment experience in itself. The millennia-old idealistic idea of reality as *maya*, or illusion, is brought to stark, riveting life by the Wachowski Brothers in a movie that hit popular culture like a much-needed slap in the face with its message of "Wake up!"

Our hero, Neo (Keanu Reeves), is stuck in the illusion of the Matrix, a literal slave to his thoughts about reality. He suspects there is something missing in his understanding, but he is not sure what. Then the mysterious Morpheus (Laurence Fishburne) offers him a way out—the recognition of the truth. It is offered as a choice available to everyone.

Neo chooses truth and is released from the Matrix in a squirm-inducing sequence that illuminates how ugly it is to be enslaved by illusion. Now free to move about an admittedly scary reality, Neo is nevertheless determined to help others win their liberation as well. But first, he must learn to navigate the illusory world in order to reach the people that need rescuing, and battle bad guys that he knows are not truly real.

In the story, set in a world that mirrors Eastern philosophy even as it parallels the Jesus story, Neo is called "The One," the subject of prophecy, the man who must sacrifice himself to win the salvation of humanity, a man who dies in the illusory world yet is resurrected by love. East meets West in this astonishing film, which understands freedom as a violent fight against the cruel oppression of ego and illusion.

2. Star Wars Trilogy, Episodes IV, V & VI

Who doesn't remember the first thrill of seeing George Lucas' *Star Wars*, being swept away into a galaxy far, far away, to a world that was completely unknown and original and yet somehow very familiar?

In the world's most popular movie series ever—which is explicitly based on Joseph Campbell's "Hero's Journey" archetype—a small band of rebels is seeking to restore freedom to the galaxy. Young Luke Skywalker (Mark Hamil) must learn to master the energy of The Force by getting in touch with his intuition and instincts in his battle against the "Dark Side"—in other words, the side of ego.

We learn that Luke's father, the "evil" Darth Vader, was once the good Jedi who turned to the Dark Side when he came to value his ego's quest for power over his soul's desire to love. In the series' second installment, *The Empire Strikes Back*, the enlightened Jedi Master Yoda, like Master Obiwan Kenobi from the first film, trains Luke in a veritable New Age course about staying in the moment, and the power of belief.

The unprecedented success of these movies shows how satisfied we are by stories that portray the inner battle we all feel between soul and ego, good and evil.

3. I Heart Huckabees

This captivating comedy swiftly and unabashedly dives into the big questions of meaning when Albert (Jason Schwarzman) a conservationist/poet hires two "existential detectives" (Dustin Hoffman and Lily Tomlin) to help him unravel a coincidence that has been bugging him. The detectives try to teach him about the big blanket of unity that connects all and encourage him to dismantle his personality. Unhappy with such abstract help, Albert bolts with a fireman in the middle of an existential breakdown (Mark Wahlberg) to become disciples of a French mistress of chaos and meaningless (Isabelle Huppert). When our two lost souls learn to make peace with paradox, we are happy for them, and for ourselves, caught up as we are in the same circumstances. The script is clever and absurd all at once, and the divine cast, which includes Jude Law and Naomi Watts, is appropriately lighthearted in unraveling such deep dilemmas. A delicious treat for those hungry for a movie with real metaphysical bite.

4. What the Bleep Do We Know?

Explicitly New Age (without using the term), this documentary/fable became a sensation in different parts of the country as a mind-blowing experience that all but required repeat viewings. In between interviews of physicists, scientists and other alleged experts questioning the nature of reality, the viewer gets a graphic introduction to "new" physics and how it all plays out in our brains, and influences the choices we make in our daily lives.

We see all this information play out through the ego-bound character of Amanda (Marlee Matlin), who is cranky from conditioning and being controlled by her negative thoughts. As we follow her through a lively and often funny story (guests at a Polish wedding dance to Robert Palmer's *Addicted to Love* while high on their own brain chemicals), she learns to become aware of the power of her thoughts. And as she struggles to learn to be nice to herself, we realize how much we are like her.

It's impossible to watch this movie and *not* feel like one has experienced surprising realizations about one's own potential. Meanwhile, the movie's cartoon rendering of brain chemicals surging around our bodies with their own mindless agenda provides liberating images that stay with you. Since seeing this movie several times, I no longer feel like a puppet on the strings of my own emotions. I have learned to wait for negative chemicals to wear off before I act. In this regard, especially, the movie was literally life-changing for me.

5. The Films of Charlie Kaufman

Just about any movie written by the brilliant Charlie Kaufman is going to be a startlingly original, funny and eye-opening experience**.** *Being John Malkovich* opens a metaphysical can of worms when married couple Craig (John Cusack) and Lottie (Cameron Diaz) find a cramped and damp portal into the consciousness of the actor John Malkovich. Lottie is liberated by the experience of being someone else (as are the lines of people paying two hundred dollars for their journey through the portal). Meanwhile, like an ego run amuck, Craig learns to control Malkovich like a puppet, leaving the poor actor buried inside his own head. A gloriously absurd tale of how we get lost inside our identity.

Adaptation is an inside-out creative look at the stories we tell ourselves and how those stories become our reality. Kaufman literally writes himself into the movie, or to be more exact, he writes two versions of himself into the movie, as he shows us how he wrestles with himself trying to write the movie he is actually in. A bracing Mobius-strip of a movie that is only a little flattened by its purposely gimmicky ending.

In *The Eternal Sunshine of the Spotless Mind*, which earned Kaufman his much-deserved Academy Award, we follow the tortured adventure of Joel (Jim Carrey) as he fights his own attempt to have his memory erased. In the effort to avoid the pain of a break-up with Clementine (Kate Winslet), Joel follows his impulsive girlfriend's example and contracts with a doctor to have all his memories of the relationship erased. It is only as he experiences each memory one last time that he begins to appreciate the moments for what they actually were, instead of the interpretation he later pinned to them. When the wiped-clean Joel and Clementine agree to give their relationship another shot, knowing that it will end up the same pleasurable-painful way, our characters make a thrilling choice to accept life and love with all its ups and downs, a choice it just so happens that we ourselves must make every day.

6. Groundhog Day

The New Age often preaches that time is an illusion, and in this delightfully literal exploration of the eternal now, the cranky and self-centered Phil Connors (Bill Murray) must relive the same Groundhog Day over and over. Sharply written and acted, we get to watch Phil go from reckless joy at the lack of consequences to suicidal despair over his inability to escape his surroundings. His efforts to control the situation and turn it to his advantage are portrayed to giddy comedic effect, but eventually, Phil learns to fully inhabit and completely appreciate the moment he is given. When he stops resisting "what is," he is not only set free within time again, but he wins the woman he could have never hoped to attract before his stay in limbo. This fantasy co-written and directed by Harold Ramis is a profound metaphysical lesson that plays as a fiendishly funny romp.

7. The Truman Show

In this beautiful movie of the "reality is not what it seems" genre, our hero Truman (Jim Carrey) is stuck in a world he believes is real, but is entirely fake, built by the god-like Christof (Ed Harris) as the world's largest movie set. Raised from birth in this fake world, Truman has always accepted the reality which he has been given, but he begins to suspect that something is not quite right.

A literal interpretation of the idealistic tenet that all of life is an illusory drama played out in the mind of god, the movie follows Truman's struggle to liberate himself from a life in which he is controlled by his fears, as well as the desires of others for him to meet their needs. In other words, Truman no longer wants to be a character in a movie, even as a star of the show. Rather, he wants to become an authentic person, living an authentic life. We cannot help but cheer for him in the end, as he risks death to sail to the edge of his known world and bravely steps out the door, past the threshold of illusion, and into the mysterious world of reality.

8. Pleasantville

A close relative of *The Truman Show*, this slow-moving but visually stunning movie is another fantasy about waking up from illusion to the beauty of reality. When two siblings (Tobey Maguire and Reese Whitherspoon) get sucked into the black-and-white TV world of fictional Pleasantville, they are received like enlightened teachers by the clueless townsfolk. Stuck in ruts of habit and trapped by fear of the unknown, the people begin to literally turn color when they awaken to their true selves. The essence of a true self remains frustratingly unclear in the movie—for some it is a burst of feeling, whether from sexual longing or from anger, for others it is a simple decision to act differently. Yet it is inarguably inspiring to watch a group of people struggle to transform themselves and their world.

9. Memento

Although this film does not present a view about the nature of reality that can be identified as New Age, it is still a dazzling time shuffle that portrays how life tumbles directly, shockingly, and pretty much meaninglessly out of this moment. Just as interestingly, it shows us how much of our sense of self (ego) is based on memory. A former cop (Guy Pearce), who lost his short-term memory at the same time his wife was murdered, is looking for revenge in spite of his formidable handicap. We see the payback unfold at the movie's start, then move backward in time as we move forward in the movie, scene by scene, loop by loop, until the beginning-at-the-end in which we see our hero choose the road he will take, even though he knows the meaning of that choice will soon be lost to him. This movie left me breathless.

10. The Wizard of Oz

One of the most beloved movies of all time, this gorgeous musical fantasy is a Jungian sojourn through the psyche of our young heroine, Dorothy Gale (Judy Garland). When a bang on the head in the middle of a tornado sends Dorothy into the land of her unconscious, she begins a heroic journey to ask the help of the Wizard of Oz to help her get back home to Kansas. Along the way, she make allies and dodges a fearsome enemy in the

Wicked Witch, and undertakes many challenges to prove herself worthy. Of course, as in all heroic journeys, Dorothy is really looking for the essence of her true self. She also gains the recognition that "there's no place like home," meaning she is exactly where she is supposed to be.

Honorable mentions

Moulin Rouge, eXistenZ, Family Man, Waking Life, Stranger Than Fiction

PART VI

What Next?

Don't waste life in doubts and fears;
spend yourself on the work before you,
well assured that the right performance
of this hour's duties will be the best preparation
for the hours or ages that follow it.

– RALPH WALDO EMERSON –

Transformation, New Age Style

Throughout these pages, I have argued that if we want to be visible and effective in the world, we spiritual idealists are going to have to surrender some of our excessive individuality and join together under a common identity. I've also argued that "New Age" appears to be the only emblem with enough recognition and stickiness factors to unite us in identity and galvanize us as a community.

Yet in the end, the name by which we call ourselves is not nearly as important as what we *do*. Ultimately, we are defined in life by our actions, not by labels or ideology. A philosophy is worthwhile only to the degree that it inspires positive action in its adherents. Which means the question of "What next?" is the most important question of all.

In the New Age, the answer to this question is as simple as it is formidable. We aim for nothing less than the physical rescue of the planet, and the spiritual rescue of all who live upon it. Not so long ago, such a declaration caused a lot of eye rolling and accusations of messianic delusions. But today with peak oil problems, terrorism, wars, and global warming an ever-accelerating reality, we don't have the luxury of eye rolling anymore. Any part of the population struggling to work together and take responsibility to avert planetary disaster should be given whatever support and encouragement they can get.

New Age idealism is very clear about what is necessary to transform society: We must recognize our unity with Spirit—and through Spirit, our unity with each other.

As we have seen from our map of spiritual growth, this recognition usually only becomes *possible* for us when we reach Stage Four in the spiral of our spiritual development, and only becomes tangibly *real* for us in Stage Five. Thus, a true transformation of society will require all of us to continue up the spiral. Not only do we have to help ourselves grow to higher stages, we also have to make it possible for everyone else to grow. We have an evolutionary imperative to help Stage One grow into Stage Two, Stage Two move up to Stage Three, and so on.

This is why an understanding of the stages of spiritual development is a vital start in the transformation of self and society. All change is preceded by a change in our mental maps. Learning to see the world from a developmental perspective is a revolutionary change that will help create the conditions for transformation.

"Awareness drives development," writes Bill Harris, founder of the Centerpointe Institute. "Whatever you are immersed in, you are unaware of, like a fish in water. But when you do become aware (if you do), your perspective changes. It expands." In other words, the more you become aware of where you sit on the spiral, the more you become aware of the stage you are in, the more likely you will be able to transcend it.

This is why it is essential for all idealists, New Age or otherwise, to become familiar with the stages of development and help make it common knowledge throughout our culture. It is essential that we all stop seeing ourselves as static entities, already fully formed, and begin to understand that we are beings meant to continually grow and evolve.

The yin and the yang of change

The New Age approach to transformation has a dual focus—interior and exterior, individual and community. We work on the big picture of changing paradigms, and changing society as a whole, through big causes such as environmentalism and the peace movement. We also work on changing the self through personal spiritual growth and study.

In the New Age of the 1970s, the big picture was definitely the star of the movement, says David Spangler. New Agers were constantly whipping up excitement for the planetary transformation looming just over the horizon. But the scale of the big picture often left many feeling overwhelmed and disempowered. That is one reason why in the 1980s, the pendulum swung the other way—toward the individual.

In fact, the pendulum swung so far to the individual that, as we have seen, it pushed us all off the edge of the movement entirely. The big picture, the exterior, got lost. Alternative spirituality is now lopsided toward the individual, and we are suffering for it.

A revitalized New Age must restore the balance between individual and community through the recognition that they are two sides of the same coin and equally important. The New Age, says Spangler, must "enable us to blend the spiritual and worldly aspects of our lives and see them as one."

Idealism contends that the source of change is the self, so we certainly need to continue to work on personal growth, to minimize the ego and connect with soul. But we must also make an effort to move beyond ourselves and connect with others, to discover ourselves in context with the greater universe.

To focus on one half of the equation at the expense of the other is like trying to walk with one leg. We won't get far. "The power to change is entwined with the power to *be* changed," Spangler adds. If we focus only on the exterior and neglect to do the inner work of spiritual development, our work for the community is hampered. If we focus only on the self we neglect to reach out to others and work for a better society, then we hamper our ability to grow personally.

In order to help ourselves to grow, we must help others to grow as well. If we are truly going to change the world for the better, we must develop a personal spirituality that is also socially engaged.

JANUARY 31, 2009

"You Know What to Do."

BLOG **Looking for the New Age**

Last November, I heard Marianne Williamson give one of the best talks I've ever heard about the moment of opportunity we now have to change the world for the better—and our obligation to take advantage of it.

After a standing ovation, a Q&A session followed and, as almost always happens after inspiring talks, someone asked: "*How* do we take advantage of this moment? What do we do next?"

Williamson's reply: "You know what to do."

I was frustrated by that answer, and I'm sure the questioner was frustrated, too. After all, if she really knew what to do, she would not have asked the question. I think many of us, maybe most of us, think about changing the world and immediately feel so overwhelmed by the enormity of all there is to do that we literally have no idea where to start.

And so we stand, hearts packed with good intentions, but at a profound loss. We are hopeful that someone, somewhere, will give us some instruction. And what do we hear from the New Age—or from "higher consciousness movement" as Williamson called it that night? We hear, "You know what to do." I bet this sends a whole lot of people back to the couch to watch TV.

Yet after mulling this over for the last few weeks, it finally hit me that in the New Age, there can be no other answer. The New Age paradigm is not a top-down enterprise. The only reason we are standing about, waiting to be given answers, is because we have been trained to it by "the system," by the old paradigm.

New Age teachers tell us again and again, do not look to teachers, do not look to leaders to save you. The New age paradigm is not a leader/follower model, it is a cooperative model in which we are expected to be self-directed, expected to take responsibility for the whole. We are expected to understand that it is our job to save ourselves.

In the context of my particular life, I am the only one who knows what I should do. And if I put myself in contact with what Emerson calls "the internal ocean," then the right answer will come. It really is a radical notion that requires our willingness to step out of the comfort zone of the old paradigm, and approach the world in a new way.

Great expectations

So let's say we do get down to the serious business of transforming self and society. How long before we make that quantum leap to a New Age and harmony for all?

Many New Age writers see a mass paradigm shift as a natural progression of our evolution toward consciousness. Some even believe it to be inevitable. They say we will progress until ego at last opens its eyes to the primacy of soul and begins acting in accordance to its unity with all. They say science and technology will open its eyes to spirit and begin trodding carefully across the planet, helping to heal the damage it once wreaked.

Of course, this idea isn't exactly original with today's New Age, or even with idealism. Michael Grosso, in the *The Millenium Myth*, says the idea that we will reach the end of history to see the dawn of a golden age has long been part of human mythologies. "At the heart of the Myth is the idea that history—Our Story—is a journey with a goal, a drama with a climax."

But while inspiring in the short run, images of magical tipping points and miraculous transformations do not serve us well for the long run. "Such images encourage unreasonable expectations that, when not fulfilled, lead to disillusionment and anger," says David Spangler.

"The New Age needs a healthy dose of realism," he continues, "particularly in grasping the depth of time, work, compassion, loving, and communication necessary to move the world into healthier and more holistic directions... We need an appropriate spirit of idealism and vision that prepares us for both the transformative leap *and* the transformative hike."

Dreaming up pictures of the future, adds Peter Block, is basically a desperate attempt "to take the uncertainty out of the future. But when we take uncertainty out, it is no longer the future. It is the present projected forward. Nothing new can come from the desire for a predictable tomorrow."

The New Age is not something we can predict for tomorrow, it is a choice we make today, a choice we live into. The place to stand is right here at hand, today, solid and substantial. Saving the world must become a way of life we choose today, not envision for tomorrow.

New Age idealism *can* change the world, but only if we commit to it as an everyday process, not a future reward. Creating the New Age is not the work of a special time, but of everyday ordinary time. It is the patient and steady work of clearing the vision, exchanging old habits for new habits that take the whole into account, and evolving up through the spiral of spiritual development.

Yes, it is sometimes difficult, Spangler added, not to "crave the great event that will liberate from the mundane." But real transformation is "not dependent on great events," but "on shifts of perception and mindfulness. When we focus too much on the great events that seem to lie on our horizons, then we overlook the immediate events through which the New Age may be seeking to enter our lives."

The source of change

In any effort to change the world, we can all agree there is an overwhelming amount to *do*. Wars need to be stopped, the environment needs to be protected, the hungry need to be fed. With so many tasks before us needing urgent attention, how do we know where to start?

The great changers of history, those who are celebrated far and wide for transforming their one corner of the world, tell us that change starts with the self. To create a "beloved community," wrote Martin Luther King, "will require a qualitative change in our souls as well as a quantitative change in our lives."

King followed the example of Gandhi, who realized, said one of his biographers, "a person can be an 'instrument of peace,' a catalyst of understanding, by getting himself out of the way," by "reducing himself to zero." In other words, Gandhi was able to be so effective in the world because he was able to set aside his ego and connect with the unity of soul.

All doing flows from being. Yes, feeding the hungry is a vital task, and one we must undertake immediately, along with other good works. But even if I spent my every waking moment collecting food for the hungry, I'd never gather enough food to feed them all. Widespread hunger is a symptom of a defective society that doesn't recognize its unity, a society that believes it is the natural order of things to marginalize the many in order to increase the wealth and privilege of the few.

If we are to truly end hunger, we must transform ourselves, and the belief systems we hold that create hunger.

"The only conceivable way of bringing about a reconstruction of our world on new lines is first of all to become new men ourselves under the old circumstances, and then as a society in a new frame of mind," wrote Nobel Peace Prize winner Albert Schweitzer. "Everything else is more or less wasted labor, because we are thereby building not on the spirit, but on what is merely external."

By changing ourselves, we really do lay the foundation for changing the world. The real question is, how do we change ourselves?

A number of idealistic traditions tell us that personal change is the result of five disciplines:

1) contemplative practice
2) study and knowledge
3) spiritual community
4) right behavior
5) good works

Each of these disciplines is equally important in bringing about our transformation, both on a personal and collective level, and if we ignore any one area, we will inhibit conditions for true growth. But if we work with these disciplines consistently over time, with true commitment, we may find ourselves undergoing a very great transformation indeed.

"I have not a shadow of a doubt that any man or woman can achieve what I have," wrote Gandhi, "if he or she would make the same effort and cultivate the same hope and faith."

21 Contemplative Practice: The Technology of Transformation

There is a vast difference between having knowledge and living from that knowledge. Ralph Waldo Emerson, one of the most wise and knowledgeable men of the nineteenth century, lamented the "double-consciousness" of his idealism, which allowed him to see universal truths without giving him the daily means to live those truths. "I wish to exchange this flash-of-lightning faith for continuous daylight, this fever-glow for a benign climate." He wished, he continued, to reconcile his "two lives," the one of his ego, the other of his soul.

For thousands of years, countless monks, mystics, and teachers have been telling us that the way to heal the painful breach between ego and soul, illusion and reality, is through meditation or other contemplative practice. More recently, advances in brain imaging technology and developmental psychology have provided solid evidence of meditation's ability to rewire the brain and how we see.

Both science and religion end up telling us the same thing: with consistent stillness, we create a space of freedom from the tyranny of ego-thoughts, a space that allows us to recognize the quiet soul.

In the New Age, the vital first step for all efforts at transformation, whether of self or society, is to develop a regular contemplative practice. If we ignore this step, then all our good intentions simply bog down in the perennial struggle of being human—or being "meat," as Wilber bluntly puts it. Indeed, as Wilber goes on to say, the main reason that Western idealism has not yet lived up to its promise to transform societies is because, in the past, it failed to "develop any truly contemplative practices... to reproduce in consciousness the transpersonal insights and intuition of its founders."

According to idealism's founders, the purpose of life is the evolution toward greater consciousness. And for eons, consciousness evolved on its own, on its own unhurried time frame. But the more we have come to understand how consciousness unfolds, the more we have been able to help along our own growth, and the faster we humans have advanced through the different stages of spiritual development.

Not surprisingly, meditation and/or contemplative prayer has proven to be the most effective way to move oneself up the spiral of development. In his foreword to the book *Translucent Revolution*, Wilber writes that if you take up meditation, "then you are given, say, the Loevinger test, a very famous and well-documented test of developmental stages... It's not uncommon to find the percentage of the population at Loevinger's two highest stages (versions of integral), which is normally about 5 percent, goes to nearly 40 percent after four years of meditation."

No other growth technique of any kind, Wilber adds, can offer one such an accelerated rate of development.

Choose the contemplative method that best suits you, and commit to doing it, even if only a few minutes a day. Let others know you practice and how it impacts you. Help build a culture that makes room for reflection, a culture that is grounded in the wisdom of stillness.

The tree of practices

One of my favorite resources on the Web is The Center for Contemplative Mind in Society (contemplativemind.org). Their site provides a helpful chart, The Tree of Practices, which divides contemplative practice into the following categories:

Stillness: Most sitting meditation or any contemplative silence and breathing

Movement: Walking meditation, Qigong, T'ai Chi, yoga, labyrinth walking

Prayer or Generative Practice: Centering Prayer, the Lord's Prayer, mantras, rosaries, lovingkindness meditation

Creation Process: chanting, singing, journaling, art

Ritual: Sabbath rituals, vision quests, sweat lodges, ceremonies, altar-building

Activist: volunteering, pilgrimages, vigils/marches

You can find great support in developing a spiritual practice by joining a progressive church, such as Unity or Unitarian Universalist, or a contemplative group that forms around a Buddhist Temple or Zen Center, or Christian monasteries and retreat centers. But you can certainly learn a lot on your own from the Internet or one of many hundreds of books on meditating.

Obviously, the social ramifications of regular contemplative practice are huge, but so are the personal benefits. Daily meditation calms the mind, increases self-understanding and mental health, sharpens focus, develops creativity, reduces stress, eases anxiety, improves physical health, encourages compassion for oneself and others, and enriches your relationship with the world around you.

Finding peace with lack of time

Sitting meditation is probably the most direct and effective practice for spiritual growth, but not everyone is temperamentally suited to it. Or, if you're like me, with a full-time job, plus an extra part-time job (writing this book), plus volunteer work, plus three kids, a husband, a house, two cats and a dog—well, it's usually impossible to get two minutes to myself, and when I do, those minutes are not usually quiet. My life is gloriously, ridiculously full to the bursting, and I am able to formally sit only a few times a week, and even then not for very long.

In the meantime, I grab every opportunity I can for meditating while moving. I walk my dog every evening, and try to keep my focus on each step. I do qigong movements in the morning and some yoga stretches at night, and try to keep my focus on my breath. I remind myself at different points in the day—while in the shower, or doing dishes, or sitting at a red light, or standing in line at the store—to stay mindful and present with what I am doing. And I am starting to come back to prayer, meditative Centering Prayer as developed by Father Thomas Keating, as a way to "consent to the action of the Lord," and more deeply connect with the personal dimension of the divine.

It is the best I can do, and while I have experienced many wonderful and calming benefits from my patched-together method, I admit it is not the regular and committed practice I long for. I sometimes feel cheated by circumstances, and I despair that I will never be able to achieve true inner understanding of reality.

Yet, thanks to my study, I also know that the most effective way to clear my vision is to accept my life as it is today in all its crowded, noisy, too-much-to-do splendor. We must remember, said Chogyam Trungpa, that one state is no better than the other.

"Chaotic situations must not be rejected," he wrote. "Nor must we regard them as regressive, as a return to confusion. We must respect whatever happens to our state of mind...Any state of mind must be regarded as a workable situation."

Spiritual growth is the result of practice, but that practice does not necessarily have to be the practice of formal sitting meditation. There are no specific means or practices that can bring one closer to reality, says Alan Watts, "for every such device is artfulness...There is no way to where we are, and whoever seeks one finds only a slick wall of granite without passage or foothold. Yogas, prayers, therapies and spiritual exercises are at root only elaborate postponements of the recognition that there is nothing to be grasped and no way to grasp it."

When all is said and done, the most important form of spiritual practice is daily living. And while meditation practice is undeniably the most effective way to dial down the noisy ego long enough to hear the truth within us, it does not follow that we can't hear any truth without it. Intuition of truth has a way of slipping through the cracks in even the thickest wall of thought. And a shift in perspective is all it takes to open a crack. Meanwhile, a consistent daily effort to be mindful and present in your daily life will help those cracks to widen.

In the end, whether you are able to formally meditate or choose some other contemplative practice or ritual, there is one way to measure whether you are succeeding in true self-realization: when your practice moves you beyond yourself to take action in the greater world.

22 Feed Your Head: Study and Knowledge

Knowledge is power. To be in possession of true facts is to be more effective at reaching any goal, in all things, but especially in spiritual growth. Indeed, the word education is from the Latin, *ex ducere,* which means to be led out. Study and learning leads us out of the suffering caused by ignorance.

Studying to attain knowledge is probably the easiest—and most immediately rewarding—discipline in the effort to transform the self. It's often hard to haul oneself off the couch to volunteer for good works. It's also difficult to find time to meditate on a regular basis, still more difficult to actually sit there and work with the jumpy mind.

But head out to the store or library for a book? Nothing hard about that. In fact, for many of us, studying is so satisfying, it's all we want to do, and there are hundreds of publishers out there working hard to serve a thriving New Age book market. I myself have a little book addiction and my shelves hold books it will take me years to get around to reading.

Yet studying is only one part of the wisdom equation. Knowledge, after all, is *interpreted* information. In his essay "Toward Wisdom," Copthorne Macdonald says, "If the perspective or conceptual model through which we interpret our data is inappropriate, or flawed, then our knowledge is flawed and will lead us astray... The task of becoming wise is not one of absorbing more information, more raw facts; it is to put the facts into appropriate contexts, to view them from more helpful perspectives."

In Buddhism, the right view or correct view is considered the forerunner, or prerequisite, of all the other steps in the Noble Eightfold Path to enlightenment. As Tibetan master Traleg Kyabgon Rinpoche writes in his book, *Mind At Ease*, "We cannot simply practice meditation and hope for the best; we need a conceptual framework that is based on a correct view... We need to have a comprehensive view of our human nature, our place in the scheme of things and our relationship to the world in which we live and to our fellow sentient beings."

Before we can fully benefit from meditation or study, we must make sure our conceptual model of reality is as accurate as possible, giving us a means to judge whatever information we encounter. In the early twenty-first century, the most complete model of reality is undoubtedly Integral Theory, which includes a detailed understanding of spiritual stages and Spiral Dynamics. It also features Wilber's AQAL model, which explains how all our experience of life unfolds in four quadrants—I (self and consciousness), it (brain and organism), we (culture and worldview) and its (social system and environment). (For more on Integral Theory, see Wilber's many books or visit integrallife.com.)

With a good framework to build upon, we can flesh out our understanding with further study. As Socrates and many others have pointed out, in order to move toward true wisdom, one must begin with philosophy.

The study of philosophy

A good philosophical foundation helps us put all the facts we learn in proper context. It also helps us learn how our context can shape the facts.

Part IV of this book is a basic primer on the philosophy of idealism as interpreted by the New Age, along with a list of must-read authors and books popular in the movement.

But the most interesting reading is found in the works of the giants of idealistic thought. Eastern idealism begins with *The Bhagavad Gita* and *The Tao Te Ching* and extends all the way through D. T. Suzuki and Alan Watts.

In Western philosophy, you could start with Plato and Plotinus or the great European idealists of the eighteenth and nineteenth centuries such as Berkley, Spinoza, Hegel, Schelling, or Kant (although if you can grasp a good fraction of Kant, you are ahead of me). I have also learned much from turn-of-the century idealists I dug out of my local university library, such as William Ernest Hocking and F. H. Bradley and the dazzling genius Henri Bergson.

My favorite idealists, however, are the Transcendentalists—Ralph Waldo Emerson and Henry David Thoreau. (If I could only take one book with me to a desert island, it would be the collected works of Emerson.)

The New Age movement, however, has never been content to look at one side of things. Besides philosophy, New Age thought embraces many other disciplines as well, and I have gained invaluable perspective by delving into the classics on comparative religions and spirituality (William James, *The Varieties of Religious Experience*; Huston Smith, *The Religions of Man*), mythology (anything by Joseph Campbell), psychology (Carl Jung, Abraham Maslow, Carl Rogers), or physics (David Bohm).

The more well-researched your philosophy and knowledge of life, the stronger the foundation for your beliefs. And solid beliefs that actually match reality can sustain you remarkably well through the chaotic ride called life.

So read and study to your heart's content. Nothing else can open your mind quite so quickly and easily. And although studying is no substitute for contemplative practice, and can only take you so far in the recognition of reality, it moves you along the biggest leg of the journey.

Many interesting papers and ideas can be found at the Collective Wisdom Initiative: collectivewisdominitiative.org.

For a more complete list of New Age and spiritual authors, and to read excerpts of their work, visit spiritsite.com

You will also find a full list of links to spiritual education, spiritual magazines, and other resources for study and knowledge at my site: newagepride.org.

23 Become Part of the New Age Community

The importance of community in the transformation of self and society has already been taken up in Chapter 8, but here we'll talk about specific ways to form community and why it is an especially urgent effort for those of us of a "spiritual but not religious" bent.

Whether we identify ourselves as New Age or not, we spiritual idealists do not often discuss our belief system with others who might not think the same. We are a "live and let live" bunch, we see faith and belief as a private matter, and we don't want to impose our views on people. We may actually live next door to a New Ager, or work at the next cubicle to one, or sit on the same bench with a like-minded person at our kids' Little League games week after week, and never even know it.

Our reticence to identify ourselves means that most New Age-style believers, unless they live somewhere like Sedona or Santa Cruz, are missing out on the life-enriching experience of belonging to a spiritual community. I grew up going to the Vermont Avenue Church of Christ every Sunday, and all these many years since leaving the church, I feel the loss of regular fellowship. But how silly to feel so alone when there are so many of us with the same set of ideals, the same hopes and dreams.

We need to ask ourselves, is it really best to forsake the warmth of companionship on the journey, or support and encouragement when the road gets rough? It would be tempting to answer this question with a quick "no" and move on, but that would do a disservice to the complexity of the typical New Age idealist. We are, as we've seen, a famously independent bunch, most of us very self-sufficient and content with the solitary path. I suspect many if not most New Agers are like me, fairly introverted, and initially attracted to this path precisely *because* it allows us to wander on our own. While isolation is not always comfortable, and can often be lonely, it can still be preferable to the discomforts of trying to fit oneself into a community of other people.

Yet, as we've also seen, discomfort with community is often the pain of an ego that doesn't want its control of the self jeopardized. Which is not to say that solitude doesn't have an important place in spiritual life; silence and solitude both bestow a great many gifts on us. But it is to say that just because one can be comfortable in isolation doesn't mean it is always wise. Community is about more than companionship, which we may or may not feel we need. It's also about gaining self-knowledge, something we all most definitely need, for self-knowledge is the foundation of all spiritual growth.

We can sit in meditation for years, watching our own thoughts, and still be relative strangers to ourselves. But spend time with other people, and our deepest thoughts, feelings, insecurities, and judgments rise up almost immediately. Our interaction with other people serves as our clearest mirror. I don't know how many times I have been uncertain how I feel about an issue or event until I hear myself explaining it to someone else. Through interaction with others, we come to know our own minds.

In Buddhism, the community ofbelievers is known as a *sangha*. I once read that a *sangha* is like a bag ofbarley, the husks fall away and the grains rub together, polishing each other. In community, we help each other become "more" ourselves—that is, more soul, less ego—thanks to a group interaction that prevents the ego from puffing up on too much of its own thoughts.

We also gain access to wisdom through other members of the group. No matter what challenges we face, there is always someone who has been through something similar and can provide insight or help us see things from a different perspective. The more we talk to people about our spiritual questions, the more we will avoid getting lost in error, and the more we will stay focused on what's real. A spiritual community also allows us to encounter others who are further along the path, others who can inspire us by showing us what a life aligned with spirit looks like.

But beyond all the benefits to self, we have seen that intentional "bridging" community is the primary doorway to a transformed society. All our work on the self through study and contemplation is meant to be preface to the real work of connecting with others, and together building a community that works for everyone.

How to create community

We need spiritual community in order to truly grow in spirit. But we 'spiritual but not religious' are unlikely to find much of it unless we take on a common identity—a New Age identity—and make it a point to build "bonding" social capital. And if we hope to do more than help ourselves, if we indeed hope to create a better world, we also need to work on "bridging" social capital. "We need," says sociologist Robert Putnam, "to fortify our resolve as individuals to reconnect."

- **Identify Yourself (bonding)**

1. When spiritual subjects come up in conversation, talk about what you believe and what the New Age means to you. You might stumble across fellow New Agers in the most unexpected

places. And even if you don't, since so few people even know what the New Age stands for other than the pop culture connotation of "woo-woo stuff," you might be surprised how many people are curious or even eager to talk about it and ask questions.

2. Wear a New Age t-shirt or emblem. Or, sport a New Age bumper sticker on your car. Make it easy for other New Agers to recognize and connect with you. A large selection is available at www.newagepride.org

♦ **Reach Out to Others (bridging)**

1. Join an established spiritual center: Connect with others at a Buddhist Temple or spiritually progressive church such as Unitarian Universalist, Unity, Church of Religious Science or Kabbalah Center. Many of the more mainstream Christian churches can be very liberal and a good place to discover other idealists. (See Progressive Christianity: religioustolerance.org/prog_chr.htm)
2. Connect through the Internet: The Internet is the single best community-creating medium since the invention of the town square. Get online, begin connecting with other spiritual idealists through Internet-based coalitions, groups, and blogs. One of my favorite groups is a network that combines spirituality with political action. The Network of Spiritual Progressives boasts many local chapters. Visit spiritualprogressives.org.

   If you can't find a group that feels right to you, then start your own. To help you find or facilitate any group, visit Meet Up, a networking Web site, at meetup.org.

Start a Circle

"The small group is the unit of transformation and container for the experience of belonging," writes Peter Block. "The future is created one room at a time, one gathering at a time."

Of course, New Age thinkers have long advocated circles as the most powerful way to gather and not only support personal growth, but the mutual growth of those in the circle and beyond. According to Jean Shinoda Bolen in *The Millionth Circle*, these small gatherings are based on a simple hypothesis: "When a critical number of people change how they think and behave, the culture does also, and a new era begins."

Bolen suggests that when enough circles are convened as spiritual centers of peace and growth and love, then, like ripples reaching out and intersecting in a million directions, we will be able to transform the fabric of society and be able to truly create a world that works for everyone.

Yet, it is essential to understand that circles are not only about solving social problems, says David Bohm. Dialogue in circles will also change us as individuals "in relation to the cosmic. Such an energy has been called 'communion'...the root of which means 'to participate.'" The idea, he adds, is to partake of whole, "not merely the whole group, but the *whole*."

Create a space, an actual circle of chairs, then issue an invitation to people you know in person, by phone, by email. Or to people you don't know by advertisement online, on a bulletin board at a yoga studio or a New Age store or in an alternative periodical. Most circle veterans say anywhere from 12 to 20 people is ideal. Then sit down together and start a conversation—a real conversation of depth that "creates a new story for the planet," in the words of Marianne Williamson.

Conversations for circles

When gathering a circle, Peter Block recommends that each group meeting have nothing to do with information and answers, but everything to do with questioning and listening. "The nature of the questions we ask either keeps the existing system in place, or brings an alternative future into the room."

Answers, says Block, shut down the discussion, and shut the future down with them. Questions, however, create the space for something new to emerge.

David Bohm also points to the importance of creating an open space to allow for whatever arises—all our assumptions and opinions. We need to be able to speak them without defending them, and be able to hear them without judgment. "If we can see what all of our opinions mean, then we are sharing a common content, even if we don't agree entirely... By looking at everything together, the content of our consciousness is essentially the same, and a participatory consciousness becomes possible...[and] we may then move more creatively in a different direction." We may then move toward shared meaning, to coherence, to community.

Block identifies six necessary conversations we should have in the forming stage of any circle. These conversations are centered on questions which engage us with each other in an intimate way, and invite us to co-create a future possibility. His invaluable book, *Community: A Sense Belonging*, explores small group interaction in great detail and provides whole lists of questions and suggestions. If you do want to convene a New Age circle—and I hope you do—his book is essential reading, along with David Bohm's *On Dialogue*. In the meantime, here is a brief outline of Block's suggestions:

♦ **Conversation One: The Invitation**

You invite to the room those you believe need to have a voice in your community. Try to invite a cross section of people from different disciplines, different backgrounds. It is not just a request to attend, says Block, "but a call to create an alternative future." **Example question**: To what extent are you here by choice?

♦ **Conversation Two: Possibility**

"The communal possibility comes into being through individual public declarations of possibility," says Block. We don't want to

focus on problems; rather, we want to declare the future we want to live into, the world we want to inhabit.
Example question: What do we want to create together that would make a difference?

♦ Conversation Three: Ownership

"We need to believe in the possibility that this community, this society, is ours to create," Block continues. "People best create what they own." We need to ask questions that lead us to take responsibility, accept accountability.
Example questions: To what extent are you invested in the well-being of the whole? What have I done to contribute to the situation I hope to change?

♦ Conversation Four: Dissent

We need to be able to hear dissent without defense. "Without doubt," Block says, "our faith has no meaning, no substance; it is purchased at too small a price to give it value." Protect space for the expression of people's doubts. As Block adds, we let go only those doubts we have been able to voice. The freedom to say "no, thank you," is the beginning of the conversation for commitment.
Example questions: What doubts or reservations do you have? What resentments do you hold?

♦ Conversation Five: Commitment

A promise made with no expectation of return, independent of approval or reciprocity, takes barter out of the conversation, says Block. "It is one thing to set a goal or objective, but something more personal to use the language of promise, [which is] a sacred form of expression." We need to ask each other questions that help us connect to our desire and intention to commit to a better world.
Example questions: What price am I willing to pay for the success of the whole? What promise am I willing to make to create an alternative future?

- **Conversation Six: Gifts**

"In community-building, rather than focus on our deficiencies and weaknesses, which will most likely not go away," Block continues, we need to focus on the gifts we bring to the group, and seek ways to capitalize on them.
Example question: What gift have you received from others in your group?

Although we gather and converse in the context of a wider social movement, we cannot judge the effectiveness of our circle by what is happening in the larger world. It is important to keep our attention focused within the room, within the circle, and not become obsessed with the scale and speed of our efforts. "Scale and speed and practicality are always coded arguments for keeping the existing system in place," says Block.

He advises us to set aside concerns for scale and speed, and train ourselves on what is happening in the room, here and now. "Something shifts on a large scale only after a long period of small steps, organized around small groups patient enough to learn and experiment and learn again."

Circle activities

Beyond essential conversations, circles give us the opportunity to engage each other in activities that move us toward connecting and relating, and building bridges toward greater social capital. Many circles organize themselves around different interests, themes, or goals:

- A study circle or book circle that focuses on spiritual or progressive books.
- A movie club where you get together to watch a spiritual movie or progressive documentary.
- A "New Church a Month" club for spiritual explorers and seekers, where once a month you visit a different church and soak

in a new version of wisdom. Or, meet and try reading from a different holy book.

- Start a "Wine and Spirit" club. Get together with a bottle of wine and spiritual conversation.
- Start a "Serving Others" group. Get together with other New Age idealists to focus on service as a spiritual path. Organize fundraisers for charity to serve local families in need. Gather clothes and blankets for homeless shelters, or food for local food banks. Organize volunteers for civic projects, community clean up projects, youth after school activities or whatever else needs attention in your community.
- Start a "New Age Politics" group. Gather to help address issues of progressive politics, on both the local and national level. For instance, your group can join the fight to save a local stream or watershed in the spring, and work to elect a progressive candidate in the fall. Investigate what your government is doing. Locate your progressive representatives, then help them achieve their goals even as you enlist them to help you with yours.

Circle Resources

Community: The Structure of Belonging by Peter Block (designedlearning.com)
On Dialgue by David Bohm
The Millionth Circle by Jean Shinoda Bolen (millionthcircle.org)
Circles of Change (spritinaction.net)
Stone Circles (stonecircles.org)

24 Do the Right Thing

When we think of right behavior, the first thing that probably comes to mind is a list of "thou shalt nots." But interestingly, we don't see a lot of "don't" lists in the New Age. Once one embraces idealistic principles, morality is no longer troublesome, but a natural condition. If we know that we are all equally divine, all of us One with God, then it becomes unthinkable to harm another human being—whether by lying, cheating, stealing, killing. If we know the earth to be another manifestation of God, then we feel a reverence for all life and respect for nature.

So the don'ts are easy. What is more far more difficult is to rouse ourselves for the do's.

I don't know how many times I've tossed an aluminum can toward the recycle bin in my house, missed, and the can landed in the trash instead. Not wanting to get up to switch the can from trash to recycling, I catch myself thinking, why bother, it's just one can. How much good does recycling do anyway? With something as astronomically huge as global warming breathing down our necks—digging through the garbage for one can seems ridiculously minor. But…

I usually go get the can anyway. I work to remind myself again and again, if I want to help create a different world for my children, I can't be part of the problem, I have to be part of the solution. I have to make different choices. Every day. Every time it comes up. Every can.

"As individuals, there is both little and much we can do," writes Fred Branfman in *Imagine: What America Could be in the 21st Century*. "We cannot hope to reverse the course of evolution on our own. But we can, each of us, transform ourselves. We can stop our present way of life and begin instead, on our own, to live for future generations. Our individual acts, by themselves, will change nothing. But if enough follow, our cumulative actions will transform everything, in the only way that fundamental change has ever occurred: person by person, life by life, dream by dream."

We need to make the effort to do the right thing. Yes, for it's impact on the whole, but to be frank, the size of the benefit is almost beside the point. Right behavior is ultimately a *spiritual discipline* that encourages us to step beyond our own instant gratification and ego desires.

This doesn't mean we need to weigh our lives down with tortured obligation. Or saddle ourselves with guilt for every unrecycled can. The goal is not to suffer and sacrifice oneself toward sainthood. The goal is simply to make steady progress toward right behavior that, over time, not only helps repair the world but also helps elevate our souls by placing the self in context with the whole.

Most do's are pretty much common sense, and common knowledge. Still, thanks to differences in region and culture and background, not everyone's list of do's will be the same. Hunting and killing one's own food has a different moral connotation in Alaska than it does in L.A. And "buy organic" is not going to be on the list of someone who lives in an area where organic products are not readily available. Overall, if you hear a voice in your head saying you *should* do a particular thing, like recycle aluminum cans, then that thing should probably make your own list of right behavior.

My own list has included different things at different times of my life; for example, reading to my children when they were young seemed a moral obligation. Today my list looks something like this:

1. Accept the Responsibilities of a Citizen

Vote. Beyond that, encourage everyone you know to vote. We all have friends or family who don't vote, have never voted, are a little intimidated at the thought of registering. Help them register; help them get to the polls on voting day.

Call, email or write your elected representatives, make your views known to them. Let them know you would like them to end the war in Iraq, prevent global warming, support universal health care, support equal rights for gays, support a woman's right to choose, and so forth. This responsibility is so important that I'm going to repeat it.

Call, email or write your elected representatives, make your views known to them.

You've probably heard or read this advice so many times that you automatically skip past it, without any intention of doing it. As I've said before, New Agers are a particularly "live and let live" bunch. We don't like to seem loud or intrusive, we don't like to rattle cages. And, like most Americans, we have become very cynical about politics, and sure that our representatives don't care what we think anyway.

But whether our representatives care about our opinions or not is none of our business. Our business is to do the right thing and express our opinions, even when we have handy excuses not to do it. We have a moral obligation to speak up for what is right. In fact, this obligation is so important, it gets it own bullet point.

2. Speak Up for What Is Right

We idealists, full of strong convictions and deep concern for the world, are nevertheless the most quiet group of people out there. We typically avoid public argument. We believe in tolerance and respect for differences. And so, when we hear someone rant about why they don't vote, or we get stuck in conversation with a coworker who is putting down gays or blaming illegal immigrants for their insecurities, we may stand there quietly, our only goal to get away as soon as possible.

Whenever life hands us the opportunity to speak up for truth in the face of ignorance, and we walk away because we feel the right thing to do is to be "respectful of differences," then we are confused about what is right. The right thing is always, always, to insist on the truth. We don't have to be confrontational or insulting, we don't have to speak in a way that makes the other person wrong about their own feelings. But we do have to speak. In the words of Martin Luther King, Jr., "Our lives begin to end the day we become silent on things that matter."

I learned this most vividly from a wonderful book written by Robb Foreman Dew called *The Family Heart.* A true-blue liberal, Dew raised two sons believing she had done everything right to ensure the health and safety of her children and promote their success in life. Then she learned her oldest son was gay. Suddenly, her child was not safe anymore, but the target of unreasonable fear and prejudice by the conservative Right.

Dew became haunted by the fact that she had blithely let slurs against gays go unchallenged in her own house. These slurs had undoubtedly been absorbed by her child, and had undoubtedly at times made him feel he had no right to exist. The book follows her courageous acceptance of her responsibility for not having spoken up against this vicious prejudice in the past, and her determination to fight the silence of well-meaning people that allows prejudice to survive.

The book changed my life. I will never be silent again when I encounter ignorance or harmful opinion. We must hold to the truth, and speak up for what is right.

3. Go Green

Change to fluorescent bulbs, conserve, recycle, don't spill toxins down your drain, ride a bike or walk instead of driving, buy a hybrid instead of a gas guzzler, buy reusable shopping bags, buy bulk foods instead of heavily packaged foods, support alternative energy. There are all kinds of things you can do, most of them fairly simple, that will help you cause less harm to the planet, and help steer the culture toward green priorities.

Yet beyond that, says Stephanie Kaza in *Mindfully Green*, going green can be a spiritual path in itself in which we change our entire relationship to the planet and to each other. It can bring up all kinds of valuable questions about what kind of role we wish to play in our time here. "If we engage green living in more depth, it becomes an expression of our deepest moral values," writes Kaza, and "this shift in thinking can be quite profound."

4. Take Care of Yourself

In any truly integral approach to self-development, one doesn't just develop the spirit and the mind, one makes an effort to develop and care for the body as well. After all, it is difficult to grow spiritually if you feel like crap, or you're continually battling illness and disease.

This important little "do" is usually fairly high on a New Agers list, as evidenced by the boom in yoga studios, alternative health clinics, and holistic living magazines. We've come far in learning how much some exercise and a few daily fruits and veggies can improve one's feeling of well-being.

But taking care of yourself has a moral element as well. If you get cancer or diabetes from bad lifestyle choices, you drive up the cost of health care for everyone. The cost of health care is one of the biggest drains on our economy. By making good health a personal priority, you help foster a culture of health and well-being for everyone.

Eat healthy, don't smoke, get moving. If you're not in the habit yet, keep trying. Help build a culture of valuing health.

5. Enlighten Your Spending

In a capitalistic society such as ours, change follows the flow of dollars, and you can create a market for change with your spending faster than any government mandate could do it.

Buy a hybrid vehicle. Buy solar panels to help provide power for your home. Buy florescent bulbs. Buy recycled. Buy organic. Try alternative medicine options. Buy alternative energy from your public utility if they give you the option.

Beyond boosting healthy products and services, you can also help support companies that donate to progressives. After the 2004 elections, Buy Blue was started to provide information to consumers so that they can "vote with their wallets to support businesses that abide by sustainability, workers' rights, environmental standards, and corporate transparency."

For example, Wal-Mart gave 82 percent of its political contributions to Republicans. Costco gave 95 percent to Democrats. Which superstore should you patronize? Meanwhile, Hyatt Hotels gave 94 percent of its contributions to Democrats, rival Marriott give 82 percent to Republicans. Where would you stay? Levi's gives 100 percent of their contributions to Democrats.

JC Penney, Sears, Home Depot, Target and Fruit of the Loom contribute primarily to Republican campaigns. J Crew, Barnes & Noble, Calvin Klein, Foot Locker and Bed, Bath & Beyond are big Democratic contributors. Yahoo goes Republican. Google gives to Democrats. (Maybe it's time to get rid of that Yahoo account and go for gmail.)

Make it a habit to think about how you spend your money. Change always follows the flow of dollars and it is in your role as a consumer that you have the most power to transform our society.

6. Practice Random Acts of Kindness

I often think that the most impactful contribution we make to our world is simply with our attitude. We can either add negative energy to the societal mix, and bring down the level of the whole, or throw in some positive energy, and raise the level of the whole. My faith in humanity is always restored when I am in a terrible hurry and someone lets me cut in line at the grocery store. When I'm not in a hurry, I always let someone cut in front of me.

It only takes a few minutes to make the world a more hospitable place and add good vibes to the communal pot of karma. Rake the leaves in your elderly neighbor's yard, leave a big tip for your server at a restaurant, bring something tasty to work for everyone to share, pick up the litter on your street, buy a meal for the person in line behind you at the drive through, smile at a stranger. When you spread good energy around, you'll find your own feel-good levels shooting up in a virtuous circle that keeps on giving.

25 Good Works: Lending a Helping Hand

Sometimes on a Saturday, I marvel at the traffic jams and overflowing parking lots of shopping centers in my city, as my neighbors flock to buy patio furniture and cell phones and new shoes and gourmet burritos and whatever else we use to fill the nagging sense of emptiness that is part of the human condition. I always think, Man, if all this money and determination could be turned toward giving instead of getting... Then I slide my own car into a parking slot and head in to wait in line for my own burrito.

"Americans," says Marianne Williamson, "are not starving for what they don't have, but rather for what they won't give." Never were more true words spoken. Of course, many many New Age-y types are already out there, working hard to bring change to one issue or another, and in some years, this has described me. But many New Agers are *not* out there working for change, and in too many years, this has also described me.

The stereotype of the narcissistic self-absorbed New Ager is embarrassingly accurate, as any publisher of New Age books can attest. In 2006, *Publisher's Weekly* reported that even with the recent urgency of the environmental crisis, New Age publishers were having a hard time finding buyers for books which urge readers toward activism.

"Not all readers are interested in books that nudge them to look beyond their own problems," the magazine reported. Instead, the biggest New Age book of last year, make that the entire decade, was *The Secret*, a book that promised to tell us how to manipulate the universe into granting one's every desire.

It can take a lot of trial and error to learn that personal growth that does not lead us to see our unity with others is no growth at all. And even if we do get an inkling, we may assume that until we feel absolutely driven to get active in the world, we're not "there" yet, and had best hunker down and keep on working on ourselves. Many of us dabble in this spiritual practice or that, exploring nothing but our own heads year after year, waiting for the urge to serve, an urge that somehow never becomes urgent enough to get us out the door.

We wait to grow in order to serve, but the irony is, we need to serve in order to grow. Martin Luther King Jr. linked "qualitative change in our souls" with "quantitative change in our lives." Spiritual growth depends on service to others perhaps even more than it depends on contemplation. The ego is a very tough customer, thick and strong. We can, and should, work on dissolving it from the inside, but we will get the job done much faster if we also work on dismantling it from the outside.

"The road to holiness must pass through the world of action," said Dag Hammarskjold. With that first step outside ourselves, the ego immediately begins to soften.

If you are not yet at the integral stage in your spiritual development, the stage in which you feel the urgent obligation toward service, then it's time to "fake it 'til you make it." Just get out there, start cultivating the habit of putting others before yourself, and with your action, you help break down the hard barrier of ego that keeps you trapped within yourself and separate from spirit.

Yes, it is hard, extremely hard, to climb over the walls of ego-apathy that keep us confined to the duties of our own lives. In my own case, I am always playing catch up and can easily convince myself I don't have a moment to spare. Especially when my children were young, I already felt self-sacrificing to the point of having nothing left to give. And we all know that even if we get out there, we are going to spend a lot of time flinging ourselves against the walls of others' apathy.

And yet, I've also learned that there is ultimately no peace in doing nothing. The problems don't go away when I close my eyes. And if I am any kind of idealist at all, I can only avoid for so long the creeping knowledge that unless I am doing something, I am part of the problem. That burden becomes quite crushing eventually. I recall going to see Al Gore's *An Inconvenient Truth*, and I was barely able to rise from my seat afterward, so heavy was the sense of responsibility in knowing I have done so little to help address the problem.

Haul yourself over that wall of apathy, find the issue that most weighs on you. Ending poverty, feeding the hungry, sheltering the homeless, addressing the global warming crisis, stopping domestic violence, improving public education, justice reform, election reform, health care—there are dozens of worthy issues that are in great need of your help, and at least one of them is likely to strike a personal chord with you.

But don't just peek at their Web site, or support them in theory. Join the group, donate some money, volunteer some time. The habit of "I can't afford it" sneaks in, but unless you're living in your car or getting "Final Notice" before your electricity is shut off, that's usually just the ego's way of refusing responsibility.

The issue of responsibility lies at the heart of all idealism. We are all unavoidably interconnected, which means we are all responsible for each other. No matter the issue, it is my job to solve it, too. And I have learned, again and again from my own intermittent forays into service that Anne Lamott is right when she says, "Love and service decrease the fear, and even sometimes change it to joy."

What a surprise to discover that even as you are steeling yourself to endure a dreaded obligation, you stumble upon a source of great happiness. Becoming active in service is about becoming "fully alive," says John Graham in *Stick Your Neck Out*. It's about "the meaning and passion you can add to your own life by getting involved." Even when confronting the biggest of challenges, Graham adds, one often feels "an energy, a sense of excitement, a deep satisfaction of being in the right place at the right time."

That, of course, is exactly how one feels when freed from the overtight confines of the ego. So do your soul a favor, do your world a favor. Volunteer, donate, get involved.

To find the best place for your donation dollars, visit Charity Navigator at charitynavigator.org.

To find volunteer opportunities, visit Web sites such as:

- change.org
- pointsoflight.org
- volunteermatch.org

A New Age Manifesto

- We recognize that the "old paradigm" represented by materialism and dualism, which sees life as a fear-based struggle for power and domination over each other and the planet, has failed us—failed us personally, failed us collectively, and failed us environmentally.
- We recognize it is time to operate from an idealistic "new paradigm" of love-based acceptance and harmony with ourselves, with each other, and with the planet that sustains us.
- We recognize that this new paradigm will evolve naturally from the correct understanding that we—along with everything else in the universe—are manifestations of One Spirit, and that we are all interconnected parts of this greater divine whole.
- We recognize that even though Spirit is immanent in the universe, Spirit also transcends the universe we can see and touch and measure, and unfolds in ways we cannot imagine.
- We recognize that the energy of Spirit can be expressed positively as love, or negatively as the fear we know as evil.
- We recognize that this shifting dark-light energy strives for greater awareness and learns through the balancing law of karma, or cause and effect.
- We recognize that many human beings throughout history have connected with and been inspired by Spirit, giving birth to many religions with a common mystical core. We believe each religion is a valid representation on the greater spectrum of truth—"many paths, one mountain"—and each has much to teach us.
- We recognize that human beings have evolved in order to allow the universe, and thereby Spirit, to become conscious of itself.
- We recognize the key to increasing awareness of our place and purpose here is through contemplative practice.
- We recognize that the next crucial step in our evolution is to accept our responsibility for co-creating a new age of social harmony and a sustainable future for all.

PART VII

The Horizon

*The outcome of the world, the gates of the future,
the entry into the super-human—these are not thrown
open to a few of the privileged nor to one chosen people
at the exclusion of all others. They will only open
in an advance of all together, in a direction
which all together can join and find completion
in a spiritual renovation of earth.*

— PIERRE TIELHARD DE CHARDIN —

26 On Saving the World

In the late 1990s, I lived in Oregon and worked for my county in a new youth drug and alcohol prevention program that co-ordinated the efforts of many different agencies. A few months into the job, I attended a prevention conference, and in one of the workshops, we were asked to introduce ourselves and explain why we were there. Most people said things like, "My boss sent me," or "I want to learn more about being racially sensitive," things like that. I stood up and bluntly said, "I'm here because I want to save the world."

A long moment of uncomfortable silence and blank stares greeted this. The facilitator said, "Isn't that nice," her condescending tone unmistakable, then moved on. Even in a group of teachers and social workers, my statement smacked of naïve 1960s hippie-style idealism, or worse—embarrassing 1980s New Age-style utopian blather.

Back when the New Age first appeared on the cultural radar, many a New Age writer waxed rhapsodic over what a New Age of harmony would look like. War and hunger and disease would be a distant memory, the air would be bright and clean, birds would sing in abundant trees, and people would hop in their solar-fueled cars and head off to perform meaningful jobs wearing blissful smiles of inner peace.

Now let's compare that with reality in 2009: The nightly news shows us death tolls from bombs (many of them ours) exploding all over the Middle East and Europe, experts setting the odds on terrorists exploding nuclear devices here in America, as well as the acute suffering of refugees from famines and wars and disease. Here in the U.S., people are losing their jobs, losing their homes, and living in their cars, while entire cities run dry of gas and our government is bailing out Wall Street to avoid complete economic collapse. Meanwhile, we are absorbing one climactic catastrophe after the next—freak storms and yearly hundred-year floods and wildfires and hurricanes—while ice shelves the size of Long Island collapse into oceans with vast dead zones of floating garbage.

No wonder people like me who prattle on about saving the world get blank stares and condescension.

Idealism, writes Todd Gitlin in his wonderful book, *Letters to a Young Activist*, can actually shield the status quo by appearing so "exotic" that it renounces any hope of serious influence and "leaves center stage to the tough guys of realism."

He's absolutely right. Yet at the same time, it is only very tough and hard realism that allows us to recognize that if we do not change the course of society, it is going to collapse in on us and kill us all—or at least make life so miserable and desperate and marginal that it won't be worth living. Those who don't recognize that are the true, out-of-touch dreamers.

Of course, from the universe's perspective, this might all be a moot point.

Shiva's dance

As I near the end of this book, I realize that I have been writing on the assumption that most idealists care deeply about changing the course of events—that we very much *want* to save the world. I've also been writing on the even bigger assumption that we have some kind of choice in the matter. The latter assumption especially may have no basis in reality.

Many spiritual teachers are quick to point out that we have no permanent right to existence, and that the universe may decide the human experiment was a spectacular failure and should probably be allowed to self-destruct. After all, from the view of the Absolute, we are just one cycle out of an infinite many in the continuous rising and falling of being unfolding.

Eastern cosmology in particular is based on the knowledge that reality *depends* on the fluctuation between creation and destruction, the on-off pulsation between life and death. This idea is personified by the Hindu god Shiva, who continually destroys and recreates the physical universe with his dance. This concept of the universal dynamic of fluctuation is why, back in the 1970s, the marvelous Alan Watts glossed over the possibility of nuclear disaster as a silly "fascination with doom." He said the proper spiritual attitude toward a fiery end should be, "Why bother about that? Because if it happens, it's just another fluctuation."

Yet this openness to disaster is not as fatalistic as it sounds. As Watts continues, "If you realize that it doesn't really matter if the whole human race blows itself up, then there's a chance you won't do it." A fascination with our impending doom makes us panicky, he added, and it is the people who are in a panic who are most likely to "push the button." In other words, only by embracing our fate do we gain the ability to change it. (Perhaps this is why the dancing Shiva is not only known as the "Great Destroyer," but also the "Bringer of Happiness.")

Today, with terrorism and global warming added to the nuclear threat, we have even more reason to expect that a cataclysmic end may be unavoidable. And so we find popular teachers like Ken Wilber and Deepak Chopra engaging in a dialogue in which they both acknowledge that from the Absolute perspective, it doesn't matter in the least whether we figure out how to save ourselves or not. And yet, they are also quick to add that from the Absolute perspective, we finally see how much saving ourselves really *does* matter on the Relative Plane. After all, the entire reason the Absolute gives birth to the Relative is to discover what we will make of it.

True, we may make hash of it, and as Watts and Wilber would both say, "That's fine." Destruction will engulf us once more, and from those ashes, the Absolute will create us relative creatures once more, and presumably again and again until we get it right. Until we learn to cherish the opportunity granted to us on the relative plane, the opportunity to taste, to touch, to feel, and to reach out to each other in love.

I believe the Absolute spins the beautiful world into existence, and then evolves us here to find out whether we will care enough about ourselves and each other to save it. Ultimately, the outcome does not matter, yet ultimately, that is what we are here to do.

This has ever been the paradox of the human condition: We are both grounded in the unchanging Absolute, yet draw breath from the ever-changing Relative.

From the Absolute perspective, we do not have a choice in the world's fate, while from the Relative perspective, the choice is always ours, and always important. So I shall go back and rest on the assumption of the Relative, that it *is* in our power to save the world, through the only medium that can heal the rift between Absolute and Relative—through love. I am also going to rest on the assumption that we idealists care deeply about making it happen.

Indeed, if we want our children and grandchildren to have a chance at life as we understand it, we are going to have to *insist* on saving the world, no matter how much condescension we encounter, "using the language of healing and relatedness without embarrassment," in the words of Peter Block.

Yet, Gitlin is surely right in that we must also be careful to ground this language in reality. "Resist the temptation to think you are ushering in an earthly paradise," he warns. "Fantasies of an ideal realm will not do. The place to stand must always be solid, substantial, right here at hand."

So then, realistically speaking, what would a New Age and a saved world actually look like?

How A Paradigm Change Works

My all-time favorite analogy of how a new paradigm can help us solve our tangled mess of complicated and seemingly impossible to solve issues like global warming and health care and public education comes from a book called *Society's Breakthrough!* by Jim Rough. He begins with the familiar example of the three blind men who come across an elephant. The first blind man comes into contact with the elephant's legs and declares an elephant similar to a tree trunk. The second blind man gets hold of the tail and decides an elephant is like a rope. The third blind man puts his hands on the trunk and believes an elephant to be like a snake. From here, Rough continues:

> Pretend for a minute that the elephant is restless, causing problems for each of the men. The tree-like legs are stepping all over the vegetables in the garden; the rope-like tail is whipping the blind man in the face; the snake-like trunk is destroying the nearby bush. Not understanding the whole system, each man then works hard to solve his particular problem. One tries to turn the legs into posts, by heaping dirt around them. Another attempts to cut off the rope-tail. The third squirts poison at the snake-trunk to protect himself. The elephant, of course, doesn't benefit from any of these actions, nor do the men.

Of course, as Rough points out, this is exactly how our old paradigm politics approaches our problems today, "as though they are separate and as though we could use methods of control to fix them." But if we were to start looking at these problems from the perspective of a holistic new paradigm, we could then see the whole system, the whole elephant so to speak, and then "respond intelligently."

We might, for example, put a pile of food nearby to compel the elephant to simply move to a better spot. And say the elephant did indeed move away. Our seemingly separate and overwhelming problems would be solved almost effortlessly, all on their own. But as Rough adds, such a simple whole system answer would likely be resisted by the blind men. "Even though each may care deeply about the problem he addresses and wants it solved, the narrowness of his perspective may cause him to believe the new solution is irrelevant and resist it. What value could there be, they might all exclaim, in putting a pile of hay nearby? After all, each is an expert in his field of study and all agree there is no value to this new idea."

Watch Congress in action on CSPAN for awhile, and you will certainly see some blind men and women, our old paradigm legislators, railing against whole system solutions—the only solutions that will work—as nonsense. But as long as we stay in the context of the old paradigm, our societal problems and threats to the future will remain impossibly difficult to solve. The only way to respond intelligently to issues like global warming and health care and public education is to make the leap to a new, holistic perspective.

Choosing the future

Back in the 1980s, I confess I was one of those who believed that awareness was building throughout the whole of the population.

I believed this growing awareness would, at any moment, build to the critical point that would allow us to see ourselves in each other, allow us to lay down our weapons and begin caring for each other, allow peace and prosperity to reign—and solar-fueled cars to zip along the highways. In other words, this awareness would allow us to save the world without too much effort on our part.

It was not such a crazy notion; after all, I was only 20 years old and in my short lifetime, society had advanced in huge stunning leaps—with civil rights and the peace movement and the women's movement and men walking about on the moon. What reason did I have to expect that all that progress, however chaotic, would come to a screeching halt?

Now that I have a better grasp on history, and a better understanding of the dialectic of progress, I understand why there hasn't been many stunning leaps of late. (The exception: Electing our first black president in 2008 was about as stunning as it gets.) I still believe that human beings are meant to evolve in awareness, and that this will happen on its own, in fits and starts as it always has. The problem, of course, is that the normal pace of evolving awareness is lagging behind the pace of societal breakdown from the failures of the old paradigm. Human consciousness is not evolving nearly as fast as the planet is degenerating in its ability to sustain us.

Clearly, we long ago sailed past our chance to create utopia, and now it is simply a matter of surviving long enough to fight another day. This might be one of our first critical junctures in history where it could go either way, (the dawning of the nuclear age being the very first), but this is certainly not our last critical juncture. Life on this increasingly crowded planet will likely always be teetering on the brink of disaster—and the efforts of idealists will always be our only hope of keeping us all from crashing over the edge.

And whatever a real New Age might look like, we're certainly not going to get there in one glorious moment. There will be no magic tipping point when we will finally be able sit back with a

"Whew! Mission accomplished." Rather, every moment will continue to be critical, and I imagine a New Age-saved world will look very much like the world today.

The news will still be full of stories of violence and bombs exploding, stories of Third World countries struggling to pull themselves up from chaos to order, and stories of terrible weather as the climate absorbs the damage done over the past two hundred years. Our politicians will still do epic battle in Washington, police will still arrest criminals, people will still go to church and grope their way toward God, and our children will still go to school and be under too much influence from Hollywood and the celebrity culture.

In a realistic New Age, most of our problems will not disappear. But there will be subtle differences. You might not be able to put your finger on it, but the panicked bite of the times will be gone. Instead of inching closer to disaster, we will be inching away from it, and you will start to see glimpses of it here and there. A story about soldiers coming home and the lessening of anti-American sentiment around the world. A story about crime rates falling now that we have a new focus on restorative justice and rehabilitation. A story about high school dropout rates falling and college enrollments going up because tax dollars that used to go prisons are now going to public schools. A story about unemployment being at its lowest point in thirty years thanks to the explosion in green jobs and the alternative fuels industry.

You may also notice a few new spiritual centers popping up in your town, and some of your friends trying out meditation or yoga, and seeming less stressed. Another friend might invite you to do some volunteer work with her at a homeless shelter one night a week. Your drive to work will suddenly seem faster because more companies are encouraging their employees to telecommute. And then one day you will see it—a cute little solar-fueled car zipping by...

Or maybe it won't look like that at all. Who knows how a New Age will really unfold? And does it matter? Ultimately, the New Age is not something we can predict for tomorrow, it is a choice we make today, "a choice we live into," says Peter Block. The place to stand is right here at hand, today, solid and substantial. Saving the world must become a way of life we choose today, not envision for tomorrow. It must become a way of understanding oneself in relation to the world today, and every day.

Still, I have not addressed the question of *how* the New Age can change the world. What makes me or any New Ager so sure that idealism holds the means to a better-world end?

Paradigms, old and new

One thing, and one thing only, defines the meaning of your life, forms the basis for your decisions, and guides your contribution to the choices made by your society. And that one thing is your philosophy about reality, your metaphysics. It is your set of beliefs about why you are here on this planet and what you're supposed to accomplish while you are here.

We all have a philosophy, there's no way around it. And that philosophy determines what we do with our hours and days, how we spend our money, how we vote, how we support this issue or that, how loudly or quietly we support it, how responsible we feel for each other, how likely we are to get involved.

And as true as this is on the individual level, it is even more true on the collective level. Our collective philosophy gives us the basis for collective policy decisions, lets us know whether or not we should go to war or cut down trees or invest in schools or regulate markets or rehabilitate criminals.

Today, our collective philosophy in America is largely determined by the longstanding paradigms of authoritarian dualism and capitalistic materialism. Most people would agree that the policy decisions coming from these two paradigms have not been healthy for people *or* planet. (Not exactly true, the old paradigm works fabulously for the rich, but even they won't be able to escape the effects of global warming or nuclear disaster.)

With the old paradigms failing us so spectacularly, we are clearly in urgent need of a new paradigm to guide us to better choices for self, society, and planet. "For this we know about the mysterious ways of the paradigm," writes Professor Michael Nagler. "No alternative, no shift. No matter how outmoded the old paradigm has become, no matter how dangerous, there must be an alternative before one can abandon it."

The New Age provides a fully formed alternative—an idealistic paradigm that has been tested throughout many centuries of spiritual practice, and has been sharpened and refined in these last decades of scientific advance and study. This paradigm provides us with a new, commonsense way of approaching problems in which our unity, interdependence, and the well-being of the whole point us to obvious solutions.

For decades now, idealistic writers of every stripe, from many different fields, have been arguing and begging and pleading for a wider adoption of this paradigm. Yet the truth is, we don't *all* have to become idealists in order to save the world. Most people, in fact, are not ready to embrace the idealistic paradigm, for as we know from our map of spiritual development, we can't get to Stage Four idealism without first evolving from Stage One chaos to Stage Two order to Stage Three skepticism.

So we don't need just one world-saving paradigm, we need the structures of a number of increasingly evolved paradigms that allow movement up the spiral of growth through all the stages. Which means our problem is not that there aren't enough idealists (although more would certainly be better); our problem is that we idealists are so invisible, so isolated, so lost from each other, that the paradigm we champion has become inaccessible.

FEBRUARY 17, 2009

Barack Obama is not the answer

BLOG
Looking for the New Age

I thank all the gods and goddesses that Barack Obama is now our president and not another conservative. I believe he represents our one slim hope of turning our Titanic-nation away from the melting iceberg that looms before us. Yet at the same time, his election increases the danger for us, as he himself admits. His election makes it easy to believe the bulk of the work is now going to be done for us.

Someone said to me today, The New Age is already here, see look, there's a black man in the White House, the world has changed. The tired old ways are crumbling, she said. A new paradigm is no longer an ideal that we need to name and talk about, she said, because it is already "a living, breathing way of being."

I first wanted to weep. And then to ask, what world are you living in? (As it turns out, she lives in the luxe world of Santa Barbara, California, where the New Age does indeed live and breathe in fine health.)

Not that I don't marvel at how far we've come. I do believe in celebrating the good news, and focusing on the strides we have made toward the positive. Oh, how I believe in that. But I also know that good news can lull us, can make us feel finished, can hypnotize us into a trance of complacency.

The old paradigm—including corporate control of our way of life—is not crumbling nearly as fast as we think. True, it is more transparently ineffective than ever, but that doesn't mean it is slumping off in defeat. There are way more people working to rescue it than there are people working to construct a new paradigm. Barack Obama himself is trying to shore up the structures of the old paradigm with his Wall Street bailout plans, with his new stimulus bill.

We cannot rest just because Obama is in the White House. He is stuck working within the context of the old paradigm as much as any of us, and he will stay stuck unless we the people create a new context for him. This is the moment to get in gear, identify with each other, connect to each other, talk to each other, start building social capital. We need to consistently and ardently articulate a new paradigm all over the land today, and every day. Until we truly begin to long for it. Until we start picking up the phone and writing letters and emails to our representatives to insist on it. Until we find ourselves going out the door to start working for it.

You are pretty hard on yourself, and on the New Age community, said another friend who read part of this book. I know why she said that. The New Age has trained us to be so very gentle with ourselves, we become alarmed at any kind of self-criticism.

Stop beating yourself up! we cry. Yet if any group of people needs a good hard shaking out of apathy, it is we idealists, who dream so beautifully, yet in these last few decades, act so infrequently.

History has shown us again how change is won, and it is always through tough, persistent and even life-risking work against astronomical odds. It is work not just privately discussed, but publicly insisted upon in every corner. Look at the revolutionaries who founded this nation. Look at the abolitionists who ended slavery. Look at the workers who faced down exploitive corporations to win labor rights. Look at the suffragettes who won the vote for women. Look at the civil rights workers who ended segregation. Look at the peace marchers who helped end the war in Vietnam. They stood up, they spoke out, they fought, and they never gave up.

Yes we have come so very far. It takes one's breath away really. But there is still so far to go. The evolutionary journey is not finished—and it is our turn to take over the work. We have to shake off the trance of thinking change happens on its own. Or that Obama is going to take care of it for us.

Opening up the spiral

As the most public and popular form of Stage Four idealism available to us over the last forty years, the New Age long formed a vital bridge between Stages Three and Five. Unfortunately, the New Age as a recognizable, cohesive movement dropped off the cultural radar, was kicked to the side, and as I've argued in these pages, our spiritual evolution has suffered as a result. Most of us who grew into Stage Four have bogged down here, year after year, decade after decade.

The fact is, without a strong and vital New Age movement, the spiral breaks down and our evolution remains unfinished. Those ready to grow from Stage Three skepticism are unable to find a well-marked and respected path toward idealism, and they either stagger off on an uncertain hunt for it hidden in pockets of the culture, or more likely, they stay unsatisfied in Stage Three. Meanwhile, those of us in Stage Four have no solid structure beneath us to support growth and movement, and no particular philosophy to point the way beyond to Stage Five integralism. We are alone, isolated, stuck—and blocking the spiral for all others trying to find their way.

It seems clear that without New Age-style idealism to provide a prominent alternative paradigm, we *all* end up stuck, no matter which stage of the spiral currently dictates our worldview. In my opinion, bringing the New Age back not only *can* save the world, it may, in fact, be the *only* way to save the world—by giving us the means to unstick ourselves and restart our collective evolution.

You can help rebuild a strong and proud New Age by declaring yourself a part of it. In identifying with the movement, and living by its principles, you can create a connection in the social field that will strengthen around you and support your growth and that of many others. In identifying with the New Age, you can help restore a most vital piece of infrastructure on the spiral of development which holds the flow of all of humanity.

I invite you to join me in risking condescension, and start speaking in "the language of healing and relatedness without embarrassment." I invite you stand up in front of the room and say, "I'm New Age, and I'm here to save the world."

27 The Opportune Moment

I have been working on these pages for months, years, reading everything I can find about the New Age movement and its dramatic rise and fall in our culture. I have studied its philosophy, its meaning, and its promise as a vehicle for transformation. And now that I am resting my case, I cannot help but wonder—how practical is this effort?

Have I been toiling on a pipe dream, or is a New Age revival a real possibility?

On one hand, it will be a tremendous uphill battle to rekindle a movement and a label that many assume to be extinct. Sometimes I feel that trying to talk people into bringing the New Age back is no more sensible than trying to get one of my favorite TV shows back on the air. The kids on *The Brady Bunch* are all grown up and have moved on, as well they should.

On the other hand, rekindling the movement could be far easier than we might expect. After all, the idealistic movement formerly known as the New Age did not really die. There are still just as many idealists in the world going quietly about their lives, working to live up to their ideals. We merely stopped calling the movement the New Age and, without a name for it, stopped thinking about it as a collective force at all. But the movement is still all around us, burgeoning with potential.

William Irwin Thompson suggested that even though the New Age has "desiccated," there is every reason to believe that, like a tightly-packed spore that goes underground for the winter, it will make itself known again. Even when there is no aboveground evidence that there is anything there, he writes, as soon as a new opportune moment arrives, then wham! The hidden and underground mushrooms will spring up everywhere, and we will again have the opportunity to be part of a movement that can change lives and save the world.

I believe Thompson is right, and the New Age movement is still with us, mostly private and anonymous, but thriving in its own underground fashion. Although, in describing it in this way, I do not mean to discount the thousands of wonderful people and their organizations who daily strive to be visible and aboveground in the work of planetary transformation. We are lucky to have them, and if you know which magazines to buy, or which Web sites to visit, you can find these forward-thinking people and organizations without too much trouble. Yet, the fact remains, the movement's essential ideas rarely pop up in our broader public discourse, and the movement's ideological core lives almost entirely below society's noisy surface.

Of course, today's version of the New Age movement, whether above the ground or below, is very different than the movement that burst so colorfully pell-mell onto the scene in the 1980s. The faddish exterior has been scuffed away by the well-aimed slings and arrows of its critics. We thankfully no longer hear much from trance channelers or those who tell tales of a past life on Atlantis. To be New Age is no longer to be part of an entertaining or hot trend.

But as Ann Powers writes of alternative bohemian culture, "That its façade is out of fashion makes it easier to get to what's inside." Like bohemia, the New Age movement is no longer "a show staged for others." There is a lot less anything-goes silliness, and a lot more time-tested and truly helpful ideas to ground us and guide us. Most of us have read quite a few books now—we have experimented, contemplated, meditated and practiced. We have taken many wrong roads, and also stumbled upon many right ones.

In other words, the New Age has grown up and now represents a more enlightened spirituality, which takes into account knowledge of spiritual stages and our evolutionary development, as well as a spirituality more balanced between the individual and the community. We are now much better prepared, as Powers adds, "to confront and reinvigorate the premises of society."

I believe the opportune moment is upon us. Our society is clearly ready to shift right now, today—more than at any time in decades. Progressives quite suddenly have control of the White House and Congress. The ground has shifted beneath us, said Barack Obama in his inauguration speech, and the time has come to put away childish things, "to reaffirm our enduring spirit; to choose our better history."

Still, I keep asking myself, is a revival really possible?

In the end, no matter how certain I feel that the troubled world is waiting for us, hoping for us, rooting for us to discover our purpose, I admit that I don't really know what the world thinks or hopes for. I only know what I think and hope for the world.

I don't know how sound my arguments, how far away from reality, or how close. I don't know what lies in people's hearts, or what they think is possible. I don't know whether I am just like every other Stage Two blind-faith believer, preaching my little New Age gospel, so certain that if only the world would come round to seeing things my way, we'd all be saved from the disaster that looms.

Yet as David Spangler writes, "One does not manage the New Age. It is not a product that we create. It is a process in which we participate." It is a process to which, he adds, we must surrender.

So here I sit in Phoenix, Arizona, trying to surrender to what is, trying to detach from my hope that there are thousands of idealists out there, tens of thousands, hundreds of thousands, more—who will read these words and say, yes! Just what I've been thinking! Yes, this is just what we need to do! Identify ourselves, reach out to each other, help each other grow in spirit, help each other reach the next stage of development, help each other work for the transformation of society. Help each other, period.

I don't know if such a thing is possible. I write as if we all somehow have a choice in this, when I believe the concept of choice is largely illusion. All our thoughts, feelings, ideas, beliefs, and impulses are all formed by circuitry in our brains over which we have no control, are all formed by life. "Something very vast is living you, doing you," write the sages.

Life happens, events unfold, and we trail after them, dreaming up stories to explain them, dreaming up movements and meaning. But surely, this no accident. Surely, this is what we are here to do, to dream up a life of love and meaning out of the chaos tumbling willy nilly from the void.

In the story I have dreamed for myself, I am New Age and will continue to be, whether history whisks it off into the dim past or not. And if your life allows you the choice, I invite you to dream this story with me. I invite you to stand up for the New Age as well, wherever you are, today, now.

The opportune moment is upon us. It is time to claim the power of our identity. It is time to set aside ego, and recognize soul. It is time to open up the spiral of development, move from differentiation to integration, from individuality to collectivity.

It is time to give birth to a genuine New Age, with the power to transform not only ourselves, but our world.

Acknowledgments

As I've been inching this book toward print over the course of many years, through alternating stages of ambivalence and obsession, I am indebted to a number of people who helped and encouraged me in my hours of labor.

I am most indebted, literally and figuratively, to certain ex-husbands, who supported me financially and/or emotionally during different drafts and versions of this book. So I thank you Bill and Joe. And to Rhyse, most especially, my gratitude flows.

Of course, I must also thank my children—Scott, Natalie, and Evyn—who have managed to grow up despite an ever-distracted mother. They, more than any other, have shaped my feelings about life and made the grandiose notion of "saving the world" a personal and urgent priority for me.

Susan Ray at Moment Point Press bought an early incarnation of this book and let me know there is a worthy idea or two here, for which I am grateful.

I am also grateful to the many people who stumbled across my Web site during the years it was under construction, people who took the time to write me and let me know they felt I was on the right track. Their words often inspired me to return to the project after I'd abandoned it for the umpteenth time.

Yet there was one email in particular that came unexpected from a voice I have long revered, an email which uplifted me and gave me the gift of seeing this project with new eyes. I therefore dub David Spangler my official fairy godfather and thank him from the bottom of my heart for reaching out to me, and for generously agreeing to write the foreword for this book. I must also thank him for several decades of enlightenment and inspiration, especially the inspiration I took from the final chapter of his 1997 book, *A Pilgrim in Aquarius*, a chapter called "Reclaiming the New Age," a chapter which clearly took root in my mind and eventually grew into the first half of *Unfinished Evolution*.

I effusively thank the architects of the physical book you hold in your hands: Gail Kearns of To Press and Beyond for advice and patient editing and, even more important, optimism; Diane McIntosh for a cover design that made me gasp out loud when I first saw it; and John McKercher for beautifully typesetting all the many different elements I envisioned.

This book would not exist, nor would most of my thoughts, without the work of many of the geniuses of idealism in all its different forms. I liberally quoted all my favorites here, but relied on one to ridiculous excess. So Ken Wilber, I thank you for illuminating strings of words so perfectly put that I could not bear to paraphrase them. And in those instances I may have used them in ways you would not agree with, I ask forgiveness.

About the Author

TEENA BOOTH is a mother of three, and writer of novels (*Falling From Fire*), TV movies (*A Little Thing Called Murder, The Natalee Holloway Story, Fab Five: The Texas Cheerleader Scandal, Sex & Lies in Sin City, The Wronged Man*), and the founder of a New Age Web site, newagepride.org.

She was born and raised in Los Angeles, the oldest child of the very beautiful news reporter and actress Carol McEvoy. Teena, along with her two sisters, grew up in two very different worlds at once. During the week, they lived with their mother in the anything-goes hippie world of 1970s L.A. On weekends and summers they lived with their great-grandmother in a religion-soaked house with prayers before supper and bed, and a requirement to memorize Bible verses. This unique upbringing left Teena with a deep appreciation of relative truth and an ability to tolerate paradox.

After a stab at community college, Teena joined the U.S. Air Force to see the world, and have adventures (and because the government paid for more college.) At the end of her tour of duty, she became a mother to her first son, Scott. When he was four months old, Scott's father was killed in a motorcycle accident, leaving twenty-two-year-old Teena to raise their child alone.

A quick sidetrip into the U.S. Coast Guard (it was harder than it looked) was followed by a new marriage and the arrival of her daughter Natalie. Raising children, writing several not-very-good novels, doing volunteer work in obsessive spurts, reading Emerson and Alan Watts, and walking in the woods of Northern California and Oregon kept her busy through another marriage and the birth of her third child, Evyn.

Once she moved to Phoenix, Arizona, her writing skills had improved enough to land her jobs as a journalist, then editor of a trade magazine, and on to editor of a legal newspaper. She sold her first novel, *Falling From Fire*, to Random House in 2002. That same year, her screenplay *Showstopper*—a script she wrote to come to terms with the suicide of her very beautiful mother—won a Chesterfield Screenwriting Fellowship. She spent a year commuting back and forth to L.A., learning the art of screenwriting. Not long afterward, she got her first assignment from Lifetime Television to adapt a true-crime book into a script, and a TV movie writing career was launched.

Today, Teena still lives in Phoenix with a half-husband (long story), her three exceptionally cool and attractive children, two cats, a dog, and a gerbil. And, after seeing some of the world, having many adventures, and having most all of her dreams come true, she still carries with her a deep appreciation of relative truth and the ability to tolerate paradox.

You may contact her at *teenabooth@newagepride.org.*

Bibliography

Bergson, Henri. *The Creative Mind: An Introduction to Metaphysics*. The Wisdom Library, 1946.

Block, Peter. *Community: The Structure of Belonging*. Berrett-Kohler, 2008.

Bohm, David. *On Dialogue*. Routledge 2nd Edition, 2004.

Bohm, David. *Wholeness and the Implicate Order*. Routledge & Kegan Paul, 1980.

Bolen, Jean Shinoda. *The Millionth Circle: How to Change Ourselves and The World*. Conari Press, 1999.

Campbell, Joseph. *A Joseph Campbell Companion*. HarperCollins, 1981.

Campbell, Joseph. *The Hero With a Thousand Faces*. Princeton University Press, 1949.

Campbell, Joseph. *Myths to Live By*. Bantam Books, 1973.

Campbell, Joseph. *The Power of Myth*. Doubleday, 1988.

Capra, Fritjof. *The Tao of Physics: An Exploration of the Parallels Between Modern Physics and Eastern Mysticism*. Shambhala, 1975.

Carse, James. P. *Breakfast at the Victory: The Mysticism of Ordinary Experience*. Harper San Francisco, 1994.

Dumoulin, Heinrich. *Zen Enlightenment: Origins and Meaning*. Weatherhill, 1979.

Durant, Will. *The Story of Philosophy, The Lives and Opinions of the World's Greatest Philosophers*. Simon & Schuster, 1961.

Durant, Will. *The Pleasures of Philosophy: A Survey of Human Life and Destiny*. Simon & Schuster, 1929.

Earth Works Action Network. *50 Simple Things You Can Do to Fight the Right*. Earth Works Press, 2006.

Emerson, Ralph Waldo. *Emerson: Essays and Lectures*. Library of America Press Syndicate, 1983.

Ferguson, Marilyn. *The Aquarian Conspiracy: Personal and Social Transformation in Our Time*. Jeremy P. Tarcher, 1981.

Frazier, Kendrich (ed.). *The Hundredth Monkey and Other Paradigms of the Paranormal*. Prometheus Books, 1991.

Gandhi, Mohandas K. *The Essential Gandhi: An Anthology of His Writings on His Life, Work and Ideas*, (Louis Fischer, ed.). Vintage Books, 1962.

Gitlin, Todd. *Letters to a Young Activist*. Basic Books, 2003.

Graham, John. *Stick Your Neck Out: A Street-Smart Guide for Creating Change in Your Community and Beyond*. Berrett-Kohler, 1995.

Grosso, Michael. *The Millenium Myth: Love and Death at the End of Time*. Quest Books, 1995.

Hazen, Don and Lakshmi Chaudhry (eds.). *Start Making Sense: Turning the Lessons of Election 2004 Into Winning Progressive Politics*. Chelsea Green Publishing, 2005.

Harris, Sam. *The End of Faith: Religion, Terror and the Future of Reason*. W. W. Norton & Co., 2005.

Heelas, Paul. *The New Age Movement: Religion, Culture and Society in the Age of Postmodernity*. Wiley-Blackwell, 1996.

Herbert, Nick. *Elemental Mind: Human Consciousness and the New Physics*. Dutton 1993.

Horwitz, Claudia. *The Spiritual Activist: Practices to Transform Your Life, Your Work, and Your World*. Penguin Compass, 2002.

Houston, Jean. *The Search for the Beloved: Journeys in Sacred Philosophy*. Jeremy P. Tarcher, 1987.

Huxley, Aldous. *The Perennial Philosophy*. Harper & Brothers, 1945.

Jung, Carl. *Man and His Symbols*. Doubleday & Co., 1964.

Jung, Carl. *Psychological Reflections*. Harper & Brothers, 1961.

Kaminer, Wendy. *Sleeping With Extra-Terrestrials: The Rise of Irrationalism and Perils of Piety*. Pantheon Books, 1999.

Kelly, Mary Olsen, (ed.). *The Fireside Treasury of Light: An Anthology of the Best in New Age Literature*. Simon & Schuster, 1990.

Krishnamurti, J. *The Only Revolution*. Harper & Row, 1970.

Lakoff, George. *The Political Mind: Why You Can't Understand 21st-Century American Politics with an 18th-Century Brain*. Viking, 2008.

Lerner, Michael. *The Left Hand of God: Taking Back Our Country From the Religious Right*. Harper San Francisco, 2006.

Lewis, James R. and J. Gordon Melton, (ed.). *Perspectives on the New Age*. State University of New York Press, 1992.

Lipton, Bruce H. *The Biology of Belief: Unleashing the Power of Consciousness, Matter & Miracles*. Mountain of Love/Elite Books, 2005.

Melton, J. Gordon. *New Age Almanac*. Visible Ink Press, 1991.

Moore, Thomas (ed.). *The Education of the Heart*. HarperCollins, 1996.

Murchie, Guy. *The Seven Mysteries of Life: An Exploration in Science and Philosophy*. Houghton Mifflin, 1978.

Muses, Charles (ed.). *Consciousness and Reality*. Outerbridge & Lazard, 1972.

Peck, M. Scott. *The Road Less Traveled*. Simon & Schuster, 1978.

Plato. *The Republic*. Penguin Classics, 2007.

Powers, Ann. *Weird Like Us: My Bohemian America*. Simon & Schuster, 2000.

Ray, Paul H. and Sherry Ruth Anderson. *The Cultural Creatives: How 50 Million People are Changing the World*. Harmony Books, 2000.

Rough, Jim. *Society's Breakthrough! Releasing Essential Wisdom and Virtue in All the People*. 1st Books, 2002.

Schweitzer, Albert. *The Light Within Us*. The Philosophical Library, 1959.

Senge, Peter, C. Otto Scharmer, Joseph Jaworski, and Betty Sue Flowers. *Presence: An Exploration of Profound Change in People, Organizations and Society*. Doubleday Business, 2005.

Smith, Huston. *The Religions of Man*. Harper & Brothers, 1958.

Smith, Huston. *Forgotten Truth: The Common Vision of the World's Religions*. Harper San Francisco, 1992.

Sobel, Eliezer. *The 99th Monkey: A Spiritual Journalist's Misadventures with Gurus, Messiahs, Sex, Psychedelics, and Other Consciousness-Raising Experiences*. Santa Monica Press, 2008.

Spangler, David. *A Pilgrim in Aquarius*. Findhorn Press. 1997.

Spangler, David, and William Irwin Thompson. *Reimagination of the*

World: A Critique of the New Age, Science, and Popular Culture. Bear & Company.1991.

Sutcliffe, Steven J. *Children of the New Age: A History of Spiritual Practices*. Routledge, 2003.

Taylor, Jill Bolte. *My Stroke of Insight: A Brain Scientist's Personal Journey*. Viking, 2008.

Thoreau, Henry David. *The Heart of Thoreau's Journals*, (Odell Shepard, ed.). Dover Publications, 1961.

Thoreau, Henry David. *Walden and Other Writings of Henry David Thoreau*. Random House, 1937.

Tollifson, Joan. *Awake in the Heartland, The Ecstasy of What Is.* Non-Duality Press, 2006.

Trungpa, Chogyam. *Cutting Through Spiritual Materialism*. Shambhala, 1973.

Trungpa, Chogyam. *The Myth of Freedom and the Way of Meditation*. Shambhala, 2005.

Watts, Alan. *Behold the Spirit: A Study in the Necessity of Mystical Religion*. Vintage Books, 1971.

Watts, Alan. *Does It Matter? Essays on Man's Relation to Materiality.* Vintage Books, 1971.

Watts, Alan. *This is It and Other Essays on Zen and Spiritual Experience.* Vintage Books, 1973.

Watts, Alan. *The Way of Zen*. Pantheon Books, 1957.

Watts, Alan. *The Wisdom of Insecurity: A Message for an Age of Anxiety.* Pantheon Books, 1951.

Whybrow, Peter C. *American Mania: When More Is Not Enough.* W. W. Norton, 2006.

Wilber, Ken. *Boomeritis: A Novel That Will Set You Free*. Shambhala, 2002.

Wilber, Ken. *Integral Spirituality: A Startling New Role for Religion in the Modern and Postmodern World.* Integral Books, 2007.

Wilber, Ken. *Sex, Ecology & Spirituality: The Spirit of Evolution.* Shambhala, 1995.

Wilber, Ken. *The Spectrum of Consciousness*. Quest Books, 1977.

Williamson, Marianne. *The Age of Miracles: Embracing the New Midlife.* Hay House, 2008.

Index